# HISTORY, EDUCATION, AND THE SCHOOLS

# History, Education, and the Schools

William J. Reese

HISTORY, EDUCATION, AND THE SCHOOLS
Jacket photograph courtesy of Herbert M. Kliebard, Rural school, ca. 1895.

First published in 2007 by
PALGRAVE MACMILLAN™
175 Fifth Avenue, New York, N.Y. 10010 and
Houndmills, Basingstoke, Hampshire, England RG21 6XS
Companies and representatives throughout the world.

PALGRAVE MACMILLAN is the global academic imprint of the Palgrave Macmillan division of St. Martin's Press, LLC and of Palgrave Macmillan Ltd. Macmillan® is a registered trademark in the United States, United Kingdom and other countries. Palgrave is a registered trademark in the European Union and other countries.

ISBN-13: 978–1–4039–7744–1
ISBN-10: 1–4039–7744–5

Library of Congress Cataloging-in-Publication Data

Reese, William J., 1951–
     History, education, and the schools / William J. Reese.
        p. cm.
     Includes bibliographical references and index.
     ISBN (invalid )1–4039–7744–8 (alk. paper)
        1. Education—United States—History. 2. Postmodernism and education. 3. History—Methodology. I. Title.

LA212.R424 2007
370.973—dc22                                               2006050982

A catalogue record for this book is available from the British Library.

Design by Newgen Imaging Systems (P) Ltd., Chennai, India.

First edition: April 2007

10 9 8 7 6 5 4 3 2 1

Printed in the United States of America.

*To Richard and Averil Aldrich, for their kindness,*
*generosity, and friendship*

# Contents

## Part IV  The Fate of the Public Schools

# List of Figures

# Acknowledgments

"If wishes were horses, beggars would ride," Mother Goose reminds us. I'm very grateful to friends and benefactors who have kept me on my toes, but made my scholarly travels possible and joyful. Richard Aldrich, Karen Benjamin, Mary Ann Dzuback, Barry Franklin, Story Matkin-Rawn, B. Edward McClellan, David McDonald, Adam Nelson, Chris Ogren, Jeremi Suri, and Marc VanOverbeke kindly read drafts of this manuscript and provided detailed, constructive criticisms that noticeably improved my thinking and writing. Karl Shoemaker offered very helpful commentary on my chapters on the nature of history and on Christian day schools. Conversations with Bob Orsi enriched my understanding of American religious history. I appreciate the generosity of these outstanding scholars and friends. My editor, Amanda Johnson, a friend to my field of study and a pleasure to work with, has been kind and encouraging, and Emily Leithauser has similarly been enormously helpful and thoughtful.

Historians have often traveled light, but my academic journeys were generously supported by various foundations and two great public universities. Grants from the Spencer Foundation, the Profitt Foundation at Indiana University at Bloomington, and from the University of Wisconsin-Madison Graduate School helped expedite my research. At Wisconsin, a special thank you to my former Dean, Chuck Read, and to Dean Martin Cadwallader of the Graduate School.

The chapters in this book all have previously appeared in a different form in edited books or journals. I am therefore grateful to the journals *Education Research and Perspectives*, *Educational Theory*, and *History of Education* as well as to Taylor & Francis, Thompson Publications, the National Council of Teachers of Mathematics, and the University of Missouri Press for permission to draw upon this work. Full citations precede the relevant chapter endnotes. I am also grateful to those who listened to and commented on earlier drafts of these chapters in public presentations. Some of the central ideas in chapter 3 were presented in a lecture at the Missouri Botanical Gardens in the fall of 2000. And graduate students kindly invited me to present some of the ideas from chapter 8 to the Wisconsin-Spencer Lecture Series on Education at the University of Wisconsin-Madison in 2004.

# Introduction

According to Greek mythology, Jupiter and Mnemosyne gave birth to nine daughters, each with a special responsibility to promote learning and song and, in the case of Clio, memory. Jupiter was ultimately deposed as ruler of the earth, but the muse of history enjoyed a happier fate. Through the ages, Clio was honored in poetry and prose, paintings, and public art. Often she was depicted with a scroll and books, the historian's armament. An American poet in the early nineteenth century was moved to write:

> Majestic Clio touched her silver wire,
> And through time's lengthened vista moved a train,
> In dignity sublime;—the patriot's fire
> Kindled its torch in heaven's resplendent ray,
> And 'mid contention rose to Heaven again.[1]

The muse still lights the way. "What is Past is Prologue," reads the inscription on the imposing Muse of History that greets visitors at the entrance to the National Archives in Washington, DC. Historians have replaced scrolls with computers and can read books on-line, but the impulse to remember the past, whether in our thoughts or on paper, remains ever powerful in all societies.[2]

*History, Education, and the Schools* explores the nature and purpose of history and the evolution of key aspects of public and private schools in America. Two of the chapters were conceived in the mid- to late 1980s, and the rest after 1998. It was a period that witnessed momentous social changes whose impact on history and historical sensibility was profound. Since the early 1980s America has continued its political shift rightward; left-wing fantasies of worldwide revolution have evaporated, and market and communications revolutions and the attendant global economy have come to dominate the postmodern, postcommunist world. Even before the seemingly endless war on terror that followed the tragedies of September 11, 2001, many citizens, including academics and public intellectuals, shared a haunting sense that the present was strikingly different from a slowly departing "modern" age when, according to many critics, industrialism, colonialism, and imperialism had defined Western culture. To some soothsayers, the events of 1989—the democracy movements in Tiananmen Square and the dismantling of the Berlin Wall—pointed to the end of a world that had stretched forward from the French Revolution and the Enlightenment, and the beginning of another.

Blessed with the advantage of distance, time, and better historical records, the next generation of scholars may better understand how to think about the recent past. For a historian who has lived through this period, however, the present moment is an appropriate time to take stock and reflect upon one's labors. *History, Education, and the Schools* is divided into four parts, with two chapters apiece. The first chapter analyzes the history of historical writing from antiquity to the postmodern present. It explores the rise of the idea of history in Western culture as well as recent developments in the study of American history, when postmodern critics reopened old debates about the nature and purpose of historical scholarship. While this chapter traces the origins of history as a professional calling, the next one examines a more humble but not less important profession, education. It probes the history of educational research, specifically research on public education, in the twentieth century. Among education's many social functions, its utility has always been prized in America. The chapter tries to find an answer to the question: Has educational research had an appreciable impact on public school practices?

Part II examines the evolution of public education in the nineteenth century. It focuses on cities, opening with a case study of the public schools of St. Louis, Missouri. Throughout the post—World War II period, citizens often described urban schools as deeply troubled. In a land of verdant hills and productive farms, cities had long seemed threatening and forbidding, despite their being centers of culture and achievement. Because of their innovative programs and leadership, the public schools of St. Louis once attracted visitors and attention from throughout the Western world. Some visited the local high school, one of the many educational innovations of the nineteenth century born in response to a variety of urban problems and educational needs. Often called the "people's college," the early American high school is the subject of a separate chapter. To unearth the values that permeated secondary instruction, the chapter explores what pupils read and studied across the curriculum, highlighting the boundaries of acceptable knowledge, especially views of political economy in a period of dramatic socioeconomic change.

Part III shifts the reader's attention from the public schools, which most pupils in America still attend, to the history of private education. Like urban schools, the place of private schools in the social order has been hotly debated over the last quarter century. The opening chapter examines the history of public and private education over a long time span, beginning with the colonial period and culminating in the 2002 U.S. Supreme Court decision that ruled in favor of public funding of church-based schools in Cleveland. (The city, it seems, remains central to educational innovation.) The next chapter moves from the general to the specific, focusing on the history of Christian day schools since the 1960s. It analyzes why many evangelical and fundamentalist Christians abandoned the public schools and also enables readers to experience vicariously the inner world of fundamentalist education. Christian schools are a notable expression of parental dissent against modernity and of emerging criticisms of the "public school monopoly," and school choice, variously defined. Today school choice enjoys almost universal assent.

The final section of this book returns the reader to a consideration of the place of public schools in American culture. Private and public schools have always had a symbiotic relationship, so they cannot be fully understood in isolation. The past generation witnessed growing public support for private schools and choice in general. As President Ronald Reagan famously proclaimed in his inaugural address in 1981—a time of high inflation, unemployment, budget deficits, and familiar complaints about ineffective schools—government was the cause of and not the solution to the nation's ills. Reagan often questioned the role of the public sphere in the common welfare. In what ways, however, had schools in the past contributed to the common good? What gains and losses accrued from the creation of a single system of public schools? Why did so many people in the late twentieth century find public education wanting and favor choices both within and outside of the system? The concluding chapter also covers broad historical terrain. Since numerous citizens, including parents, politicians, and pundits, regularly assail public education, why do so many people still believe the system can be reformed and labor to do so?

A final note: While I have preserved some of the original tone and style of these chapters, they first came to life as independent essays. Thanks to the benefits of further research, reading, and reflection, I have not only revised and rewritten them, but also forged some connections among them. Concentrating on a few interrelated topics, the book rests on a simple faith that the past is still prologue and that history is the best guide to understanding how our world and its educational arrangements came to be. The present makes little sense without knowledge of the past. As Clio's admirers over the centuries have realized, history liberates us from an excessive preoccupation with ourselves by expanding our intellectual vistas. Otherwise, as it has been often said, one remains a child and never grows up.[3]

# Part I

# History and Its Uses

# Chapter 1

# On the Nature and Purpose of History

What is history? Since its emergence as a distinctive intellectual pursuit among the Greeks in the fifth century BCE, writers from a variety of backgrounds have tried to answer that question. To study, record, and educate others about the past seems so obvious to modern sensibility that it almost seems unnecessary to comment upon. In fact, the significance of the rise of history as a unique type of inquiry—related to but different from chronicles, storytelling, myths, and other ways of memorializing the past—can easily be underestimated. We assume today that acquiring knowledge of history, either for pleasure or for more utilitarian ends such as judging events and seeking "truth," has some place in our lives, however vaguely the need may be articulated. Everyone, for example, has seen a movie where a character temporarily has lost his or her memory. This is a horrifying thought, since without a sense of the past, the present and future seem unnavigable. The same is true of any culture or society. While professionally trained historians routinely argue among themselves about the fine points of historical research in academic journals and seminars, citizens from all walks of life employ history—verifiable or invented, etched through a mixture of sources and means into personal or collective consciousness—to guide their thinking and behavior.[1]

Examples of the uses of history abound in our times. When the Smithsonian Institution in the mid-1990s planned an exhibit of the *Enola Gay*, which decades before had dropped the atomic bomb on Japan, outraged veteran groups lobbied politicians to kill the proposal, which they believed criticized America and overly empathized with a former enemy. Those who fought in World War II and conservative activists who had never served in the armed forces invoked an image of the past to influence the outcome of the decision. History serves many masters. Who has not read an editorial or heard a speech that pointed to declining standards in modern education, claiming that the schools were once better, that a return to basics, to standards, to whatever once was superior could fix whatever ails them? Debates over welfare reform, affirmative action, or reparations from the federal government to African Americans for the horror of slavery, all make an appeal to history.

Citizens will never agree about the nature and purpose of history, since it encompasses all that has ever happened and since perspective is shaped by present concerns and hopes for the future; history is not simply a string of facts commonly agreed upon. Historians cannot capture the past truthfully to everyone's satisfaction any more than photographers can frame a subject without some angle of personal vision. Neither historians nor photographers simply record an image; both try to understand or see some essential part of a larger whole that is beyond capturing in its totality. History remains the central way to understand how individuals and society change over time, providing a kind of perspective unavailable in any other discipline or body of knowledge. This has been true from ancient times to the postmodern present, as the history of Western historical thought reveals. "The study of history," as Donald R. Kelley has persuasively argued, "is always renewing itself, but it is nonetheless, unavoidably but appropriately, bound to its past."[2]

Herodotus of Halicarnassus (ca. 484–425 BCE), whose account of the Persian Wars is generally regarded as the first major work of Western history, eloquently explained why history should be written. Yet even this master of prose, still often remembered as "the father of history," was dismissed by some critics in the ancient world as "the father of lies." At the time, various literary forms, especially the epic poems immortalized by Homer, competed to help shape memories of the past. Homer answered the call of the Muse, but Herodotus responded to the human need to remember in a different way. In the opening lines of *The Histories*, he told his readers that "his *Researches* are here set down to preserve the memory of the past by putting on record the astonishing achievements both of our own and other peoples; and more particularly to show how they came into conflict." Defined as "inquiry," "investigation," and "research" in Greek, *history* became for Herodotus and later historians a disputed but central means to perpetuate the memory of the great deeds of important men. The range of subjects deemed legitimate fields of study within history would expand enormously over the centuries, including especially recent times; yet even Herodotus had a remarkable curiosity about the customs, religious beliefs, and myths of the people he met in his travels and learned about through conversation and interviews. Herodotus and a handful of other ancient writers took painstaking efforts to not simply tell important stories—the heart of epic poetry—but to investigate the past with an eye toward accuracy, to separate when possible, truth from myth, and to link evidence into a prose narrative that described men's motives and influence on notable events. Most importantly, while drawing upon oral traditions, myths, and almost exclusively nonwritten sources, Herodotus made humans, not the gods, the center of inquiry.[3]

Written history had an implicit educational function as it emerged in societies dominated by spoken rather than written words. If the most important deeds of men were worth remembering and recording, what role would the deeds play in people's lives? Did history, for example, have predictive power? That question especially interested Thucydides (460?–400? BCE), who followed in Herodotus's footsteps and hoped to leave an indelible imprint on historical writing. Few ancient writers took up his challenge to write history with such concern for accuracy; his was nevertheless an important contribution to a way of thinking and writing about the past. *The Peloponnesian War*, which examined the conflict between Athens and Sparta, focused not on the remote past like Herodotus's history, but on a recent event, one in which the Athenian author participated. Like Herodotus, Thucydides studied war and politics, both of which remained the central focus of history until modern times.

Certain that he was witnessing "the greatest movement [the war] yet known in history," Thucydides was less interested than Herodotus in the customs, religious practices, and cultural beliefs of different peoples, and he claimed to be more scrupulous than his predecessor in getting the facts straight. "The way that most men deal with traditions, even traditions of their own country," he warned, "is to receive them all alike as they are delivered, without applying any critical test whatever." He worried about the accuracy of what informants told him and of the speeches he heard and recorded for posterity. Thucydides nevertheless believed that knowing history could help predict the future, a point disputed then and ever since. Many (though hardly all) ancient writers had a cyclical rather than a linear view of time. "The absence of romance in my history will, I fear, detract somewhat from its interest," Thucydides realized, "but if it be judged useful by those inquirers who desire an exact knowledge of the past as an aid in the interpretation of the future, which in the course of human things must resemble it if it does not reflect it, I shall be content." He also wrote not "to win the applause of the moment, but as a possession for all time."[4]

Only a handful of writers in the ancient world drew upon the inspiration provided in the famous histories by Herodotus and Thucydides. As G. R. Elton remarked in *The Practice of History*, these few were nonetheless distinguished by their accomplishments. Polybius (ca. 198–117 BCE), a native Greek captured by the barbarians (the Romans), became one of antiquity's famed historians, who repeated an already popular notion that "men have no more ready corrective of conduct than knowledge of the past." In fact, he argued that "the soundest education and training for a life of active politics is the study of History, and that the surest and indeed the only method of learning how to bear bravely the vicissitudes of fortune, is to recall the calamities of others." The thought was so commonplace among his contemporaries that he doubted he had "to repeat what has been so well and so often said." His writings tried to explain Rome's meteoric rise as it conquered its neighbors and much of the known world. Other talented writers would emerge in the Roman era to write history. Yet the subject paled in significance compared to rhetoric, poetry, and other forms of expression that kept a view of the past alive but often lacked the sense of history exhibited by Herodotus and Thucydides.[5]

As Moses I. Finley reminds us, myths taught and learned through speeches and oral histories, usually in the form of epic poems, more commonly provided ancient societies with a sense of timeless facts. Myths were not rooted in any definite place or time, but they still taught essential moral truths and the pains and pitfalls of life, thus providing continuity between those who lived in some unspecified but distant past and the present. Even today, whether written by amateurs or professionals, history offers many readers similar psychic nourishment. By learning the art of rhetoric, still so integral to effective historical writing today, students of the past learned to make allusions to historical events, heroic deeds, and mythological images to bolster their historical arguments. Indeed, the use of colorful stories and selective history to suit political or religious ends is nothing new.[6]

Greek and Roman authors often wrote insightful interpretations of the past, but these lacked the appeal of oral traditions and traditional ways of seeing and understanding what came before. No less a figure than Aristotle (384–322 BCE) helped seal the second-class status of history by comparing it unfavorably with poetry. In the *Poetics*, he explained that the poet was superior to the historian, since the former described what "might happen" and the latter, what actually happened. Even if one put Herodotus's history into verse, Aristotle pointed out, it would still be history, not poetry; it dealt with particular events, while poetry "is something more philosophic and of graver import than history, since its statements are of the nature rather of universals, whereas those of history are singulars." Thus the attractions of myths and oral traditions remained powerful.[7]

Among various Roman writers, history held an important, though not a superior, place in the world of knowledge and politics. As Ronald Mellor explains, most of the historians were senators who were primarily interested in politics and wrote mostly for each other. They were more parochial in their tastes than earlier Greek writers such as Herodotus and Thucydides, who showed genuine interest in both sides on the battlefield. Roman historians focused on the rise, progress, and ultimate corruption of the Roman republic and empire; they often tied history more closely to rhetoric and recognized its utility for orators and its overall intrinsic pleasure. Marcus Tullius Cicero (106–43 BCE), famously wrote that "to be ignorant of what occurred before you were born is to remain always a child. For what is the worth of human life, unless it is woven into the life of our ancestors by the records of history. Moreover," he emphasized, "the mention of antiquity and the citation of examples give the speech authority and credibility as well as affording the highest pleasure to the audience." Cicero eloquently concluded that because history "bears witness to the passing of the ages, sheds light upon reality, gives life to recollection and guidance to human existence, and brings tidings of ancient days, whose voice, but the orator's, can entrust her to immortality?"[8]

As Thucydides had shown, history provided examples, warnings, and lessons. The patriot opposing the *Enola Gay* exhibit, the reformer who thinks schools once were better, the parent who believes children once had better manners, the politician who invokes an image from the past in defense of controversial legislation, the book club member who devours the latest purchase for enlightenment and pleasure—all pay homage to Cicero's insights into the multiple uses of history. Among other things, history helped preserve diverse truths, inform and guide the orator and politician, and thus serve the present while offering "tidings of ancient days."

The fall of Rome in the fifth century CE and the rise of Christianity brought momentous changes to the idea of history. While the dramatic story of the rise and fall of their empire understandably appealed to Roman authors, Christian scholars embraced a new sense about time, about the relation between past and present, and about the meaning of history. Ancient writers had believed that history served various purposes and that gods intervened to shape the fate of humankind, but an emerging Judeo-Christian tradition viewed human history as inextricably bound by a divine plan, guided by one God. However imprecise the dating of the event, God had cast man out of the Garden of Eden; man's fall into a state of sin forever shaped human destiny. Providence guided history, even if His will remained inscrutable, as Christians debated how civilization emerged from the chaos and how individuals might enter the Gates of Heaven. Writings on the apostles, miracles, and the saints revealed God's active intervention in the universe and remained a common focus of church chroniclers for centuries. Eusebius (260?–340?), the early leading historian of Christianity, said that all history flowed from Providence, with Adam's fall decisively shaping everything that followed. His *Ecclesiastical History* thus proposed to explore the history of the church, "writing the successions of the sacred apostles, covering the period stretching from our Savior to ourselves," and recounting the story of those who advanced and retarded God's plan. History had a beginning, a middle, and a definite end, according to biblical teachings.[9]

During the next century Augustine of Hippo (354–430) similarly applauded history for its help "in understanding the Sacred Books" and thus in guiding more people to the City of God. Augustine battled against paganism and the claim that Jesus based his religious "maxims" on the works of Plato, which he called "utmost madness" (even though he was himself strongly influenced by neo-Platonists). Augustine observed that history—past, present, and future— conformed to God's plan, occurring in the proper "order of time, whose Creator and Administrator is God." History, properly understood, told the living "what has been done," but only God's word revealed "what should be done. History reports honestly and profitably what has been accomplished." That history provided a reliable record of the past linked some of the early pagan historians with these Christian writers. History was not simply a matter of facts but a product of interpretation, research, and inquiry, even if men of the cloth bent history in a certain direction.[10]

Even before the fall of Rome, Christian writers, as part of a deep spiritual need to confirm their faith, took a special interest in understanding former times. History taught prophetic lessons about the unfolding of human development from pagan to Christian times. As Charles Homer Haskins noted in *The Renaissance of the Twelfth Century*, three main forms of historical writing predominated among medieval Christians: annals, chronicles, and the lives of saints and other key religious figures. Early Egyptians and Babylonians among others had often compiled lists of momentous events, year by year, but the Christian, antipagan polemics of the second and third centuries made the genre of historical annals serve the special interests of the church for many centuries. Following the grand achievements of Eusebius, chronicles offered more extensive descriptions of important people and events in the rise and progress of Christianity. Monks and other clerics wrote numerous histories of the lives of saints, popes, and bishops and also recorded miracles and divine prophecies, thereby preserving historical memories to help advance the faith. These common forms of historical writing continued to be popular into the early modern period; they attempted to document the progress of Christianity generally, and Catholicism in particular, from the Creation to the expulsion of Adam and Eve from the Garden of Eden, which marked the dawn of human history.[11]

The rediscovery of the writings of the ancients in the twelfth century was part of a larger efflorescence of scholarship during an age of urban growth, commerce, and intellectual curiosity that led to the founding of the first European universities. But the discovery of pagan wisdom, especially Aristotle's works, did not overturn dominant Christian ideas about the nature of history. Instead of placing man at the center of history, Catholic scholars still viewed history as an unfolding Providential plan leading the faithful to the Celestial City. As Augustine had taught centuries earlier, history was a battle between good and evil, pagan and Christian. Pagan writings were ultimately absorbed into Christian theology, most notably by Thomas Aquinas, but the flurry of renewed interest in the ancient world did not mean a preoccupation with the ethical views or historical lessons of Herodotus or Thucydides.[12]

Throughout the ancient and medieval periods, then, history served multiple purposes and addressed diverse human needs. Herodotus and Thucydides had elevated the quality and rigor of historical analysis, though their approach to the past never competed very effectively with the higher appeal of poetry, rhetoric, science, and philosophy. History remained a branch of literature and rhetoric and, to Aristotle and his followers in antiquity, inferior to poetry. Roman writers emphasized the memorable deeds of important men, focusing their attention on war and politics, the republic and empire, and affairs of state. Christian writers added a new dimension to the writing of history, linking it to the fate of mankind, rooted in biblical teachings, prophecies, and divine purpose. But history was not included in the medieval university curriculum, the quadrivium or trivium. Only in the nineteenth century, far in the future, would history rise to elevated importance in the university, where it would gain professional status and gradually loosen its ties to religion.

During the flowering of the Renaissance in the fourteenth and fifteenth centuries, when humanistic interest in ancient writers again bloomed, history was newly praised, in the manner of Cicero, for its broad utility, moral lessons, and pleasures for the reader, challenging but hardly superseding the dominance of theologically oriented history. Secular histories, such as those of the Italian city states, appeared, but so did the familiar annals, chronicles, and stories about popes and monarchs within a Christian interpretive framework. Most histories reflected a religious point of view that was only reinforced by the religious wars that followed the Protestant Reformation of the sixteenth century. Whether conceived by Protestants or Catholics, many histories assumed that Divine Providence determined human destiny. Both the Christian humanist Erasmus and his rival Martin Luther were fascinated with history, returning to ancient texts and languages to unearth the meaning of the past and God's role in history. Yet history remained a minor branch of study within the curriculum, taught largely as a branch of theology in the universities that were themselves growing in number and usually sponsored and controlled by church and state. Only during the Enlightenment of the seventeenth and especially eighteenth centuries would more secular, often anticlerical authors and philosophes popularize new ideas about historical scholarship. By then, many learned Western Europeans perceived history as divided into new divisions—ancient, medieval, and the "modern" period—the last word being coined in the sixteenth century and indicative of a new consciousness about time. This cultivated a new awareness about historical change and about the historian's role in interpreting it.[13]

Drawing upon the rising faith in science earlier promoted by such intellectual lights as Francis Bacon and Isaac Newton, Enlightenment writers of the late eighteenth century exalted the power of the human mind to unlock the mysteries of the universe. Christian thinkers in the medieval period such as Peter Abelard and Thomas Aquinas had championed reason as compatible with faith, despite powerful opponents who saw them as mutually exclusive. To Voltaire and skeptical French philosophes, however, most history had been a series of errors, led by the designing aims of church and state. While praising Herodotus and Thucydides for their contributions to the study of history, especially their commitment to accuracy and search for truth, Voltaire believed in the late 1770s that "one requires of modern historians more details, better founded facts, more precise dates, better authorities, and more attention to usages, laws, manners, commerce, finances, agriculture, and population." Historical writing, he insisted, should encompass the ordinary as well as memorable deeds of people, and he rejected supernatural explanations for the nature and meaning of the universe. Eighteenth-century intellectuals shared this avid interest in history, offering philosophers concrete examples of past behavior as they pondered the essence of human nature. Montesquieu, Edward Gibbon, and other contemporaries studied the ancient past, notably basing their histories on a range of primary sources and offering biting appraisals of the role of Christianity in the collapse of the Roman empire.[14]

By the time of the American and French Revolutions, a host of writers had increasingly started to believe in progress and had removed God from the center of human existence. As in any era of dramatic change, the idea of history and its uses was the subject of considerable debate. America's Founding Fathers, for example, were often serious students of history, and classical writers shaped their views on human nature, ethics, and government. Ideas drawn from the European Enlightenment had a decisive impact on American intellectual thought. The French skeptics had less influence than the moral philosophers and political economists from Scotland, home to a more moderate brand of Enlightenment thinking. To Adam Smith, the rise of free trade and capitalist enterprise marked a decisive break from the past, deepening an awareness of the ubiquity of change in the modern world. While countless histories of the early nineteenth century remained infused with theistic assumptions, a spirit of unfettered inquiry and faith in the life of the mind spread within Enlightened circles. Efforts to develop a scientific, not theistic, foundation for politics, morals, and economic relations proliferated. And by the mid-nineteenth century, amid increasing efforts to make history more scientific, where the accumulation of facts might reveal the truths of history (and perhaps the laws underlying them), the reputation of Francis Bacon soared. Only hard, empirical facts were the basis of science, said his interpreters, and the reduction of Bacon's thought to empirical investigation fed an evident American passion for the practical and suspicion of grand theories and speculative thought.[15]

In a handful of advanced centers of study in Europe such as the universities, history gained a strong foothold. The University of Berlin, dedicated to the study of the humanistic sciences, appointed a chair of history as early as 1810, and the Sorbonne followed suit two years later. The English universities lagged behind their European counterparts, but by the 1880s they as well as American universities were becoming transformed by exciting developments in the German states. The most popular historians earlier in the century were amateurs and patricians with a patriotic, romantic, highly nationalistic tone to their works. However, in the United States, they were soon replaced by professional historians, increasingly lodged in the universities, and a similar process was underway in Western Europe. History written increasingly by experts for experts was undeniably rising in importance. Inspired by the example of Germany, whose universities had trained several thousand Americans in various graduate studies by the end of the century, professionals here and abroad vowed to make history into a veritable science.[16]

As professional historians embraced the scientific method and thoroughgoing empiricism, they sometimes found themselves buried under a mountain of facts from the archives and research libraries. Unable to imitate the methods and procedures of laboratory scientists, historians nevertheless embraced objectivity and science and tried to apply them to history. Monarchists and republicans, Marxists and their opponents, all saw value in the effort. The most famous contribution to the writing of scientific history, based on the discovery of universal laws, came not from a university-based historian, but from a political revolutionary with a keen sense of the past. Rejecting German idealist philosophy, Karl Marx, by mid-century, conceived of a revolutionary, materialistic interpretation of human history, as full of prophetic language as the religious evangelicals of his day. Through the struggles of competing social classes, history would lead to the Promised Land, not to a heaven above but one on earth in which the state withered away and a working man's paradise flourished. Most academics enthralled by scientific history offered less prophecy and fewer apocalyptic claims. Many dry-as-dust treatises poured out of the universities (few with a Marxist bent) and they only seemed to prove that history was a specialized form of inquiry, mostly (still) oriented toward politics, affairs of state, and war.[17]

Science had magnetic attractions to the scholars who built the historical profession. As the Industrial Revolution transformed economic and social life and the discoveries of Charles Darwin undermined theistic views of human origins, science became a powerful intellectual presence throughout the Western world. Science became a central part of the modern belief system. Leopold von Ranke, who assumed the chair of history at Berlin in 1825, held that history should be written in an objective and scientific manner; otherwise scholars could not accurately recreate "what really happened" in the past. As Peter Novick and Georg Iggers explain, the famous historian had actually written that scholars should discover what had "essentially" happened, but leaders of an emerging historical profession heard what they wanted. Ranke's philosophy of history was in fact rooted in German idealism, not in a materialist conception of life or Baconian empiricism. But Ranke's influence remained considerable in shaping an emerging historical ideal about science and objectivity.[18]

Offering graduate course work very inexpensively and with few European rivals engaged in innovative research, the German universities revolutionized the study of history. Americans flocked to Berlin, Göttingen, Heidelberg, and other schools to study the new approaches to historical scholarship. Philology, numismatics, and other innovative research tools inspired and broadened historical investigation, and German mentors labored to make history a professional undertaking. They taught research students in the new graduate departments to base their work on a solid foundation of fact, derived from painstaking work in primary documents in the state archives. Meeting in seminars under the direction of a professor trained in the new scientific methods, where their work would be discussed, criticized, and perfected, graduate students would systematically and rigorously sift through original sources to build an empirical foundation of knowledge, perhaps leading to the discovery of universal laws that governed history.

What was happening to the study of history in the nineteenth century was hardly unique. Knowledge was increasingly becoming specialized in the research universities, and other new disciplines such as economics, sociology, and political science, all vied for their place as social sciences in the newly transformed state universities such as Michigan and Wisconsin and new private ones such as The Johns Hopkins University and the University of Chicago. Critics said that history, for centuries written by amateurs, was now retreating behind monastic-like university walls, as scholars created their own historical journals and professional associations and increasingly communicated with each other rather than to the public. The most popular American historians of the nineteenth century, including Francis Parkman, wrote for a broad lay audience, not other historians, but the trend toward greater professionalization was clear. By the early twentieth century, to become a historian required graduate training, and to win an appointment at a reputable university, a Ph.D. Himself a well-known historian of the American West, Theodore Roosevelt regarded the new scholars as "little pedants" whose work lacked literary merit or appeal.[19]

As Bonnie G. Smith and other scholars demonstrate, professional-ization strengthened male control over historical scholarship and mar-ginalized women who wrote about the past. In Europe and America, the world of the professional historian became virtually all-male. Women were often denied admission to graduate studies or treated as second-class citizens. Those completing their degrees were often unable to secure academic posts. Men regarded women as too emo-tional or intuitive to engage in the rigors of scientific training or the quest for "objectivity." Whether or not women held advanced degrees, they were stigmatized as amateurs who too often focused on biographies, domestic life, and everyday matters in their scholarly writing, and not on the real stuff of history, politics and statecraft. As Smith explains, male scholars arrogantly assumed that they alone could seek transcendent truths and understanding by applying scien-tific methods in their search for the relevant facts of history.[20]

The nineteenth century nevertheless had proven critical in the shaping of modern historical scholarship. It had added the claim, soon disputed if not destroyed in the next century, that historians had the capacity to study the past in a dispassionate, objective way, scientifi-cally gathering facts to tell the truth about history. It mattered not that Ranke had been misunderstood in translation; though he did train some American students, he had already retired from teaching before throngs of them arrived at the German universities. Faith in scientific objectivity nevertheless seemed to carry the day in the fledgling profession. Facts, facts, and facts were the gateway to knowl-edge in this age of Gradgrind. While the excitement generated by the new research ideals was real, former students often described their his-torical training as tedious and their classroom instruction as dull. On the American side, the German influence was profound, as research seminars and graduate study became common late in the century. The history seminar, said a leading German-trained scholar at Johns Hopkins, was nothing less than a "laboratory of scientific truth." Another professor compared it to the chemical laboratory. Whether the scientific ideal would actually triumph in historical scholarship as the new century dawned was uncertain. But the seminar became a mainstay in graduate study, as Hopkins alumni, including Frederick Jackson Turner at the University of Wisconsin, helped make it essential to advanced study.[21]

By the early 1900s, leading historians within the university shared some basic norms about their craft. As Peter Novick explains, scholars were committed in general to objectivity, though its precise meaning was muddled both in theory and in practice. American historians,

**Figure 1.1** Graduate Study at the University of Wisconsin: Frederick Jackson Turner's History Seminar, ca. 1893–1894

Courtesy: Wisconsin Historical Society Image ID Whi-1910

drawing upon hallowed Western traditions, assumed that facts were discovered, not invented; that history was an empirical science, not a theoretical or a speculative enterprise; that history was distinguishable from literature or poetry; that the mind was capable of separating facts from fictions; and that language accurately represented the reality uncovered through the rigorous pursuit of primary sources. All of this was questioned within the historical profession in the early twentieth century and assailed by critics of modernism after the 1960s. But these guiding assumptions helped bind the historical profession in its founding era.[22]

Despite hosannas in praise of the scientific ideal, the notion that one could know history dispassionately and accurately gradually started losing credibility. By the late nineteenth century, European writers such as Friedrich Nietzsche began to question the notion of progress; he would become very influential in shaping postmodern critics of the Enlightenment and historical study by the 1960s. Some contemporary scholars pointed out that even the doyen of scientific history, Ranke, despite his well-publicized claim that historians should omit value judgments from their scholarship, had a romantic view of history, which he thought culminated in the perfection of the state. By the late nineteenth century other observers realized that history was not really a science, at least as laboratory-based scientists used the word, and scholars increasingly used the term to mean they approached sources in a systematic, rigorous, and critical manner. In a general way, Herodotus and Thucydides had said as much about historical inquiry centuries before access to written sources in archives existed. And anyone who read the typical school book would have hardly seen objectivity in action. History textbooks in America's expanding public school system mixed fanciful tales about George Washington and the apple tree with patriotic, nationalistic stories about 1776 and the treachery of Benedict Arnold, further undermining the notion that history was objective, value free, or scientific.[23]

Moreover, historians seemed to behave subjectively whenever duty called. When the Franco-Prussian War broke out in 1871 and when World War I engulfed the Western world, scholars on each side usually failed to view the behavior of enemy nations dispassionately; they seemed no more objective or neutral than anyone else, reminiscent of the critics who said that Herodotus and Thucydides often took sides in their famous histories. Faith in progress and Western civilization received a fatal blow on the battlefields of Europe, and cracks within the American historical profession about the supposedly scientific nature of history widened dramatically in the early decades of the twentieth century. Whether history could be objective or scientific soon attracted some of the most creative thinkers within the American historical profession. As Richard Hofstadter explains, these historians had grown up in a time of momentous change, which reoriented their thinking about the nature and purpose of history. Just as nineteenth-century professional historians who endorsed scientific and objective history had been shaped by romanticism and nationalism, the dramatic changes producing modernity influenced a new generation of American academics. The closing of the frontier line in the 1890s, the rise of industrial capitalism, the expansion of immigration, and the growth of the city transformed the nation; the boundaries of thinking about what is history correspondingly changed and widened. Huge debates erupted on both sides of the Atlantic about why one should read, write, or care about history and whether it was in any sense a science.[24]

By the early twentieth century, a few very prominent historians called for a more activist history in which present concerns openly guided research. Professors later taught their students to call these writers "presentist," since they were so concerned with the here-and-now that they blurred the distinction between past and present and failed to see the past on its own terms. To this generation of progressive historians, however, scholarship could help reform society by exposing the forces of conservatism and by promoting greater awareness about the age-old, continuing struggles of working people and political activists to build a more democratic society. The leading activist among the progressives was Charles A. Beard, who famously criticized the Founding Fathers and the Constitution, which he saw as part of a counterrevolution motivated by the economic self-interest of the American elite. Beard became the leading historian of his generation and principal advocate of what became known as historical relativism, the view that all historians write from a frame of reference influenced by an ever-changing climate of opinion.[25]

Beard and his contemporaries eloquently raised many significant questions about the nature of history, issues that remain central to historical research. Should present concerns about social improvement guide the questions asked about the past? Is it possible for historians to be objective? How do theory and methodology influence one's capacity to see the past as it once existed? In what sense is history a science? Revisiting the debates of the early decades of the twentieth century illuminates issues on which scholars still differ.

An early Progressive statement about the purposes of history appeared in James Harvey Robinson's *The New History*, published in 1912. Earning graduate degrees at Harvard and the University of

Freiburg and a reputation early in his career for hard-nosed empiricism, Robinson opened his book by criticizing the common notion that history was only about politics, foreign policy, and statecraft. He called for the use of historical sources beyond state archives, the official but hardly the only repositories of evidence on what happened in the past. History of the "common man" required a broadened perspective. Why not study "rude flint hatchets" or "a mortgage on an Assyrian tile," or "describe the over-short pastry to which Charles V was addicted to his undoing," he asked. Robinson had sent a memorable shot across the bow of traditional historiography, and it helped inspire a raft of works in social history in the interwar period.[26]

Could historians imitate the methods of the scientist, and in Baconian fashion gather enough facts to build a comprehensive and accurate understanding of the past? Reminding his readers of how the specter of Ranke, with his authoritative claims about science and the power of "facts," haunted the historical imagination, Robinson pointed out that scholars could not possibly master the sheer "quantity of facts," themselves "so heterogeneous in their character as to invite a great variety of interpretations." For history "must always remain, from the standpoint of the astronomer, physicist, or chemist, a highly inexact and fragmentary body of knowledge. This is due mainly to the fact that it concerns itself with man, his devious ways and wandering desires, which it seems hopeless at present to bring within the compass of clearly defined laws of any kind." As Robinson told big-city school superintendents at a meeting of the National Education Association in 1910, "each age has a perfect right to select from the annals of mankind those facts that seem to have a particular bearing on the matters it has at heart." Asked what sort of history was most appropriate for students in industrial education classes, he told the educators that "there are no clearly defined 'elements' in the study of history, as there are in arithmetic."[27]

A handful of historians before World War I dismissed the standard claims about objectivity and science in the profession, but the majority continued to believe that history dealt with hard facts, that literature was fiction and history nonfiction, that the past was real and distinguishable from the present, and that the historian could perceive the difference and accurately reconstruct the same. This seemed less tenable after Robinson and others started to pick away at what once seemed to be granite-like assumptions. Carl L. Becker and Charles Beard would write powerful indictments of scientific history in the 1920s and especially in the 1930s, shattering whatever consensus about historical scholarship might have existed. The weakening of the idea of progress following World War I, the rise of relativistic thinking in philosophy and other disciplines, and simply the reaction of maturing scholars such as Becker and Beard to the intellectual nostrums of their youth placed the champions of scientific history on the defensive, though they were hardly in full retreat.[28]

"What Are Historical Facts?" asked Becker in a paper of that title before the American Historical Association in 1926. Becker opened his address with the statement that every historian knows that history deals with facts, with "hard" facts, "cold" facts, nothing but a "solid foundation of fact." Were facts really so solid and tangible? Even an apparently simple statement of fact—"In the year 49 BC Caesar crossed the Rubicon"—was more complicated than it appeared. By the statement one did not really mean that Caesar crossed it alone; it also failed to exhaust all the thoughts and actions that led to that moment, so "a thousand and one lesser 'facts' went to make up the one simple fact that Caesar crossed the Rubicon," which turns out to be a generalization as much as a simple factual statement. Was not a fact a symbol of something important to someone interpreting the past, more than a hard substance like a brick? Facts, Becker continued, come alive only in the historian's imagination, which means all of them live not only in the past but in the present, too. The present guides what historians want to know about the past, and each generation, shaped by contemporary needs, inevitably asks different sorts of questions about what came before. Echoing Robinson and others, Becker added that historians cannot learn or know all the facts, so inevitably there is a process of selection at work, however much one tries to claim otherwise. History, he concluded, offered individuals a way to expand their perspectives on life and the world around them. It served no purpose if history was a body of facts "lying dead in the records. . . . They become historical facts, capable of doing work, of making a difference, only when someone, you or I, brings them alive in our minds by means of pictures, images, or ideas of the actual occurrence."[29]

The full-scale assault on objectivity came in the 1930s, in presidential addresses before the American Historical Association by Becker and by his fellow progressive iconoclast, Charles Beard. In 1931, Becker built upon earlier themes in his controversial address, "Everyman His Own Historian," there describing history as an "imaginative creation" shaped by a particular "climate of opinion" and by "practical or emotional needs" and "aesthetic tastes." And in a book destined to become a classic, *The Heavenly City of the Eighteenth-Century Philosophers* (1932), he again denied the existence of objectivity, seeing historical writing as inevitably shaped by the contemporary climate of opinion and the needs of the present. History, he wrote, "is not an objective reality, but only an imaginative reconstruction of vanished events," and "the pattern that appears useful and agreeable to one generation is never entirely so to the next." Voltaire's witty comment that "history is only a pack of tricks we play on the dead" was truer than its author realized. Becker doubted "that these tricks do the dead any harm, and it is certain that they do us much good. At best they help us to master our own difficulties; at worst they help us to endure them by nourishing the hope of a more resplendent future." It seemed clear that "every age is bound, in spite of itself, to make the dead perform whatever tricks it finds necessary for its own peace of mind."[30]

As the most famous and respected historian of his times, Beard similarly opened up a floodgate of controversy and criticism in a presidential address entitled "Written History as an Act of Faith." As Peter Novick explains, Beard had not been a thoroughgoing relativist before World War I and was best known for his revisionist interpretation of the origins of the Constitution; he resigned from Columbia University to protest the firing of colleagues during World War I. Like Robinson and a handful of other scholars, Beard believed that history had an essential role to play in social reform. Knowing history helped improve one's understanding of life and in the process contributed to social and economic progress. In a long and distinguished career, largely spent outside of academe, he epitomized the activist left-liberal scholar, critical of the abuses of capitalism but confident of the possibility of human betterment. War had dimmed but not destroyed that confidence, as he spoke to the American Historical Association in the depths of the Depression in 1934.[31]

"History has been called a science, an art, an illustration of theology, a phase of philosophy, a branch of literature," Beard told his listeners as he opened his address. "It is none of these things, or all of them combined." Beard distinguished between actual history, what happened in the past, and written history, which was the historian's best attempt at understanding what happened. While many historians claimed that history was a science, "every historian knows that his colleagues have been influenced in their selection and ordering of materials by their biases, prejudices, beliefs, affections, general upbringing, particularly social and economic. . . ." Historians arranged facts in this way or that, as "an act of choice, conviction, and interpretation respecting values," reflecting a particular frame of reference or point of view. There was not simply some objective reality out there, totally separate from the mind of the knower, waiting to be discovered. Science offered many undeniable benefits to humankind, but the methods of a chemist or physicist were not really suitable or actually followed by historians. The historian's "faith is at bottom a conviction that something true can be known about the movement of history and his conviction is a subjective decision, not a purely objective discovery." Historians had to have command over the sources but also recognize that in the final analysis writing history was fundamentally an act of faith.[32]

Critics assailed Becker, Beard, and other advocates of relativism for their presentism and questioned their basic philosophical and epistemological assumptions. They had become intellectual giants in the field of history and now questioned its guiding assumptions, forcing many to consider new ways of thinking about the past. They grappled with still unresolvable issues surrounding the nature of history. To many it appeared that their radical views erased the boundaries between knower and known, fact and fiction, truth and myth, and past and present. On both sides of the Atlantic, scholars attacked these aging progressives, though most historians continued writing history as if the debate never happened.

Reacting to the growing attempts to use history to understand the present, Herbert Butterfield, a young English historian, criticized the tunnel vision of historians who reduced the past to the needs of the present. In *The Whig Interpretation of History* (1931), Butterfield emphasized that the past was unlike the present and that it was the task of the historian to understand it on its own terms. Too often in the search for distant precedents to modern developments the crooked roads of the past that led to the present were made straight, distorting history. In the next decade the British philosopher and historian, R. G. Collingwood, whose widely read book, *The Idea of History*, appeared posthumously in 1946, offered a partial resolution to the debate. Collingwood shared the progressive view that written history was what contemporaries thought about the past, different from the past itself, which was irretrievable in any absolute sense; but he reaffirmed the older claim that history was scientific in the familiar sense that historians rigorously, critically, and systematically explored the documents of the past and tried to reenact in their minds the past thoughts and actions of those from a different age. Collingwood thus made historians uncomfortable with the notion of relativism to realize that a broad scientific approach nonetheless supported their labors.[33]

The decades that followed World War II, however, seemed to confirm the view of the historical relativists that each generation writes its own history. Debates resurfaced concerning whether historians should study common people or elites, seek truth or improve society, embrace art and literature or science and objectivity. Whether amateurs or professionals, historians would also continue to hold broad views on their calling. Without question, however, the horrors of World War II further undermined any uncritical faith in science, human rationality, and the ubiquity of progress. Marc Bloch, the prominent French historian who was tortured and executed by the Nazis for his work in the resistance, wrote in his posthumously published book, *The Craft of History* (1953), that the nineteenth-century search for a truly scientific history had failed. History was a science, since scholars examined documents systematically and critically, but otherwise had little in common with it. Whether history was an art or a science increasingly seemed like a tiresome, dead-end debate. Many historians believed that they wrote from a particular frame of reference and point of view. "Nowadays, at all events, the great majority of working historians are aware that certainty in history is beyond the grasp of the human mind," wrote one well-known European historian in 1955. "Not only is the multitude of facts staggering, but their nature is acknowledged to be elusive." By the early 1960s, the prominent English historian, J. H. Plumb, feared that the abandonment of most of the main tenets of the Enlightenment—a faith in science, progress, human reason, and thus certainty—led not simply to relativism but to nihilism.[34]

While historical relativism in various degrees seemed victorious, many American scholars of the 1950s rejected the progressive view of history associated with writers such as Charles Beard since the turn of the century. During the decade, a largely Republican era of expanding economies, suburbia, and the cold war, a so-called consensus school of American history emerged that rejected the progressive claim that history was a product of competition between contending forces; instead, whether or not they were pleased with their findings, leading historians argued that consensus characterized American history. Americans shared a broad faith in private property, capitalism, a Creator, and nonideological politics; even the Civil War was interpreted as consensus politics, since both sides fought over their interpretation of an equally venerated document, the Constitution. In the 1960s, a period of social and political activism that witnessed a huge expansion of higher education and the size of the historical profession, these writers were criticized as defenders of the status quo and conservative politics. A new generation of scholars revived some of the key progressive assumptions about the purposes of history. Social history, which would flourish until the last decade of the century, would briefly restore, especially among economic historians and historical demographers, some hope for a scientific history. With the rise of postmodernist critiques, however, assaults on objectivity, drawing frequently upon Thomas S. Kuhn's influential book, *The Structure of Scientific Revolutions* (1962), intensified.[35]

The widening of the scope of historical studies in the 1960s was remarkable. While enrollments in history courses and the humanities generally declined, a new cohort of historians realized some of the old dreams of Robinson's "new history." Many scholars wrote very conventional narratives on war, politics, and foreign policy, but the range of historical study expanded. It is difficult to generalize confidently about the work of thousands of scholars, but a few trends were clear. A number of historians resurrected a Beardian approach to history, seeing conflict as central to historical analysis and history as a guide for social action—understandable in the age of the civil rights movement, the antiwar movement, and then the women's movement, gay and lesbian movements, and so forth. Beard had rejected Marx, whose popularity increased among many radical scholars; and women, African Americans, native Americans, and others pressed for entry into the profession through admission to graduate school and often researched and wrote about their own groups, hitherto ignored in mainstream scholarship. Writing history from the bottom up, to use the popular phrase of the times, was easier said than done, but more and more social histories attempted to present the world through the eyes of workers, women's activists, slaves, immigrants, children, and other marginalized groups. With old roots in European and American scholarship, social history flourished as never before in the 1960s and 1970s.[36]

Never a monolithic enterprise, social history became an important part of American historical scholarship, embracing a variety of subjects and critical perspectives on the nation's past. Some scholars took their cues from the contemporary civil rights movement, trying to write a "usable" past, such as reconstructing the origins of nineteenth-century feminism, abolitionism, or the ongoing struggles of Indians or immigrants. More historians than before drew upon the social sciences to recast their understanding of the past. Most notably, cliometricians transformed economic history, offering a more "scientific" approach through the use of sophisticated quantitative methods and theoretical models. Even social historians, however, largely proved the rule that most historians are fairly unsophisticated in matters of theory and method. As Paul Conkin and Roland

Stromberg noted in *The Heritage and Challenge of History* (1971), historical scholarship has been "influenced more by the events of this century than by philosophical ideas or other intellectual formulations. . . . Left to their own devices, historians are seldom very theoretical or philosophical." A number of historians did draw upon more theories, models, and examples from other disciplines, especially in the years after this book appeared. At the same time, many historians remained suspicious of theory, certain of its limitations and lukewarm about dissolving the lines separating established disciplines. Since at least the time of Aristotle, and especially since the formative years of the profession in the nineteenth century, historians had regarded their labors as distinct from poetry, literature, theology, and philosophy. To this day, they have sometimes utilized theories and models after they have been discredited, even abandoned, by their discipline of origin.[37]

Histories of Western thought commonly note that Americans are averse to metaphysics and prefer the practical over the cerebral. So it is not surprising that the two most prominent books that debated the nature of history in the 1960s were by two scholars in England: Edward Hallett Carr and Geoffrey Elton. In *What is History?* (1961), Carr articulated well the relativist arguments that had matured on both sides of the Atlantic since the turn of the century. While Carr later maintained that objectivity of a sort was possible, he ridiculed the proposition in his primer on historical scholarship. "The historian is necessarily selective," said Carr, sounding much like Becker and Beard decades earlier. But most historians, he affirmed, still believed in the existence of "a hard core of historical facts existing objectively and independently of the interpretation of the historian . . . a preposterous fallacy, but one which is very hard to eradicate." Somewhat inconsistently, Carr both criticized those who thought all views of history were equally valid and then affirmed that historians followed some procedures akin to the scientist. But overall, *What is History?* presented the relativist claims for a new generation of historians coming of age in the 1960s.[38]

In a well-known response to Carr in *The Practice of History* (1967), Elton defended the unfashionable belief that historians could write about the past objectively. Acknowledging the impossibility of knowing the past or the truth completely, given the paucity of extant sources and limitations of the human mind, he believed that historians nevertheless substantially agreed about many significant facts and events. That historians admittedly chose certain facts over others in their writing did not dim Elton's faith in objectivity, since the process, he said, was not random but followed well-known rules: "The historian's method does not give him the powers of a god but it reduces the effects of human frailty and creates a formidable foundation of certainty beneath the errors and disputes which will never cease." According to him, knowing the sources well and critically appraising them "are the basic requirements of a reliable historiography."[39]

Looking back at this once-prominent debate on objectivity, postmodern critics of the late twentieth century only saw misguided scholars unable to see that history was a highly relativistic, nonscientific enterprise. By the 1960s and 1970s, developments in linguistics, literary theory, psychology, and anthropology helped alter the focus of the standard historical discussion. Postmodernists questioned a key assumption about history: that it was distinct from literature, as fact was from fiction, and truth from falsehood or myth. Writing from many different angles of vision, disciplinary perspectives, levels of self-criticism, and depth of charity toward others, critics helped reinvigorate scholarly debate about the meaning and character of history. The most bombastic claims to revelation by some postmodernists—who sometimes, ironically, defended relativism as an absolute—annoyed some historians and sometimes touched a tender nerve. But most historians were familiar with older disputes about relativism and, in a basic way, agreed upon the epistemological tenets of their discipline. Many simply ignored the theoretical debates about what discourse analysis, deconstruction, or literary criticism might mean for the profession.

It is difficult to say how many historians regarded themselves as "postmodern." And there is no simple way to trace postmodern influence, since it was never a single, coherent movement. At the same time, many of its adherents shared some broadly articulated norms and perspectives. Postmodern writers typically questioned Enlightenment faith in progress, science, and reason and pointed to the many horrors of twentieth-century life, from everyday institutions such as schools and mental hospitals that stripped people of their freedom to wars that used science and technology as instruments of death. Postmodern writers were often critical of many things—racism, war, colonialism, oppressive family arrangements—more confidently saying what they were against than coherently saying what they were for. Their prose was often turgid. Moreover, to their embarrassment, some postmodern scholars unknowingly embraced intellectuals or academics later exposed as Nazis or Nazi sympathizers; much less controversially, postmodern critics of conventional norms of historical practice were attracted to a range of literary critics, philosophers such as Michel Foucault, cultural anthropologists such as Clifford Geertz, and the literary scholar Hayden White.[40]

Called the "patron saint" of postmodernist historians by some and "the daddy" of the movement by Geoffrey Elton, White helped introduce the "linguistic turn" to the historical community and helped popularize a postmodern approach to the past. White's *Metahistory*, published in 1973 when scholarship in social history was in high gear, tapped the insights of literary theory in a study of European historical thought in the nineteenth century. During that century, historical writing that was largely produced by amateurs without professional training reached an expanding market of readers, as literacy and print culture grew in tandem. By the late twentieth century, however, White believed that historians lived in a "state of conceptual anarchy," since they still embraced outdated notions of science and art drawn from the last century. Having severed their ties with literature, they had also lost their ability to communicate with a wide audience. White noted that history was inevitably a literary subject and that historians often employed familiar tropes, such as the rise and fall of a particular movement, in their representation of the past. They framed stories that resembled the structure of novels yet stubbornly denied that the line between fact and fiction was imaginary. White urged historians to reconnect history with literature, recognize the fictional elements of much that passed for history, learn more about theory, epistemology, and the innovative methods of other disciplines, and realize there was no such thing as truth.[41]

According to White, there were multiple readings of all events, and, as Nietzsche wrote, only multiple truths. The distance and the discontinuities now separating our world and the past meant that historians had a special obligation to help people understand the here-and-now through a broadened perspective. To study the past for its own sake, White warned in 1978, would ensure history's irrelevance, as its declining course enrollments portended. "In the world in which we daily live," wrote White in *Tropics of Discourse*, "anyone who studies the past as an end in itself must appear to be either an antiquarian, fleeing from the problems of the present into a purely personal past, or a kind of cultural necrophile, that is, one who finds in the dead and dying a value he can never find in the living."[42]

Various social historians in the 1960s and 1970s with little interest in postmodernism unintentionally contributed to this general indictment of historical scholarship. Many of their histories, after all, examined outcast groups in local settings; insisting that history must be "multivocal" and "decentered" became a cliché in postmodern theory. Social historians studied oppressed and marginalized groups as well as identity politics; a preoccupation with history's "victims" also became an enduring theme among postmodernists and modernists alike. By focusing on the histories of previously ignored or victimized groups, Western imperialism, and related subjects, many historians with conventional views about the writing of history thus contributed to the emerging postmodern turn. Most professional historians, as conservative scholars complained, were liberals and relativists anyway, and social historians routinely described the past as contested terrain, a site of diverse perspectives, and serviceable to contemporary political causes. Few historians in the 1960s and 1970s believed they could write a grand narrative of the past once all the facts were in; quantitative history, home to some sophisticated theorists and social scientists, was briefly fashionable but soon lived on the periphery.[43]

In the 1990s, various postmodernists continued to hammer away at traditional assumptions underlying the historian's craft. They drew upon a host of theories and disciplines—from linguistics to literary theory, anthropology to psychology—in an overall critique of historical thinking. Nearly all writers pointed to the impossibility of discovering anything resembling historical truth through objective methods. Oddly enough, many critics seemed unaware of the inroads already made by historical relativism since the 1930s. But the notion that historians needed conversion to new ways of looking at their discipline grew popular. According to Keith Jenkins in *Re-Thinking History* (1991), history was not about truth but was a "discourse," indeed "a shifting discourse constructed by historians," whose writings are imprisoned in a specific time, context, and ideological framework. "History is a discourse, a language game," in which claims about the superiority of one historical interpretation over another reflected the power of those dominating the debate. Arising out of the Enlightenment, modern historical scholarship artificially separated fact and fiction, literature and history, and knower and known. Historians forgot that their profession was itself a historical creation and as practiced had become an anachronistic discourse.[44]

In a later volume, Jenkins reiterated and augmented these criticisms on history's nature and purpose in postmodern life. Erasing the overt differences Carr and Elton saw between themselves, he labeled them out-of-date modernists and uncritically embraced postmodern writers such as Hayden White. According to Jenkins, historians had to stop worrying about the proper interpretation of the past and simply choose whatever postmodern discourses seemed suitable, whatever "readings, positionings, perspectives, constructions" were personally fulfilling or appropriate. Modernism was dead, so historians, as White claimed, should realize they could only offer "interpretive emplotments," literary and poetic constructions of the past, possible only by eliminating opposing constructs such as fact and fiction. Language could not capture reality (which is never independent of the observer anyway); facts are selected to fit current needs and the disposition of the author; and since facts can never be fully or adequately known, history remains but a shifting discourse. Firm definitions of history were impossible in the unstable sands of postmodernity, but Jenkins nonetheless concluded that history "is arguably a verbal artifact, a narrative prose discourse of which, après White, the content is as much invented as found, and which is constructed by present-minded, ideologically positioned workers (historians and those acting as if they were historians) operating at various levels of reflexivity, such a discourse, to appear relatively plausible, looking simultaneously towards the once real events and situations of the past and towards the narrative type 'mythoi' common—albeit it on a dominant-marginal spectrum—in any given social formation." Only through "ideological positionings, tropes, emplotments, argumentative modes" could the past be conceived and written by historians, who could not escape the prejudices of their times and their own world views.[45]

How have historians reacted to such criticisms? In defense of postmodern criticisms of "the traditional historian" in 1996, Beverley Southgate believed that historians simply had trouble accepting the notion that their histories lacked any objective validity. Numerous psychologists, linguists, and literary theorists had demonstrated that objectivity was an illusion, that what we see, the words we use, and the plots we concoct are partial and never true or accurate by some absolute measure. But "the instinct of historians has often been to close ranks and defend their old territory." Some pro-Tory historians including Geoffrey Elton did indeed offer intemperate replies to the "theory mongers," relativists, and nihilists. Annoyed by the postmodern stereotypes of historians as "positivitistic troglodytes," the English historian Lawrence Stone accepted the benefits of the linguistic turn and other insights from various fields but similarly objected "to the work of historians bedazzled by the lures of 'discourse'" that assumed an "autonomy" and became "a historical factor in its own right." Stone also denied that facts and fiction were identical and that "there is no reality out there which is anything but a subjective creation of the historian" conjured up by language. This defense of traditional views (by a scholar who had notably drawn upon the social sciences in his own scholarship) was precisely what postmodernists would have predicted.[46]

Not surprisingly, the wholesale assault on familiar professional norms in the study of history generated some heated debates on different aspects of the postmodern critique. Historians have long warned about the evils of presentism, anachronism, and an overreliance on theories and models drawn from other disciplines. That has not stopped many of them, however, from borrowing concepts and methods from another's workshop if they seemed helpful in improving their craft. Most historians are relativists, understanding that each generation asks its own pressing questions about the past, just as postmodernists are doing, and that the methods employed, words used, and questions asked are divined by humans, not gods, and thus fallible. But the prevailing norms of professional scholarship and foundational ideas of the craft seem remarkably secure: that the past is different from the present; that even imperfectly understood knowledge is better than the alternative in understanding the past and helping guide us to the future; that truth and falsehood can be discerned; that language despite its limitations can fairly well describe a reality that is independent of the observer; and that there remains a distinction, as Aristotle claimed, between the purely imaginative and poetic (of what might happen) and the historically specific (what has happened). Bernard Bailyn reminds historians that one can refute a historical fact but not a novel.[47]

The postmodern challenge has been prominent enough to capture the attention of historians, though scholars such as Ernest Breisach note that the harvest of major postmodern histories has been remarkably thin compared with the shelves of books on theory. Nonetheless, postmodern criticisms of convention have undoubtedly encouraged some historians to reflect on the nature of historical writing, if only to affirm some commonly accepted beliefs. For example, in *Telling the Truth About History* (1994), Joyce Appleby, Lynn Hunt, and Margaret Jacob applauded the new ways of seeing, the new subject matter, the new approaches to historical understanding that have arisen thanks to the rise of social history and to the recent wave of critics. Subjects that were marginal before the 1960s such as women's history, ethnic history, and African American history have been raised to new importance, as a new generation dedicated to civil rights entered graduate schools and joined the profession. Like many historians, however, the authors criticized those who condemn the Enlightenment for its absolute faith in science, rationality, and progress on one hand but who, on the other, seem oblivious to the absolutism of "subjectivity and relativism." While there will always be a plurality of interpretations about the past and differing perspectives (hardly an original insight to historians), relativism can easily slip into nihilism and affirm the views of those who suggest, for example, that the Holocaust never occurred. Despite our imperfect ways of thinking, understanding, and expressing ourselves through language, many truthful facts may actually exist in the world, from the process of evolution to learning to read and write to the reality of death camps. The inability to know the whole truth about anything hardly precludes historians from saying "meaningfully true things about the world." Just because humans write narratives "does not make them equally fictitious or mythical." One strives for accuracy, for the highest degree of objectivity and truth possible.[48]

At the dawn of the twenty-first century, we stand too close to the scene to have any perspective on the ultimate contributions, for good or ill, of postmodernism to the theory and practice of history. As a result of new insights drawn from different theories, methods, and disciplines, history will remain subject to intense debates and criticisms as long as there are historians and readers of their work. Herodotus and Thucydides helped lay the classical foundations of historical scholarship in the Western world, and critics in their day and in the generations to come sometimes applauded their efforts while simultaneously doubting their reliability. History cannot be written once and for all for the ages, yet it remains the most important path to collective memory for each generation. Through the centuries historians have engaged in numerous debates about the purposes and uses of history, whether previous writers had gotten the story or truths of the past right, and whether new questions about the past would enable humanity to cope with the here-and-now and to help guide it to the future.

Modernists and postmodernists, for all their differences, agree that history has always been subject to reinterpretation and has always served many masters. History has been written to justify the worst offenses of church and state in the Euro-American past and to fulfill the highest humanistic aspirations, even when writers could not agree upon the precise nature of the craft, the ability of its practitioners to discern the past accurately, or its capacity to teach moral lessons. As Cicero wrote centuries ago, those who write history seem intuitively to understand that ignorance of the past is disabling. Its utility ranges from a politician trying to seal an argument to those who simply find pleasure in hearing about and remembering the events of the past. From antiquity to the postmodern present, the historian "bears witness to the passing of the ages, sheds light upon reality, gives life to recollection and guidance to human existence, and brings tidings of ancient days."[49]

The past has always held multiple claims upon the historian. *History, Education, and the Schools* tries to understand the past on its own terms while providing perspective on contemporary issues and public policies. Policy makers, taxpayers, and scholars alike wonder whether we learn much from the past. At a time when access to quality schools matters more than ever before for adult success, why has educational research often seemed trivial and without merit? At a time when politicians and citizens routinely condemn public schools in general and urban schools in particular, and when private schools are often held in higher esteem, can the historian help illuminate present concerns with light from the past? Does knowledge of American history help explain why Americans continually seek to reform the schools–over and over again? What historians want to know about the past remains very much tied to questions that matter today.

# Chapter 2

# What History Teaches about the Impact of Educational Research on Practice

Since antiquity, history has served a variety of human needs. At different times and places, written history has promised to teach moral lessons, guide political decision making, honor a heavenly Creator, and buttress the claims of church and state, or simply record memories of times past. These multiple uses of history remain evident today. Histories are often on the bestseller lists, especially biographies of the Founding Fathers. Interest in Benjamin Franklin, Thomas Jefferson, and a range of presidents seems undiminished. Bookstores at the mall stock shelves of volumes on the Civil War, World War II, and military history. Millions of Americans visit historical sites and museums and many participate in Civil War battle reenactments, and they also watch the History Channel (more wars and battles, mostly) and the "American Experience" series on the Public Broadcasting System. The crotchety Henry Ford told a newspaper reporter in 1916 that history "means nothing to me." "History is more or less bunk." Yet the popular Henry Ford Museum and Greenfield Village, which opened in the 1930s, became a testimony to his growing interest in the past. In its diverse forms, history has not lost its appeal.[1]

Historians are paid to keep their eyes on the past, not on the present, and their works are obviously written and read for a variety of reasons. This chapter tries to answer a simple historical question: over the course of the twentieth century, has research made any difference in shaping everyday policy and practice in the public schools? The question is easier to ask than to answer. Whether reading the daily press or interacting with their peers, professors of education commonly hear that the connection between education-related research and school improvement is ambiguous, elusive, perhaps nonexistent. As a contributor to the *Journal of Negro Education* claimed in 1976, "it should come as no surprise to anyone familiar with the subject, that the history of research in education is replete with dismal instances of irrelevance and confusion." Twenty years later, sociologist Maureen T. Hallinan aptly wrote that "researchers claim that the findings of their studies are ignored or misinterpreted by school personnel, while educators argue that much research is incomprehensible or irrelevant to their concerns." All of this echoed the sentiments of the superintendent of public schools in Baltimore, Maryland, a century earlier. "Educational literature," he believed, "is distasteful to the great majority even of enlightened mankind, and recommendations embodied in a report are apt to be regarded as perfunctory exercises, rarely read and still more rarely remembered."[2]

Critics within and outside the academy often heap scorn on "education" research, yet precisely how research and practice are intertwined is itself a fascinating subject that history might illuminate. To understand better the interrelationship between educational research and school practice, this chapter pursues the following strategy. First it explores some of the best attempts within the educational research community before the 1950s to take stock of its own history. Most of these scholars were not trained as historians, but they had a keen interest in the evolution of their profession. History became for them a way to legitimate their place in the academy and world of scholarship and educational leadership within a suspect profession. Then the chapter examines some of the works of historical scholarship published since the early 1970s that helps improve our understanding of the research-practice conundrum, and how factors other than research—such as ideology and politics—may have been more influential in shaping educational policymaking. The extant literature by historians is not vast, but it reveals the practical and methodological problems involved in addressing a simple question: how has research shaped educational practice?

Any historical study of the link between educational research and practice must begin by exploring the early decades of the twentieth century. During the Progressive Era (ca. 1890–1920) the field of education, like other emerging areas of academic study, sought professional status and a secure home in the emerging research university. Education was swept along by new intellectual currents that elevated the authority of experts above amateurs by promoting the spread of "scientific" research methods. Symbolized best by the survey method and expressed most visibly in the widening use of intelligence and achievement tests in the public schools, scientific approaches quickly dominated education research. Academics within newly formed departments or schools of education in the expanding university system and experts laboring in various educational research bureaus struggled to give their work legitimacy. They sought a "one best way" to study the manifold problems of teaching and learning and to undermine the appeal of alternative approaches. The lure of "science" was powerful in American intellectual circles and its hegemony within graduate studies in education on many university campuses was largely unchallenged until the final decades of the twentieth century.[3]

The intrepid historian can find in the stacks of many university libraries articles and books that appeared in the early decades of the twentieth century that studied the nature of educational research, including its origins, contours, and connections to public school practices. Nearly all of these scholarly works underscored the powerful influence that psychology (rather than philosophy, history, or other disciplines) had in shaping the dominant norms of "educational science," the foundations of educational research. They reflected well the spirit of the times. As many historians have noted, the Progressive Era was the great age of scientific management in business as well as in the schools, and most early chroniclers of the evolution of education research applauded these developments. As corporations supplanted small businesses to become the heart of a growing industrial economy, schools became increasingly consolidated, standardized, and removed from lay control. This was well symbolized through numerous interlocking changes: the elimination of ward representation on city school boards, the prominence of the social elite (especially leading business people and various professionals) on newly centralized boards, and the rising power of expertise within the schools, epitomized by superintendents who preached the gospel of social and business efficiency. Most apparent at first in northern cities where industry was concentrated, these consolidating trends shaped the new bureaucratic and professional infrastructure of schooling that became common everywhere. The spread of towns and cities allowed new ways of organizing and administering the public school system—models that ultimately spread to the countryside as rural schools consolidated.[4]

Research proliferated on every conceivable aspect of education and schooling after 1900, so one can only describe and assess a fraction of this literature. There were innumerable studies of school finance, building construction, teacher pay, school board organization and administration, school tests, and other aspects of formal education.

Many research studies supported a host of new policy ideas—such as how to fund schools better or more equitably, or how to improve the teaching of particular subjects—yet often failed to explain how these ideas would be implemented. Researchers commonly used the survey as a tool to measure change within the schools with scientific objectivity to help lift educational study from its amateur status and contribute to social reform and educational improvement. Surveys were empirical investigations of various aspects of school practices. Books, journal articles, and conference reports to varying degrees addressed the question of how research influenced practice.[5]

An essay published in 1945 by J. Cayce Morrison provides a useful starting point to understand the early assessment of the linkages between research and practice in the history of American education. Morrison was the Assistant Commissioner for Research for the State Education Department in New York, and he addressed the major concerns of prominent researchers before mid-century. The essay appeared in the yearbook of the National Society for the Study of Education, a prestigious publication from the University of Chicago that disseminated scholarly research in the fledgling world of professional education. Written in the waning years of the New Deal when discussions of "planning" were still in the air, Morrison's essay tried to reconstruct the history of educational research and to account for its enormous expansion in mid-twentieth century. Morrison did not doubt that research had a direct tie to practice, but he ultimately concluded that much of it was useless. "Education for the years ahead must be characterized by more rigorous thinking, bold experimentation, and scientific appraisal," Morrison claimed on the opening page of his essay. "A résumé of the problems confronting education is appropriate to a consideration of the role research will play in the impending reconstruction of education."[6]

Since the early twentieth century, educators such as Morrison had believed that "research is basic to the formulation of educational policy." Equally without question, research studies in education had exploded as "scientific" methods gained popularity in many academic fields. In the nineteenth century, the study of education was the province of amateurs and those without graduate training (just being conceived and institutionalized late in the century). By the 1920s, however, research occurred at multiple sites: in research bureaus within urban school systems, in special divisions within state departments of public instruction, and at many universities, especially at leading private schools such as Teachers College, Columbia University, and at the larger state institutions. Specialized periodicals that explored virtually all educational phenomena including research abounded on the local, state, and national level. *The Review of Educational Research,* a publication of the American Educational Research Association (AERA), first appeared in 1931 and reflected this great passion for inquiry. Morrison was then a member of the executive committee of AERA, so he had an insider's view of the history he at that time chronicled. "A single issue of the *Review*," he noted, "usually lists from five hundred to a thousand separate researches. The great majority of these have appeared in print in magazine articles, doctor's dissertations, official bulletins and reports, chapters or contributions to yearbooks, and other professional publications."[7]

Even if quantity was not synonymous with quality, Morrison emphasized that scientific ideals had clearly advanced educational inquiry. By the early twentieth century, educational study boomed, inspired by the pioneering work of Joseph Mayer Rice, a pediatrician-turned-muckraker who called for more scientific studies of education, and especially by Edward L. Thorndike, the rising academic star at Teachers College, Columbia University, who helped make psychology the most important tool in empirical and scientific research. Along with other university-based researchers, Thorndike and his followers had popularized the use of statistics and social science models, promoting countless studies of school achievement, failure rates, dropouts, and other investigations amenable to scientific analysis. European developments in research also had left their mark on American academics. American educators and social scientists adapted Alfred Binet's work with exceptional children in France and pioneered the development of group intelligence tests and an array of achievement tests. Science seemed to offer the best way to understand the complexities of teaching and learning and to provide the guidance to manage and improve schools. Objective, empirical inquiry would replace guesswork and subjective methods. By the 1920s, testing, the best-studied scientific innovation, exemplified the presumably strong ties between research and practice.[8]

The application of social science and quantitative methods to the study of society and social institutions grew ever more popular in the late nineteenth century. College-educated settlement house residents in England, and then in America, used surveys to gather facts in studies that investigated poverty and the impact of urbanization and industrialization on immigrants, sanitation, children's health, and other social conditions. Those conducting the research were frequently not dispassionate, but often linked their research to larger goals of social reform and social uplift of the poor. In 1910, the first school survey (in Boise, Idaho) heralded a movement that would sweep across the educational landscape, exemplifying the powerful hold of science on leading educators during the Progressive Era. By the 1920s, surveys numbered in the thousands and were common not just in schools, but in industry also. Individual educators, state bureaucrats, and especially small teams of researchers under the guidance of education professors conducted these surveys that local school boards, superintendents, or civic groups initiated to study the local scene and make recommendations for improvement, including the addition of more resources for special education and vocational training. Research also proliferated, thanks to the establishment of research bureaus, in larger urban school districts and in many state departments of public instruction, even though they were often poorly funded and staffed. Again, education research leaped forward, inspired by a sometimes utopian faith in applying science to age-old pedagogical problems. There was no doubting the excitement and hopefulness of reformers, social scientists, and educators during these years. The survey of the Cleveland schools during World War I was massive, numbering well over a dozen volumes; its size was unusual, but not its presentation of statistical data in ubiquitous charts and graphs, facts and figures, to help guide the policymaker.[9]

Like many earlier studies, Morrison's otherwise useful historical survey of the rise of "scientific" educational research was vague on how research influenced practice. Following in the footsteps of Thorndike, he seemed convinced that scholars had transformed contemporary understanding of "individual differences among children," and the success of the testing movement suggested to him that research in other areas had also decisively shaped practice. Numerous studies of pupil retention and failure seemed to verify that children's individual differences (often attributed to family background and other factors) were much wider than previously assumed. As a result, Morrison accurately noted that "a period of intensive study and experimentation with the curriculum" thus emerged between 1920 and 1940. "Marked progress," he claimed, "was made in adapting the content and method of instruction to the abilities and needs of individuals; and in making the processes of education harmonize with the purposes of democracy." He lacked evidence, however, to prove that the ties between research and practice were cause-and-effect; in fact, he often undercut his own argument by complaining that education research before 1925 was often "superficial and futile." Even the long lists of publications in *The Review of Educational Research*, he admitted, disguised the reality that most scholarship examined "the minutiae of educational problems. Much of it is little more than descriptive recording of status or progress—not infrequently indifferent description. Some of it is little more than superficial analysis of trends of opinion, attitude, or practice. Some of it advances scarcely beyond the counting stage. This is too wide a gap between research at its best and much of its practice in education."[10]

Morrison reminded his readers that education, unlike industry, had few full-time researchers. Even at prestigious "research universities," faculty typically engaged in educational investigation on the side. They frequently had demanding teaching loads and other professional obligations and they depended on outside contracts to conduct surveys of local schools. Here and there, at Iowa's Child Welfare Research Station or in various projects at Teachers College, for example, admirable work was being done. But too often education research was fragmentary and ill conceived, badly executed, and poorly written. Most researchers worked not like the teams found in an industrial laboratory but alone; few could hope to replicate their studies in different settings. No classroom was exactly like another, and education research was very limited in its influence. Morrison understood well these impediments to quality within the "research community." In research bureaus in small cities, for example, the staff typically consisted of "one professional worker, sometimes with one professional assistant, a stenographer and one or more clerks. Frequently the research function is combined with some other such as statistics, instruction, curriculum, or guidance." Like their counterparts at the universities where they had trained, educational researchers completed numerous empirical studies despite these handicaps. Morrison concluded by invoking the professional's ritualistic plea for more money for more research.[11]

Morrison's often insightful analysis is illustrative of the best studies on research completed by education scholars before the 1950s. The author was not trained as a historian, but he was curious about the dramatic rise of educational science, especially the obvious impact that psychology in particular and social science in general had had on research. He was also convinced that more research monies, more applications of the scientific method (usually deemed synonymous with quantitative methods), and more scholars engaged in study would lead to the reconstruction of education and school improvement. Yet Morrison openly said that most research was weak and ineffectual. So while scientific testing, as one example, seemed influential in terms of practice, the precise ways in which research overall shaped practice were largely undocumented and remained a matter of conjecture.

To understand Morrison in his historical context, one must recall the low status accorded to education research at most universities in his day. Morrison liberally quoted Abraham Flexner from his well-known book, *Universities*, published in 1930. Flexner had helped popularize changes in modern medical education earlier in the century and was horrified at what passed for educational and social science research. The American university, he believed, was in a state of decline, thanks to the hiring of weak academics such as educationists and sociologists. Education research usually was little more than the mere gathering of information, using (and misusing) limited research tools such as questionnaires and surveys, and then equating the process with scientific study. Much education writing, he argued, was jargon-laden and littered with meaningless graphs and curves, percentages, and standard deviations, which masked the lack of knowledge or scientific method underlying the enterprise. "A very large part of the literature now emanating from departments of sociology, departments of education, social science committees, and educational commissions is absolutely without significance and without inspirational value," Flexner concluded. "It is mainly superficial; its subjects are trivial; as a rule nothing is added to the results reached by the rule of thumb or the conclusions which would be reached by ordinary common sense."[12]

Morrison basically agreed with Flexner. As an administrator of research within a state department of education, however, he believed that a better day would dawn. Cognizant of the weakness of educational research and vague about its actual influence upon practice, Morrison stood in a long and crowded line of educators who believed that the scientific study of education would ultimately prove a boon to the nation and its schools. Since the 1920s, nearly every prominent publication on educational research underscored the power of "science" in inquiry and the impact of school surveys and psychological testing in advancing scientific practices and efficiency in the schools. Like Morrison, writing near mid-century, scholars since the early 1900s usually had an uncritical faith in a fact-oriented science that would yield authoritative, objective knowledge, the key to social progress. Despite a spirited reaction in the 1920s by some scholars and public intellectuals against the misuses of intelligence testing and blind faith in science, many people nevertheless expected empirical studies to result in real reforms. A minority of education researchers dissented from this reduction of science to empiricism, and some scholars continued to draw upon other disciplines, such as history and philosophy, in their study of education and schooling. But the authority of Thorndike and his circle of scholars and students remained powerful. Recall that during the same period Carl Becker and Charles Beard also criticized "scientific methods" and the notion of objectivity, but it took decades for such iconoclasm to gain more ground either in historical or educational research.[13]

Creating a coherent narrative about its past was essential to the formation of a professional community of scholars. Every field of study coming of age in the Progressive Era competed for influence on the university campus. "Innumerable local intrigues and budgetary battles," writes historian Thomas L. Haskell, "had to be waged on campuses across the country to reshape teaching institutions to the specialized, research-oriented needs of the new disciplines." Each discipline sought legitimacy, and the scientific basis for educational improvement and management was a powerful congealing element in the low-status professions. Professionalizing fields of study such as history, itself divided over whether it was a humanistic or social science discipline, also embraced scientific norms in their quest for authority. At stake was who would have power over professional development, amateurs or experts, and what procedures, methods, and philosophies would guide legitimate research.[14]

Morrison built upon the scholarship of prominent educationists who helped give his profession an identity and a sense of its history. In 1929, Hollis Leland Caswell published one of the best appraisals of the evolution of school surveys, and it typically offered a positive image of science. A graduate of Teachers College, Columbia, Caswell understood that the educational researcher's fascination with science reflected wider trends. A report from the Russell Sage Foundation showed that nearly three thousand surveys were already in print, sponsored not only by school systems, but also by foundations, corporations, and private benefactors. The rising popularity of school surveys, Caswell said, reflected the "scientific spirit" that guided scholarship and advanced the search for "objective" truth and reliable knowledge. "Essentially the survey method is a part of the movement which is basing human thought and conduct on facts objectively measured, rather than on the assertion of authority." Whether through surveys of religion, business, schools, or municipal government, "the demand has been for facts." Facts paved the way to social improvement, and educators understandably wanted to forge the "connecting link between research and action."[15]

Caswell believed that surveys could not only be guides to action, but they also exemplified social changes that were transforming urban schools in particular. Surveys helped strengthen the status of superintendents, whose power depended upon the expansion of bureaucracies knit together by hierarchical chains of professional authority. Rule-of-thumb methods of assessing children's academic achievements, for example, gave way to a barrage of specialized tests, measurements, and instruments, as science revealed itself in educational jargon and mysterious new tools of evaluation. However bewildering to ordinary people, the Ayres's spelling scale, the Hillegas composition scale, the Courtis arithmetic scale, and the Thorndike handwriting scale became part of the modern educator's stock-in-trade and signs of educational progress. Business and professional leaders on school boards realized that ideals of scientific management were reshaping aspects of industrial life, and educational leaders similarly argued that they, too, would reshape the schools and make them more efficient and effective. Researchers had invented a brave new world of questionnaires, IQ and achievement tests, records and files, and statistical measures that reduced teaching and learning to more precise numbers, percentages, and marks. Caswell knew that this professional apparatus, promoted in the name of better schools for America's children, empowered the experts and administrators receiving graduate degrees in education. Surveys, he also realized, were fads, and their proponents sometimes exaggerated their value. As historian David B. Tyack has documented, often the research merely confirmed what sponsors of the research already wanted such as larger schools, more vocational programs, and more special education classes. But their promotion of research was vital, helping a lowly profession such as education acquire more professional legitimacy.[16]

Throughout the interwar period, educators such as Caswell who studied the foundations of educational science assumed that research inexorably led, or should lead, to improved policies and practices in the schools. They knew that much of the research lacked scientific validity, was poorly designed, and was rarely replicated even when it met basic standards of quality. The status of teachers, and teachers of teachers, was low, and knowledge in America was mostly prized if it had practical applications. What was more practical than science? Not surprisingly, graduate education departments and schools of education, struggling for survival and respect in the familiar status wars of academe, embraced a narrow empiricism. Behaviorism had more cachet among grant officers at the philanthropic foundations than philosophical musings over the meaning of education. Embracing "scientific" methods never convinced other academics of their worth, but the choices open to educational researchers seemed limited, given the context and institutional cultures in which they labored.[17]

**Figure 2.1**  Dressed in Their Sunday Best: An Ungraded School, ca. 1895
Courtesy: Herbert M. Kliebard

**Figure 2.2**  One Size Fits All: An Age-Graded Classroom on Patron's Day, Steelton, Pennsylvania, ca.1905 (From Author's Collection)

Charles H. Judd, one of Caswell's contemporaries and chair of the education department once led by John Dewey, fought an uphill battle to raise its profile at the University of Chicago. As part of that effort, Judd, who had early on championed school surveys and scientific methods among administrators, called for even broader applications of social science to enhance the quality and usefulness of educational research. Like Caswell, he too published a thoughtful analysis of the survey movement, the dominant interest of early chroniclers of educational research. His essay, which appeared in 1938, recounted how educational research before 1900 was primarily in the hands of amateurs such as Horace Mann and Henry Barnard. It was anachronistic to call these men researchers—both men were trained as lawyers and above all were publicists for public education—but Judd rightly pointed out that both had endorsed fact-finding studies of local schools. Mann, for example, lobbied for citywide tests in Boston in 1845 and published several articles on the results in the *Common School Journal*. As editor of the famed *American Journal of Education*, Barnard in turn printed innumerable empirical studies on educational developments. Like other reformers, both men also visited schools abroad and returned with glowing accounts of educational practices in Europe. Among other things they called for better professional training for teachers, enhanced state authority, and more child-centered instruction.[18]

Judd typically assumed that such lobbying had greatly influenced educational policy, but avoided explaining how this shaped practice. He also seemed unaware that elected officials at the time frequently attacked these men for trying to import foreign ideas into America. Mann and Barnard were Whigs, the party that favored the establishment of state boards of education and other centralizing reforms. Many Democrats, however, believed in limited government and doubted that Prussian models of centralized power had any place in a republic. Judd then proceeded to chronicle the ascendance of Joseph Mayer Rice, Edward L. Thorndike, and other prophets of educational science, emphasizing how faith in the "impartial judgment" of experts became commonplace in school policy in the early 1900s. A rising professionalism was becoming a familiar trope in the narrative of educational research. Surveys were assumed to have had substantial impact upon schools, but precisely how was left unexplored. Did surveys confirm what local reformers wanted to hear in the first place, before they invited the experts to town? Did "research" on local conditions really matter, and if it did, in what ways?[19]

Describing and assessing the effects of surveys was difficult, as Judd realized. After all, they existed in unbelievably large numbers. Who had ever read even a fair sampling of them? Like other scholars, Judd more effectively proved that research had exploded after 1900 than explained its effect on policymaking. Recall that by the 1930s, education research had already gained among liberal arts scholars as well as scientists a reputation for its low quality and doubtful utility; moreover, research had proliferated on so many different facets of schooling that evaluating its effects was no simple matter and rarely attempted.

In 1939, Douglas Scates, a prominent student of educational research, helped explain why evaluation of research was difficult, in an article in *The Review of Educational Research*. Scates observed that research in education was a diffuse enterprise. Since 1867, when it was formed "to collect information," the U.S. Office of Education had published reams of bulletins, articles, and facts and statistics on the schools. Various states had research bureaus of education, as did an expanding number of universities. Testing departments dedicated to vocational education and job counseling existed on many campuses and within larger school systems. Students wrote master's and dissertation theses on education, adding to the mounting pile of educational research. Quantitative studies too multiplied, thanks to the endless appeal of hard facts, and Scates affirmed that research was a bull market, whatever its meaning, value, or influence. "Research is larger than statistical work; it is something more than testing," he assured readers as he concluded his essay. "It is a continuous fact-finding, exploring, investigating service applicable to all aspects of education—administration, business management, finance, school building, transportation, curriculum, instruction, and psychological and sociological principles."[20]

Throughout the first half of the twentieth century, other education scholars interested in the history of their field routinely described the rising popularity and embrace of scientific norms, the gathering of facts, and the accumulation of empirical evidence. Books and articles, papers and invited addresses, documented the rise of an educational research community dedicated to discovering objective truths that would some day improve teaching and learning. Scholars explored the research activities, budgets, and mission of city research bureaus, state departments of public instruction, and philanthropic organizations as well as the work of university professors, professional organizations such as the National Education Association and Progressive Education Association, and the Social Science Research Council among the innumerable groups that sponsored research. The fascination with surveys did not abate. A detailed study of twelve city research bureaus in 1945 also typically concluded that research in general was a foundation for school improvement, which depended upon "objective inquiry." That same year, J. Cayce Morrison predicted that in "the future, education will be characterized by more rigorous thinking, bold experimentation, and scientific appraisal. To attain these characteristics, educational leadership will draw more and more on research."[21]

At mid-century, most educational research had much in common with social science research generally. As historian Maris A. Vinovskis has written, researchers "did not pursue large-scale, cumulative research and development projects." Research was traditionally both "fragmented and episodic," and "small case studies or occasional cross-sectional surveys" were common, unlike the larger research endeavors of later decades. A contemporary of Morrison's writing in the *Journal of Educational Sociology* in 1948 concluded that during its "fifty-year history" most educational research was limited to "quantification" and a "narrow utilitarianism. . . . Counting, measuring, correlating, and experimenting were regarded virtually as the essence of research procedure." While he lamented the appearance of "many small, inconclusive, oft-duplicated but non-definitive studies"— amounting to a high "pile of deadwood"—he and other scholars predicted a bright future for educational research.[22]

Without a doubt, education research proliferated with the expansion of higher education after World War II. School enrollments on all levels boomed and the number of published reports, bulletins, dissertations, and journal articles skyrocketed. In the 1950s and 1960s, the National Science Foundation sponsored major projects on curriculum and teaching in math, science, and the social studies, and the federal government funded research laboratories to promote better school practices. But was research overall useful or fundamental in shaping school practices? Since the 1970s, some historians of education in a broad way have helped answer that question. As educators even today, however, have considerable difficulty pinpointing the influence of research on contemporary schools, it is not surprising that historians faced some insurmountable problems when studying the issue. Histories are usually based on written records, but few of them provide direct evidence of how research shaped practice. As H. Stuart Hughes wrote over a generation ago of the general plight of historians, often there is "silence in the historical record. The result is a vast unevenness in what the historian has to work on, an *embarras de richesse* combined with and canceled out by the most distressing lacunae."[23]

Recent scholarship by several historians nevertheless offers welcome insights into the nature and import of research in the past, helping to fill important gaps in our knowledge. But there are still few book-length studies on educational research and practice similar to that of educational psychologist Robert M. W. Travers, whose history of the role of his field in the enterprise almost stands alone. Historians are increasingly interested, however, in the policy implications of their own scholarship and the conditions under which research and practice have become interconnected. Recurring efforts to reconstruct, for example, the history of teaching and classroom experiences—a daunting task, given the nature of the source materials—may shed a clearer light on the relationship between ideas and action, research and practice. But a comprehensive understanding of the subject seems unlikely to come anytime soon. Even the creation of a federal clearing house on "what works" in 2002 by the U.S. Department of Education cannot guarantee that scientifically verifiable methods and pedagogies will define future practice, or that changes in practice necessarily mean that research was the cause.[24]

It all looked simpler to the generation that helped found "educational science." In 1938, Charles H. Judd confidently predicted that the proliferation of surveys would provide later historians with a clearer sense of what really happened in the past. "The writers on the history of education," he opined, "heretofore found it necessary to depend on the writings of educational reformers and on scattered and meager data as the basis for their statements. In the future the survey reports will make possible a far more detailed treatment of school practices for this period than has ever been possible for any earlier period." Yet the reports did not speak for themselves any more than other sources on America's educational past. Much more is still known about what educational leaders said than about what teachers did, about proposals for change than about the daily realities of classrooms, about what research showed than about what actually characterized the lives of children and teachers.[25]

It is imperative to remember that, historically, educational research has not been exclusively focused on practice. Many scholars of education throughout the century studied, analyzed, and debated educational issues without making the ties between research and practice their principal concern; some also questioned the exaggerated faith in science and the testing mania in the schools. Moreover, ongoing debates about how to reconstruct the past accurately have followed the widespread abandonment of the notion of "objectivity" within the historical profession. Despite a plethora of primary sources in archives and on library shelves, historians have also dispensed with the notion that there is a science of history, that the facts speak for themselves, or that the facts speak unambiguously. Moreover, as Hughes reminded us, historians face a mountain of documents that are often mute on many issues of contemporary interest. In addition, some postmodern writers insist that historians are so enmeshed in their own language and literary conventions that their histories say more about their politics and discursive style than any supposed "past." Despite epistemological concerns, difficulties with sources, and changing philosophical viewpoints, many scholars nonetheless believe that they can legitimately reconstruct the past and that their work is not synonymous with fiction. And a number of them still try to make sense of the ties between research and practice despite the obstacles.[26]

Perhaps the most impressive article on research and practice during the past generation appeared in 1973 in the *Second Handbook of Research on Teaching*. However prosaic the title—"A History of the Impact of Research on Teaching"—its author, historian Geraldine Jonçich Clifford, provided readers with an impressive essay on a notoriously difficult subject. Clifford had already written the standard biography of Edward L. Thorndike, and her mastery of the history of his influence on educational science resonated throughout the essay. Moreover, she advanced ideas that had become more tenable by the 1960s, but would have been heretical for many education scholars earlier. To prove that research had a measurable effect on teaching, Clifford concluded, was "a near impossibility." In fact, educators seemed much better at blaming or praising a particular school practice than providing incontrovertible evidence about it. By the 1960s, educators increasingly doubted that the accumulation of research necessarily made a huge difference in school practice. Rumor, anecdote, and personal preferences had often informed educational thinking and substituted for analysis even when science was more in professional vogue. Clifford's essay, like Morrison's in 1945, is a useful point of illumination, showing how different generations of scholars envisioned the links between research and practice.[27]

As Clifford made clear, most historians who studied education traditionally wrote about the history of ideas, not school practices. America had the most decentralized system of mass education in the Western world, making research on teaching formidable. At the end of the 1930s, there were still nearly 120,000 school districts, some of which enrolled tens of thousands of pupils. Often operating on small budgets, scholars could not study many schools or individual classrooms, and they also had difficulty knowing which site was typical or which practice was informed by what specific piece (if any) of research. Did most teachers teach as they had once been taught? Did superintendents or teachers read much research, think about its implications, and try to act upon it? Clifford surveyed an incredible array of sources to show that, while previous generations of education researchers often assumed research influenced practice, this was nearly impossible to prove.

Much research was neither useful nor practical, which is something that could have been said, of course, about most disciplines or fields. But education was not a pure science but a profession, and what worked mattered most of all. Yet in reading, the most studied subject, the approximately 4,000 studies in existence in 1960 hardly confirmed which of the two leading instructional approaches—phonics-based or whole language—worked best. Did teachers and administrators hear what they wanted to believe when they read about a new "finding"? Did they use research in their work in the schools? Surveys in the 1960s showed that superintendents were not particularly aware of much research or its possible role in school improvement. Research studies were often fragmentary, limited in appeal, poorly written, and not regularly reported in teacher magazines that were not usually read by most practitioners anyway. Throughout the 1960s, "action research" was oriented toward the spread of democracy and progressive practices and was not necessarily research based, and ideology seemed to shape educational inquiry as much as anything else.[28]

Familiar problems bemoaned by an earlier generation of education scholars did not disappear after World War II. Few studies were replicated, and most researchers still labored part-time and often wrote an article or two and were never heard from again. Clifford cited William Brownell's study of arithmetic research in 1950, which "showed that 615 of 778 authors never reported more than one study, and only 53 persons reported more than three each." In 1968, AERA (American Educational Research Association, ostensibly a research group) discovered in a survey that most of its own members were not fully invested in research. In fact, the editor of *The Review of Educational Research*, echoing old complaints, said that 90 percent of what was published should have been rejected. Much so-called "research" was politically biased or rested upon opinion, supposition, or personal experience and was rarely replicable.[29]

Skepticism about the nature of education research remained powerful. In 1987, historian William R. Johnson, in an analysis of the Holmes and Carnegie reforms in teacher education, noted that education research had always had low status, widely viewed with suspicion, and mostly ignored or rejected by classroom teachers. He cited Benjamin Bloom's assertion in 1966 that, of the 70,000 studies reported in the *Educational Researcher* during the previous twenty-five years, only seventy had any real import. Which seventy would be a matter of debate, too, but the tsunami of research had not cleared away many basic controversies. Like Clifford, Johnson was critical of the familiar gap between researchers and practitioners, which an earlier generation more confidently had assumed would narrow as knowledge flowed from ivory towers downward to the schools.[30]

The distance separating research and practice also concerned leading education scholars who were not historians, as revealed in their contributions to the new edition of the *Encyclopedia of Educational Research*, an AERA publication, in 1992. Some simply stated that "research only intermittently had direct influence on policy" or that "research had little effect." Researchers moved in one direction, practitioners in another, and rarely did the two meet. Whatever the potential benefits of research for the practitioner, scholars wondered whether much "significant knowledge" existed "to transmit" to the policy maker. Studies of achievement testing found little "evidence that teachers find the information from current standardized tests particularly useful in guiding their instruction. . . . Teachers place greater reliance on their own assessments and informal observations than on information provided by standardized tests." Scholarship often came up dry on issues that raged in local school districts. Research on grade retention and social promotion, Nancy L. Karweit reported, was generally weak and "districts probably continue to retain primarily because teachers, principals, and parents believe it is in the best interests of the individual child," not because of scholarship in the field. Research on the educational effects of school integration, in turn, commonly foundered because of disagreements on how to define a racially integrated as opposed to racially mixed school. (This was a problem for sociologists, never mind the courts, and not just educators per se.) Before the 1950s, educators had more confidently assumed that more research would yield improved knowledge, but later scholars were more sober and self-critical in their assessments.[31]

In the previous generation, the debunking of the value or impact of education-based research by the public and skepticism by many academics encouraged scholars such as Clifford, Johnson, and others to try to understand the problem from the vantage point of history. Progressive Era assumptions about the value of scientific models in educational research have eroded since World War II, yet the pressures and attractions of being relevant have recently led some historians to turn their attention to more contemporary policy issues. Again, there is no huge or coherent literature by historians on how research shapes practice, but a number of scholars have written insightful books and articles on aspects of the subject.

Consider, for example, the deservedly well-known work of Larry Cuban, especially *How Teachers Taught: Constancy and Change in American Classrooms 1890–1990*, first published in 1984 and issued in a second edition in 1993. While it was not primarily a study of the relationship between research and teaching, the volume had many valuable insights into the tensions between them. *How Teachers Taught* imaginatively reconstructed not only changing theories about teaching since 1890, but also to the degree possible what actually transpired in the classroom. Like anyone doing historical research, Cuban faced the problem of discovering useful primary sources. Going to school was one of the most common experiences of children in the twentieth century, but finding direct evidence about how teachers taught them (never mind what they learned) was no simple matter. Unlike a modern ethnographer who can revisit classrooms and re-interview informants, the historian depends on extant records, and the social world of classrooms is often shrouded in mystery given the lack of suitable sources. Like many subjects in educational history, the history of teaching is still largely about the history of ideas—of what teachers were supposed to teach and how—rather than about class-room realities. By creatively examining photographs, mastering the primary sources on pedagogy, and often reading between the lines in pertinent written sources, Cuban explored the phenomena of "constancy and change" in the classroom—what remained the same and what did not—spanning over a century, itself a rare achievement.[32]

Throughout the twentieth century, all manner of ideas emanated from different places, including the university, on how teachers should teach, what they should teach, and how superiors should evaluate their labors. Ideological concerns (such as support for child-centered teaching, or back to the basics) generated more concrete proposals for the improvement of pedagogy than anything else. As Cuban demonstrated, definite changes occurred in the nature of teaching in the twentieth century, as he reemphasized in the preface to the second edition of his book. High schools usually remained teacher-centered and subject-matter based. Elementary schools, however, often became more student-centered, not always and everywhere, but increasingly so. This was not particularly due to "research," whose actual impact is elusive. For example, class sizes, especially in the elementary schools, are much smaller than they were a century ago, and this was a precondition for more child-friendly pedagogy. Smaller class sizes nevertheless resulted from agitation by teachers unions and educational professionals, not because "research" determined the outcome. By creatively exploring the tensions between policy pronouncements and school practice, *How Teachers Taught* revealed that educational policies were a mixture of ideological belief and political passion and were occasionally informed by study and research.[33]

Much writing on the history of education has been oriented toward the idea of "reform." An ill-defined but ubiquitous term (like "research"), reform exists in the eye of the beholder, but the word has been applied to so many efforts at school improvement that it is difficult to dispense with. There are numerous books on the many "reformers" throughout the past who tried to improve the schools; many of them deal at least incidentally with the subject of research and its ties to educational practice. The richest trove of relevant books deals with the early twentieth century, especially the testing movement. There are numerous books and articles on the creation and social functions of I.Q. and other school tests, biographies of Lewis Terman, Thorndike, and other advocates of educational science, and studies of related reforms such as guidance and counseling, the junior high school, and vocational education. Some touch upon the connections between research and practice, but the majority of books on school reform generally deal with politics, ideology, and issues of gender, race, and occasionally social class. In fact, the most important reform movements of the twentieth century—such as vocational education—had little to do with research but resulted from political alliances among elites who sought a more stable and compliant work force.[34]

The best single volume on the history of reform in the twentieth century is by David B. Tyack and Larry Cuban, *Tinkering Toward Utopia: A Century of Public School Reform* (1995). The authors of numerous books on different aspects of school reform, Tyack and Cuban provided a succinct analysis of the fate of several reform movements during the last century. Concerned with analyzing why certain reforms resonated with teachers and survived while others did not, the authors provided some helpful clues to the relatively minor role that research played in reform. Many innovations, as other scholars have pointed out, survived without the backing of "research." For example, the kindergarten first emerged in the mid-nineteenth century and reflected the values of romantic reformers and other enthusiasts whose religious and spiritual values nourished their passion for school improvement. When the first public kindergartens were established in St. Louis in the 1870s, they were created because of strong support by Germans on the school board, enthusiasm from the superintendent (a leading student of German idealist philosophy), and a belief (resurrected in the 1960s) that early schooling could improve the morals and academic achievement of the urban poor. Examining the genesis and fate of various reforms after the 1890s, Tyack and Cuban pointed out that those trying to change (not always improve) the schools ranged from textbook salespersons, politicians, professional altruists, and teachers, the latter often ignoring ideas from the experts that seemed utopian, muddle-headed, or just impractical. Sometimes teachers in the past took reforms hatched in universities and quietly pronounced those dead on arrival; at other times, certain reforms took hold, slowly adapted to everyday practice.[35]

Readers interested in the history of education research can also turn to the scholarship of Ellen Condliffe Lagemann. In 1989, she published a much-cited article in the *History of Education Quarterly* entitled "The Plural Worlds of Educational Research." In it she explored the broad history of research in education and focused on why the traditions of educational science promoted by Thorndike triumphed over those of John Dewey and other academics. This was a notable attempt to understand the roads not taken in educational research. In a separate article, Lagemann later underscored the wide gaps between researchers and practitioners and the common barriers separating education scholars and those in the arts and sciences. These essays were among the best yet written on the history of educational science and research traditions in American education and anticipated a landmark book on the nature of educational research over the last century. All this may be a harbinger of even more scholarship on the difficult question of how research influenced practice.[36]

A host of articles and books by historians address, usually indirectly, how research has affected practice. The topic is obviously massive, but scholars still chip away at the subject. Scholars such as Barbara Finkelstein, Kate Rousmaniere, and others investigate the history of classrooms, which inevitably opens up the question of whether research has made a decided difference on teaching and the curriculum. Historians influenced by Cuban will also study teaching and classroom pedagogy, and interest in various school reforms, which never seems to fade, should also help illuminate aspects of the issue. And, finally, a growing literature on the history of schools after World War II, and the attraction of key historians–Carl F. Kaestle, Maris A. Vinovskis, and Diane Ravitch, among others–to policy questions will enhance our knowledge about research and educational change. As historians explore in greater detail the last half-century of public education–when school enrollments often grew dramatically, federal programs expanded, and the sheer quantity of educational research exploded–we may learn more precisely how research shaped the classroom experiences of teachers and children. We may also discover that research is a weak reed compared with the sturdy influence of tradition, politics, and ideology in shaping educational policy and practice.[37]

In many respects, pinpointing and untangling the ties between research and practice demonstrate the mutually important role of intellectual and social history in understanding the nature of the modern school system. For the first half of the twentieth century, historical study offered some educators a way to elevate the status of their field, and to offer the promise that more research would improve classroom practice and educational efficiency and performance. In recent decades, however, historians interested in how research may have shaped practice have developed a more critical eye on the problem. Numerous studies written by social historians beginning in the 1960s demonstrate that many factors besides research, including race relations, gender politics, and poverty, shaped the inner workings of the nation's schools. Moreover, as Geraldine Clifford reminded readers, understanding how ideas shape behavior is an old problem in intellectual and social history and not easily resolved. Sources that directly prove influence or cause and effect are frequently elusive, no matter what the historical project. Like those who came before them, scholars always face the difficult task of discovering and appraising evidence that Clio often preserves for herself and sometimes shares reluctantly.

# Part II

# Urban Schools in the Nineteenth Century

# Chapter 3

# Public Education in St. Louis

The nineteenth century was a great age of institution building: from prisons and work houses to hospitals and asylums. For a variety of reasons, Americans turned increasingly to the power of municipalities and the state to cure the ill, punish the fallen, and educate the young. And no institution held greater hope among the citizenry for the nation's welfare and future than its growing system of public schools. Historically, schools in Europe had long been controlled by the established church, were rarely free, and were usually segregated along the lines of religion, gender, and social class. But in America, both in the countryside and in the city, free public schools became commonplace by the middle of the nineteenth century and were the place where most children (at least in the northern states) received their basic formal education. In hyperbole common to the times, the nation's most famous educational reformer, Horace Mann of Massachusetts, claimed at mid-century that free public schools were the greatest invention of the age. Along with other educators and reform-minded citizens, he believed that schools would reduce illiteracy and social strife by teaching basic knowledge, common moral beliefs, and the values needed to live harmoniously in the American republic. They would also acculturate immigrants and reduce if not eliminate poverty by teaching the work ethic and personal responsibility to every child.[1]

Americans today routinely condemn the quality of public schools in urban areas. By the late nineteenth century, however, urban schools were often regarded as the most progressive in the nation. Many citizens, including most educational leaders, routinely pointed to their innovative features: the hiring of women to teach in the elementary grades, the establishment of graded classrooms, the creation of free high schools with a broadened curriculum, and the appointment of administrators to implement new programs and policies and to make the system more publicly accountable. The one- and two-room schools found in most rural districts—so-called little red school houses—have become part of a collective nostalgia for all things small and beautiful. At the time, however, leading professional educators frequently regarded rural schools as inferior, offering a meager curriculum taught by underprepared, poorly paid teachers. The best, most ambitious rural teachers often sought positions in the cities. As numerous critics pointed out by the 1880s and 1890s, the nation's biggest cities—such as New York and Chicago—had their share of educational problems, including an inability to build enough schools to meet growing student demand, an overreliance on sing-song teaching methods, and the problems endemic to a swelling bureaucratic infrastructure. Despite these well-publicized shortcomings of large school systems, many nineteenth-century Americans nevertheless saw the cities as leading the vanguard of educational progress. And few cities in the last half of the nineteenth century garnered as much national attention for innovative leadership and school practices as St. Louis.[2]

From inauspicious beginnings, the St. Louis public schools grew dramatically and became nationally prominent after the Civil War. While only a handful of pupils entered the city's first public schools when they opened in the 1830s, over 80,000 young people did so by the turn of the twentieth century. In his masterful history of the system, Selwyn W. Troen has documented that by 1900, about 82 percent of all school children in St. Louis were enrolled in the public system, as opposed to private schools; most children attended classes at least through the grammar grades. High school enrollments also grew spectacularly in the new century. Growth was not synonymous with goodness or progress, but its celebration reflected how educational leaders evaluated the success of the system. As early as 1858, Superintendent Ira Divoll boasted that "the St. Louis Public Schools, though only in their infancy, far outnumber all the other schools of the city, and it is believed that the instruction given in them is such as commends itself to all classes of reflecting parents, and that it promotes, in no small degree, practical virtue and morality among the people." Decades later, another administrator similarly affirmed that "the great social mission of the public schools is to unite all classes of society in their rooms in the common educational preparation for life. The children of all classes, of all social ranks, of all shades of belief, affiliate during the . . . years of their school life, form ties of friendship and affection, and cultivate mutual regard and good will." Echoing sentiments educators and statesmen shared throughout the century, this administrator concluded that public schools were essential "for the perpetuity of free institutions" and the preservation of the "social and industrial order."[3]

Similar assertions were commonly registered in St. Louis and in urban systems across the nation. The public schools aimed to ensure the stability and improvement of the republic, to lessen crime and promote morality, and to reduce the tensions between rich and poor and native-born and immigrant. During Reconstruction in the late 1860s and early 1870s, Radical Republicans even lobbied for more opportunities and social justice for African Americans. But the gap between rhetoric and social practice often remained wide. Like many public institutions, schools often promised more than they could deliver. Acrimonious debates about educational policy—that the schools taught too many subjects or too few, emphasized the basics too strenuously or not enough, taught foreign languages rather than only English, or cost too much or were too penurious—surfaced periodically throughout the period. Support for the public schools, however, remained relatively strong even through hard economic times that included a depression in the 1870s, a severe turndown following recovery in the 1880s, and the onset of the nation's worst depression to date in 1893. Despite local disagreements about particular educational policies and uncertain economic conditions, the local schools often found themselves in the national spotlight.[4]

Explaining why certain educational leaders in St. Louis became national figures defies easy explanation. It resulted from a combination of chance, their ability to act creatively in propitious moments, and popular interest on a national scale in educational experiments underway in America's cities. Whatever the explanation, the St. Louis schools and the ideas of locally prominent educators were widely discussed in educational meetings, the popular press, and professional journals around the country. Most attention focused on the writings and activities of three important figures: William T. Harris, the superintendent between 1868 and 1880, who emerged as one of America's most prominent educational leaders and intellectuals; Susan Blow, who with Harris's encouragement in the 1870s helped establish the nation's first extensive system of public kindergartens; and Calvin M. Woodward, who from his post at Washington University and on the school board fought for various manual training and practical courses to better prepare young people for the workplace. Examining the key ideas of these figures in the context of their times helps illuminate the nature and character of public education after the Civil War, when attending school became a familiar experience in the lives of children.

The rise of William T. Harris became synonymous with the evolving history of the St. Louis public schools. Harris was a Connecticut Yankee, born to Calvinist parents in 1835. After attending various lower schools in the countryside and in the city, he enrolled at Yale College, still home to orthodox Protestantism. There he softened his religious faith, which remained broadly Christian, after flirting with mesmerism, the water cure, and transcendentalism. He withdrew from Yale in his junior year, heading West like many young people in search of their future. Soon the bookish Harris became one of the nation's leading exponents of German idealism. He helped form what became known as the St. Louis school of philosophy and translated Hegel's *Logic* into English. Few cities at the time could claim a philosopher king as their school superintendent. The enterprising Harris quickly climbed up the ranks from teacher to principal to superintendent. His annual reports to the school board, issued between 1869 and 1880, were lengthy, often translated into German (given the prominence of German immigrants in the city), and distributed to educational leaders across the nation. Admiring of centralized authority, he nevertheless provided considerable autonomy to local principals within the burgeoning school system. He became famous as a system builder, a defender of the humanistic purposes of public education, and a fixture on most national blue-ribbon committees that dealt with educational policy during his lifetime. After departing from St. Louis, he gained an unusual bully pulpit when he became the U.S. Commissioner of Education, serving from 1889 to 1906 under both Republican and Democratic administrations, the longest tenure of any person in that office.[5]

The post—Civil War years were exciting ones in the St. Louis schools. By the time Harris became superintendent in 1868, the basic organizational features of a fledgling bureaucracy were in place. Harris added his own unique contributions to the schools and their organization, though much had been accomplished even before his tenure. From the 1850s onward, administrators had labored to provide more uniform instruction through the adoption of age-graded classrooms, mostly taught on the elementary level by young women. The vast majority of children in St. Louis were concentrated in the elementary grades, where overcrowding was common, as in urban systems everywhere in the ensuing decades. In 1866, Superintendent Divoll emphasized the superiority of graded classes, in contrast to the typical ungraded rural school. "The advantages which will accrue from this classification of studies are obvious," he wrote. "The teacher or parent can tell the scholar's proficiency in all his studies by knowing his advancement in any one." And with more age-graded classrooms, the achievements of children of the same age in the same grade from different schools could be compared, indicating points of pride or shame. Perfectly age-graded classrooms were the ideal for every school administrator for the remainder of the century.[6] School enrollments doubled in the 1870s to about 50,000 pupils. Between 1867 and 1881, the system increased from 30 to 103 school houses, and the newest buildings (all larger than earlier ones) typically had 18 rooms. Also in this period the teaching force, whose labors were intensive, dramatically increased from 220 to nearly 1,000. In the lower grades, the school board mandated a minimum of 58 pupils per classroom, a reflection of the inability of schools to keep up with rising enrollments. Coeducation became the norm, in contrast with many private schools, and this helped reduce costs. Prominent within the expanding system was a central high school, opened in 1853. St. Louis High enrolled only a tiny percentage of the total student body but was called the "people's college" for providing free secondary education to talented pupils, who had to pass an entrance examination to gain entry. Featured in national publications such as the *American Journal of Education*, St. Louis High offered scholars a high-quality academic education and helped lure middle-class families into the system, away from competing private schools.[7]

At the time of Harris's arrival, large class sizes in the elementary and grammar level grades meant that St. Louis's schools retained their traditional reliance upon textbooks, rote memorization, and recitation, prevalent features of classrooms everywhere. Harris and others insisted that textbooks had a democratizing influence, providing each child in theory with access to the same knowledge. Given the realities of large classes, textbooks seemed the fairest and most efficient way to educate the young. John Tice, who had been the superintendent of schools in 1854, typically complained that an overreliance on textbooks had baleful effects but that requiring pupils to memorize vast quantities of material was a time-honored practice; only through daily exercise could the mind (like other muscles, it was believed) gain strength. Nonetheless, improving the mind sometimes led to inhumane pedagogy. Like many educators who followed him, Tice believed that pupils spent too much time "committing to memory whole volumes of abstract facts." In geography class they learned the "barbarous names of villages which they will never hear of after they are done reciting their lessons!"[8]

What was true of geography was true of the basic subjects: reading, writing, and arithmetic as well as history. Nineteenth-century educators throughout the nation placed an enormous emphasis on memorization and oral recitation. Pupils memorized the names of mountains and rivers, the rules of grammar, the multiplication tables, patriotic speeches, song lyrics, and much more. The goals of education were expansive, embracing moral as well as mental discipline. Teachers wanted all children to acquire not only the basic branches of knowledge, Christian morality, punctuality, and deference to authority, but also some sense of the grandeur of American history, of the nation's material wealth, and of its superiority to Europe, the countries of which the children's textbooks said were often ruled by evil monarchs, the Papacy, and aristocrats.[9]

When Harris became superintendent in 1868, he inherited a complex enterprise, one that grew larger and more complicated throughout his tenure. Like other public school leaders, Harris believed that individuals in a modern society could not rely on the traditional institutions of family and church alone to prepare children for the future. Schools in an urban industrial society had to teach everyone common values, precepts, and knowledge; otherwise he predicted social chaos and disintegration. Like Thomas Jefferson earlier and many contemporary educators, Harris wanted schools to identify and reward individual talent. This would promote social mobility and help keep America's social order fluid. Public schools also had a moral and civic obligation to teach all children, rich and poor, and native-born and immigrant, the values of a common culture. By attending school together, children would acquire a "common stock of ideas" and values, thereby reducing social tensions and strengthening the nation's civic culture. More liberal on racial matters than the times, Harris, a Republican and Union supporter, also favored racial integration that in the 1870s had few champions beyond a handful of Radical Republicans. In an ideal school system, which he knew did not exist, all children should have access to the same resources, quality teachers, and overall opportunities. Only then, in Hegelian fashion, could the tension between the individual and society resolve itself into a synthesis of social harmony, justice, and industrial progress.[10]

To Harris and most teachers, the moral aims of education were unambiguous: children were expected to be honest, hardworking, punctual, and virtuous. These time-tested values seemed particularly appropriate, he thought, in an industrial age, where showing up on time was basic to economic survival. The St. Louis schools had long banned school prayers and Bible reading, a policy Harris defended, despite recurrent sectarian attacks on the "godless" policy. Harris was especially adamant in his defense of the humanistic and intellectual purposes of public education. He believed that all children should be exposed to the canon of Western thought, widening their intellectual horizons beyond the more limited vistas of family, church, and neighborhood. All pupils should master five broad domains of knowledge: arithmetic and mathematics, which in his schema sometimes included science and taught unique ways of seeing reality; geography, which extended the visual and mental perspectives of the child; history, which showed what humans were capable of; grammar, which allowed full expression of one's views; and arts and literature which provided multiple aesthetic riches.[11]

Harris was a cosmopolitan intellectual but also an effective administrator and politician. The *St. Louis Globe-Dispatch* perceptively remarked that "Mr. Harris is a transcendental philosopher, and when he gets hold of a Philosophy of the Conditioned he can puzzle a spelling class; but when he takes hold of a plain question of fact, or explains the management of the public schools, he can satisfy the dullest intellect that his dealings with the abstruse mysteries of Kant and Hegel have not unfitted him for his practical work as a Superintendent." Harris admired German culture, especially its intellectual contributions in literature, the arts, and sciences. He worked well with German-Americans on the school board. With them he endorsed the teaching of German in the schools, which helped popularize the system, since this helped lure many immigrant children out of private academies and religious schools. Harris also pioneered in the adoption of science instruction in the elementary grades and of more rapid promotion policies; both ideas were decades ahead of the times. However, because he was identified nationally with the advancement of a humanistic course of study, he became known as a conservative. But he endorsed academics above all, and sneered at those who wanted less academics and more vocational subjects in the schools.[12]

Harris defended traditional academics but not poor, lifeless teaching. Long after he left St. Louis, he continued to criticize the mind-numbing pedagogical practices found in many schools. Yet Harris realized why traditional practices died very slowly. He knew that the pool of outstanding teachers at any given moment was not large. Moreover, he knew that teachers in St. Louis taught very large classes and faced parents who usually wanted the basics taught in familiar ways. And so teachers understandably relied heavily on custom: they assigned homework from the ubiquitous textbooks, while pupils tried to recite accurately what they learned, and both then moved on to the next lesson. While textbooks had their limitations,

Harris often defended them against romantics who wanted to dispense with them altogether; in theory, textbooks offered all children, irrespective of social background, access to the same knowledge. And, given the number of uninspiring teachers found in many schools, the textbook offered something valuable and authoritative for everyone. "The printed page," he wrote in 1870, "is the mighty Aladdin's lamp, which gives to the meanest citizen the power to lay a spell on time and space. It is the book alone that is reliable for exhaustive information." And every small step taken in mastering knowledge moved the child closer to intellectual maturity and reinforced the habit of learning on one's own.[13]

Harris's unyielding faith in the importance of academic instruction did not mean he was unaware of rising professional interest in pedagogical innovation, especially in the area of early childhood instruction. Throughout his lifetime, education had been a fertile field for reform, and many lay people and professionals had called for more humane and effective pedagogy. A public intellectual who edited a major philosophy journal, Harris studied what advanced thinkers in Europe were saying about the nature of children and how they learned. While he criticized many of the assumptions of child-centered education that arose from romanticism, he joined with others in a movement that ultimately led to the adoption of free public kindergartens in St. Louis in the early 1870s. It was the first major school system to do so on a large scale. The kindergartens ultimately faced their own political opposition and did not lead to the transformation of pedagogy in the rest of the system, but the experiment attracted considerable national and even international attention.[14]

Familiar with the child-centered educational experiments emerging in Europe, Harris encouraged a young associate named Susan Blow to study kindergarten methods. Born in St. Louis in 1843 to a rich and influential family, Blow was very religious, educated by private tutors and at an elite Eastern academy. She traveled abroad, examining kindergartens first-hand and studying the often abstruse writings of Friedrich Froebel, the German inventor of the kindergarten. The kindergarten was the leading romantic reform among contemporary educators. To many it promised for children a more relaxed and non-bookish paradise, where sympathetic female teachers would employ gentle approaches in teaching the very young. Blow's name became synonymous with the kindergarten movement in St. Louis. She believed, according to historian Barbara Beatty, that Froebel "had unlocked an ancient and secret code" about children and how they best learned. With Harris's help, Blow also published translations of

Froebel's songs and music. She was a dynamic public speaker and became a well-known author. By the turn of the century, she was a prominent defender of orthodox kindergarten practices, insisting that early childhood educators should not deviate from Froebel's original ideas.[15]

First serving as a substitute teacher, Blow ultimately supervised a large network of volunteer and then salaried kindergarten instructors in St. Louis. From a modest experiment in 1873, when the first local kindergarten opened, the innovation soon spread across the city, despite some noisy opposition to the German-inspired reform on the grounds of ideology and expense. According to Blow and Harris, kindergarten advocates elsewhere often held naive and sentimental views of children, claiming to support the creation of veritable paradises for children. Both these educators criticized these romantics and believed that taxpayers would more likely favor kindergartens as a way of teaching the very young in innovative ways while preparing them for the more structured elementary grades. Kindergartens would also serve as a bridge between the informality of the home and more formal disciplinary and learning environment of the school.[16]

Like European child-centered educators, Blow and Harris realized that the young learned through sensory experiences, not through books alone. Children in kindergartens engaged in a series of structured and graduated pedagogical exercises that Froebel had called "gifts" and "occupations." These lessons, however adapted in different classrooms, everywhere aimed to teach manual dexterity, bodily control, social cooperation, and numerous abstract concepts about space, form, and the mathematical principles that helped structure and unify the physical world. The St. Louis kindergartens did not promote unstructured play but focused on the skills and values young children needed for their intellectual and moral development. The child's garden was in reality a bit of a workshop, where children were actively involved in learning, gaining self control and the discipline needed in the elementary grades.[17]

As a result of Blow's influence, the local kindergartens grew increasingly popular and soon gained national recognition. She trained and supervised hundreds of teachers and inspired countless others through her lectures and published writings. Both Blow and Harris wanted to make public kindergartens available for all children, though they thought the poor especially needed access to them. In the early 1870s, Harris investigated the social conditions of different neighborhoods in St. Louis, noting the desperate situation of the poor, especially along the levee. He found poignant examples of

**Figure 3.1**   Learning Together in the Child's Garden: St. Louis, 1898
Courtesy: Wisconsin Historical Society Image ID Whi-41579
*Source: Forty-Ninth Report of the Public Schools of the State of Missouri* (Jefferson City: 1898)

personal misery and social despair that programs such as kindergartens might ameliorate. Like Harris, her staunch ally, Blow believed that the kindergartens might help the poor overcome some of their social disadvantages by teaching them discipline and self-control and by offering an alternative to the influence of the streets and the slum.[18]

Throughout the 1870s, critics of the kindergartens continued to question their legitimacy. They were called expensive frills that absorbed money better spent elsewhere in the schools. In his last year as superintendent, Harris nonetheless insisted that every child could benefit by attending them. "If he is a child of poverty, he is saved by the good associations and the industrial and intellectual training that he gets. If he is a child of wealth, he is saved by the kindergarten from ruin through self-indulgence and the corruption ensuing on weak management in the family." The interaction of rich and poor would thus nurture a more socially harmonious society. By 1880, even the most ill-treated group in St. Louis, African Americans, had gained access to the innovation, albeit in segregated schools. But legal challenges to the existence of free public kindergartens soon intensified.[19]

The free kindergarten experiment ended in 1883 when the courts and the state legislature forbade the use of public funds to educate children under the age of six. The kindergartens were reestablished, on a tuition basis, and the city remained well known for its faith in the power of early childhood education, despite this legal setback. Due to ill health, Blow left St. Louis in 1884 for the East Coast, where she continued to champion Froebel's philosophy. Harris's successors as superintendent, while forced to charge fees, nevertheless continued to endorse the kindergartens, whose relaxed yet structured and pleasant ambience deserved imitation throughout the elementary grades. Superintendent Edward H. Long, a firm advocate of early childhood education, insisted in 1894 that "if Froebel's methods were fully understood by all teachers of the primary and intermediate grades and were applied in giving instruction in the branches taught in these grades much more satisfactory results would be secured."[20]

Long's successor, F. Louis Soldan, claimed in 1897 that the lower grades were becoming transformed by kindergarten methods. New approaches to teaching, he said, have "brought about an education revolution by driving out the old formalism and mechanical text-book study." Even though over 10,000 children attended local public kindergartens annually by the turn of the century, Soldan nevertheless admitted in the same breath that tradition generally ruled in most elementary classrooms. Something less than a revolution had actually occurred. As in the 1850s, children still studied the basic subjects, memorized material from textbooks, and recited what they knew to teachers. "Study and recitation," Soldan reluctantly acknowledged, "are the chief activities of a child's school life."[21]

While the kindergarten had failed to transform school practice in the elementary grades, the issues raised by romantic critics had nevertheless left their mark on educational thought and ultimately led to some important curricular changes despite considerable resistance. The complaint among students that schools were often boring and unappealing was, of course, hardly news by the 1890s. Romantics and nonromantics alike, since mid-century, knew that schools were not a child's paradise, and most teachers and administrators continued to emphasize the importance of work, not play, and study, not sport. No one defended the Gradgrinds in their midst, and a succession of superintendents and other citizens in the last half of the nineteenth century complained about boring classes, dull teaching, and the resultant apathy of some teachers and many pupils. But it remained easier to complain about than eliminate the most reviled classroom practices.

The kindergarten contributed notably to the debate over how to enliven instruction and make it more meaningful to children. It promised what many reformers at the time called a "new education," one that tapped children's senses, ended their passivity, and sought ways to instruct beyond the usual trio of reading, memorizing, and reciting. Children in the kindergarten worked with clay, paints, as well as paper, played with differently sized objects, and were encouraged to cooperate and interact with each other more than was true in the higher grades. Most importantly, some educators, whether or not they read or understood Froebel's writings, were encouraged to ask more openly whether books should predominate in the schools. They wanted to make children more active in the learning process and teachers more sensitive to training their pupils' hands and bodies as well as their minds. In addition, as St. Louis became more industrial, commentators increasingly asked whether the common branches taught in the schools effectively prepared the masses of children for productive labor. This added weight to the familiar complaint that teachers and children were slaves to the textbook, which made the classroom stultifying. No wonder, said many critics, that children were often so unhappy at school that they left prematurely, without acquiring the skills necessary to succeed in the workplace.[22]

During Harris's tenure, various critics claimed that the schools should better prepare children for work, which was becoming transformed by machines and factories. Dull teaching and an exaggerated emphasis on academic subjects, they said, made the schools elitist and uninteresting to the masses of children. Most pupils left school after age 12 to work to help their families survive, leading some citizens to urge schools to offer subjects and instruction better connected to the real world. As Superintendent Long remarked in 1895, stepping down from his post, "where instruction is lifeless, monotonous, uninteresting, unprofitable, or unreasonably exacting, it becomes the instinctive tendency of a child to withdraw from school as early as he is able to prevail on his parents to let him do so. It is the child's natural protest against faulty treatment." Uninspired teaching and an outmoded curriculum, he believed, accelerated the already high withdrawal rates of children, the vast majority of whom left school as quickly as possible. Even though Long hoped that schools would become more inviting, he ultimately agreed with Harris that children needed sound academic instruction, not the practical subjects that advocates of manual training, for example, had favored since the 1870s.[23]

Identifying precisely how schools should prepare the young for the "real world" was not easy. Annoyed by those who claimed that the schools taught youth to shun common labor, Harris openly opposed all forms of vocational education, insisting that the common curriculum was the wisest and most practical education for any child. He was very suspicious of grandiose claims reformers had made on behalf of manual training after the Civil War: that it would eliminate industrial alienation, popularize school among the working classes, and end pupil boredom. Pointing to the hundreds of occupations already listed in the federal census in 1870, Harris doubted that the schools would ever train pupils well for particular jobs, even if they could identify which skills and trades to teach. Schools, he thought, should remain focused on intellectual, civic, and moral training. In addition, Harris worried about the creation of separate school curricula: academic tracks for the favored classes, and low status vocational programs for the poor. Could a ten year-old, he asked, really know anyway what he wanted to be when he grew up?[24]

The leading advocate of manual training and more practical education was Calvin M. Woodward, who became Harris's lifelong adversary and a worthy rival for influence on the local and national level. On some issues these men were in full agreement. Both opposed training pupils for specific trades and opposed vocationalism in the public schools. Both also had high praise and respect for the public schools. After that they parted ways. At a lecture at Washington University in 1873, Woodward told the audience that manual training should be part of a wider academic education, since pupils learned in more ways than from books. Invoking the image of the enterprising Abraham Lincoln and America as a land of opportunity, he said that here "there is no limit to the possible social advances of the poor man's child. A nation which bestows its highest honors on a flat-boat man and a rail-splitter of the prairie, and associates with him a man who never went to school, and whose only teacher was his wife, can not expect its sons to fetter themselves by a trade which threatens to tie them down to a life of toil and obscurity." Those trained to be shoemakers, he noted, rarely advanced to higher-skilled or better-paying jobs. While Harris dissented, Woodward remained convinced that manual education belonged in a modern academic curriculum, though they both opposed narrow job training.[25]

Born in western Massachusetts in 1834, Woodward was a star pupil, winning a scholarship to Harvard and becoming a chaired professor at Washington University at a young age. By the 1880s and 1890s, he became one of Harris's chief critics, locally and nationally. The public schools, he claimed, were too oriented around books, causing pupils to drop out prematurely. A professor of mathematics, the sciences, and engineering, Woodward railed against the classical languages and overly humanistic orientation of the city's high school. He was convinced that manual training courses would restore dignity to labor, keep young people in school longer, and have the practical benefit of preparing pupils for the world of work. He dismissed Harris's prediction that shop class would necessarily become low status, mostly serving the poor. In addition to opening a preparatory Manual Training School in 1879 at Washington University, Woodward served several terms on the school board, becoming its president in 1900. The school board and school system were increasingly won over to his views that despite his complaints were ultimately used to justify actual vocational programs.[26]

In his many books, articles, and addresses on the importance of manual training, Woodward argued that more practical courses were essential in a modern liberal curriculum. Whereas Harris assumed that manual training would become a slippery slope to a narrow vocational education, Woodward believed fairly consistently that liberal and technical education should be unified, not separated, and for everyone, not for different social classes. Like many thinkers of the age, he was convinced that the schools needed to teach eye and hand coordination and to train the body as well as the mind. He admired the message of prominent European romantics, who argued that children should be active, not passive, in the learning process, and that a diet of words alone did not satisfy the child's hunger to learn.[27]

Thanks to Harris, drawing became a subject in the elementary schools in the 1870s, and the kindergartens, with their emphasis on play and the manipulation of objects, also demonstrated the ways in which the "new education" had slowly entered the schools. Beyond this, neither Harris nor his successor, Edward Long, was willing to venture. The schools faced perennial fiscal pressures that made Woodward's lobbying on behalf of manual training programs fruitless. Moreover, until the late 1890s, the school board tended to follow the superintendent's lead on this matter, despite some support among its members for manual training. In 1883, Long emphatically denied the charge of some critics that "the tendency of modern education is to create an aversion to manual labor." How could this be true, he asked?

After all, "eighty per cent of all the pupils in these schools never advance beyond the mere rudiments of an education. They merely learn to read and write, and to use numbers in problems involving the fundamental processes of arithmetic, and then leave the schools, to pursue the vocation of their parents or some kindred occupation." If former pupils disliked manual labor, he concluded, "society is responsible for this, and not the schools. Only two out of every one hundred of our children enter the High School." And so drawing and the various exercises in the city's kindergartens would have to suffice, and public expenditures on manual training, as far as he was concerned, would have to await another day.[28]

The appointment of a new superintendent in 1895 and the election of a reform-minded school board congenial to Woodward's ideas two years later dramatically improved the prospects of manual training. Superintendent F. Louis Soldan praised the value of manual training, and while voicing (like Woodward) his opposition to a utilitarian education, endorsed the "new education" as did the school board that included Woodward as a member. Woodward had served on the board in the late 1870s, and his reelection marked the beginning of a long tenure that witnessed the adoption of manual training centers in the elementary schools and more practical courses in the high schools. Woodward persisted in his belief that a modernized curriculum would hold students in school longer. He had long espoused this view. As early as the 1870s, for example, Woodward had completed a study on the problem of early school leavers. Impressed, Harris eagerly published the study, though he disagreed with Woodward's view that manual training would correct the problem and that it belonged in the curriculum.[29]

That few pupils stayed in school beyond the ages of 12 or 13 was a source of concern to most educators after the Civil War. Harris, however, simply argued that children left for many reasons, especially economic need, and that weakening the academic curriculum was hardly a sensible solution. By the late 1890s, with Harris a fading memory and Superintendent Long retired, Woodward and others prepared the pedagogical soil for manual training and practical education. Yet no one ever had proved that such programs led to increased enrollments, more pupil satisfaction, or substantial social mobility, stock arguments among their advocates. And, to Woodward's dismay, manual training turned into narrow vocational programs in the decades that followed.

As president of the school board at the turn of the century, Woodward wrote an elaborate report on the virtues of manual training, reiterating themes from his early writings. Discounting the fear that manual training would inevitably deteriorate into low status, nonacademic programs for the poor, Woodward repeated his claim that high dropout rates would decline with the adoption of manual training courses. Parents and children, he said, wanted a more "practical education." Shop class for boys and domestic science for girls would make school more appealing and help hold them in school. After sitting through years of book-centered classrooms, children "become tired of the work they have in hand, and they see in the grades above them no sufficiently attractive features to invite them. They become discontented and neglectful; failure follows, they get behind, and then they stop." By the ages of 12–15, for example, boys often "find the restraints of the schoolroom and grounds very irksome. Many of the things they are required to do seem petty and trivial, and frequent repetitions make them intolerable." Pupils at that age had no desire to memorize more meaningless classroom assignments. Unless the curriculum changed, he said, the dropout rates would remain high.[30]

Woodward had long endorsed manual training as part of a liberal education, too long dominated, he believed, by classical languages and other useless subjects. However, an indication of the difficulties with his reform program emerged when the first manual training program began in 1890, when Edward Long was still superintendent. Like Harris, Long tended to give considerable autonomy to local principals. Long granted the request of the head of one "colored" school to establish manual training courses: but only if he could raise private funds. Obadiah M. Wood, principal of the L'Ouverture School, did so and established some programs in the use of tools and in woodworking by the early 1890s. Other courses followed, for boys and girls, setting an important precedent when Woodward and others gained control over the school board later in the decade.[31]

The introduction of manual training programs for racial minorities was a popular reform throughout the nation, made prominent by the famous black educator, Booker T. Washington. That manual training classes in St. Louis were first offered to the poorest, most despised social group in the city was nevertheless ominous. Whatever fine distinctions Woodward made between manual training and vocational education were often lost upon other citizens. While he hoped to fuse manual training and the liberal arts into a unified curriculum, many citizens in St. Louis and across the nation did not believe that wood turning or metal work was for everyone. Earlier in the nineteenth century, manual training was often touted as part of remedial training for juvenile delinquents in youth asylums, children in orphanages, and other unfortunates. African Americans in St. Louis had long fought for access to the public schools; their attendance increased in the 1860s and gained more political support during Reconstruction in the 1870s. Racially segregated schools were nevertheless the norm, and complaints about mistreatment and lack of financial support in these schools remained commonplace in the late nineteenth century. So the initial establishment of manual training in African American schools meant that such courses were always somewhat stigmatized: suitable especially for the poor, and only for other children if kept to a minimum. The experiment in the L'Ouverture School thus spoke volumes about issues of fair treatment in the schools. When manual training entered white schools, they also became the entering wedge for more vocationalism in the schools. Woodward's dream of making manual training a welcome component of an academic curriculum proved very difficult to achieve.[32]

The public schools of St. Louis thus evolved in a time of industrial growth, social conflict, and widespread disagreements over the purposes of mass education. Like other residents of their lively city, school leaders quarreled over what knowledge was of the most worth, how children should be taught, and whether there was a common curriculum best suited to the needs of children. By the turn of the century, Harris represented a past that was quickly retreating from view. Few people in the years that followed defended so well the need for academic instruction for the masses. Critics who labeled him a conservative and a system builder would forget his prescient views on the undemocratic nature of vocational education, or his defense of free high schools, coeducation, foreign language training, elementary science instruction, and more flexible promotion policies. With Susan Blow, he had pressed for innovative programs in early childhood education that proved controversial yet persevered over time. Struggling for many years in Harris's shadow as a policy maker, Calvin Woodward helped direct the schools along a different path, hoping against reality that manual training and practical education would benefit everyone and not deteriorate into class-based instruction for the city's poorest children.

Change had indeed come to the St. Louis schools. However, despite the enormous growth in the size and complexity of the system, many school practices at the turn of the century still resembled those of an earlier era. The core of the elementary school curriculum was still heavily oriented toward textbooks, study, and recitation. Child-centered pedagogy had made a dent in the system, thanks to kindergartens, even though Harris and Blow questioned the assumptions of romantic educators. More importantly, large class sizes in the elementary grades that were increasingly taught by women prevented any widespread adoption of romantic ideals. On all levels of the system, teachers remained the dominant figures in the classroom, and parents often wanted the basics taught in familiar ways. Vocationalism, however, was the new Promised Land for those convinced that common access to knowledge throughout the system was impractical and undesirable. The advent of ability grouping in the elementary grades and formal tracking in the secondary schools effectively foreclosed the notion of a common school. How children differed, and how schools should train them differently for the capitalist economy, became the key concern of the twentieth century.

By the early twentieth century, the public schools of St. Louis had a secure place in the community. They shared the task of educating the young with a variety of private secular schools and academies, parochial school systems, tutors, parents, churches, and the community in general. In the shaping of the modern public school system, Harris, Blow, and Woodward became nationally prominent and placed St. Louis on the educational map. The reforms they advocated were controversial in their time, and remain so today. Do public schools have a civic and moral responsibility to provide all children with high-quality academic instruction? What innovative programs, such as early childhood education, deserve special support, especially for children living in the most desperate social situations? Finally, since the public periodically invokes the need for more practical studies, is vocationalism a worthy goal for other people's children in the schools? Or should citizens provide the human and financial resources needed to hold urban youth to high academic standards and expectations?

# Chapter 4

# Political Economy and the High School

The creation of high schools was one of the lasting achievements of urban school reform in the nineteenth century. Boston established the first public high school in 1821, reflecting the rising influence of commercial and professional interests in educational change along the eastern seaboard. By the 1880s, free public high schools challenged the hegemony of tuition academies throughout the northern states, as their enrollments finally exceeded those of their private competitors. Their success is impossible to grasp without understanding how particular political and economic values shaped educational thought and informed classroom instructional materials and pedagogy. In contrast to public Latin grammar schools that previously prepared male youth for college via a classical curriculum, the high school was a different kind of secondary school. From the start it emphasized a modern or so-called English curriculum to educate young people for the world of work and to reinforce middle-class sensibilities. Born in an age of capitalist enterprise, high schools taught essential themes of political economy, that is, a particular way of understanding the interrelationship between state policy, the economy, and society. They taught specific values about labor, capitalism, the character of American democracy, and the cosmos, not only in classes in political economy, history, and government, but also in the entire course of study.[1]

Before trying to unravel knotty questions about ideology, curriculum, and pedagogy, one must first understand the political and economic contexts that led to the establishment of high schools. The rise of intensified market relations in the cities was basic to their development. When Boston opened its first high school in 1821, its sponsors on the school committee were prominent community leaders, including merchants, professionals, and ministers. They wanted to provide young men uninterested in college with a nonclassical though more advanced education than was then available in the primary grades. As the city fathers explained in 1823, Boston's free high school offered boys classes with "extensive and lasting utility" to prosper in a world of rapid economic change.[2]

Urban reformers elsewhere, first along the East Coast and then in growing centers of trade and commerce, heartily agreed. Appearing first in America's bustling northern cities, high schools were a product of middle-class enthusiasm for useful knowledge. They were funded by the surplus wealth generated by urban commerce and rising support for public investment in new educational institutions. As the national economy expanded and became more complex and stratified, jobs beneath the higher professions and above the swelling ranks of the unskilled seemed to multiply. Outside of the big cities, America's high schools were coeducational, and they everywhere provided an alternative to the traditional secondary school: the all-male Latin grammar school. High schools tended to imitate the curricula found in otherwise competing private academies that often offered modern subjects and grew more popular in the early national period. Like academies, the new public high schools taught not vocational subjects per se, but what was then called practical, advanced learning. A broad liberal education enabled girls to become teachers in the expanding public primary schools and boys to join the white-collar ranks as clerks, accountants, and bookkeepers. A few boys might also reach the higher professions of medicine and law. In 1848, the famous New England reformer and publicist, Henry Barnard, insisted that high schools should teach "kindred studies" that would train the mind and also expose youth to "the varied departments of domestic and inland trade, with foreign commerce, with gardening, agriculture, the manufacturing and domestic arts."[3]

Admission to high schools until the late nineteenth century was often through competitive written examinations. To take the entrance test, students had to be recommended by their grammar school principal, who had to attest to a scholar's moral fitness and scholastic achievement and potential. Admission exams—likened to the Olympic Games in some cities—reflected the broad political influence of the particular reformers who advocated free high schools. In theory, high schools were open to everyone, honoring the ideology of individual merit and personal achievement; in practice, working-class youth generally could not take advantage of the opportunity since they entered the workforce after a few years of schooling. The ethos of individual achievement in an expanding market society, so well symbolized by competitive tests, was widely embraced within school circles. It reflected a widespread faith among reformers in a republican ideology that emphasized that America had a fluid social system, one in which talent was recognized and rewarded at school and in life generally.[4]

The leading activists favoring public high schools before the Civil War were members of the Whig Party, which was formed in the early 1830s in opposition to the Jacksonian Democrats. Scholars have consistently demonstrated that support for the Whigs was strongest in areas where market relations had penetrated furthest. Party members believed most fervently in economic expansion and in certain forms of public investment: in roads, enhanced communication and transportation networks, more centralized banking, and schools. While Jacksonians frequently attracted the votes of Irish Catholic immigrants, given their emphasis on personal liberty, Whigs advocated temperance and other sober values of the native-born, Protestant middle classes. When the Whig Party collapsed and its remnants, together with various third parties, emerged as the new Republican Party in 1856, it brought to the new organization not only some of its moral fervor about personal responsibility and self-discipline, but also a faith in the power of institutions to shape the generation to follow. Despite his own meager formal education, Abraham Lincoln, a former Whig, characteristically supported public schools for helping to civilize and uplift the young. He helped carry Whig traditions about education into the Republican Party, the most visible political force in support of public schools for the remainder of the century.[5]

How did such political values and economic concerns translate into curricular and pedagogical practices? This is the most difficult part of understanding the inner workings of high schools in the nineteenth century. As numerous scholars routinely note, the history of curriculum and pedagogy is very difficult to reconstruct. The closer we get to the classroom experience, the weaker our understanding. Policy pronouncements from reformers, principals, and even teachers abound, but what actually happened in the classroom? What did young people study? What values were they taught? What they were taught is not, of course, evidence of what they learned. Approximately a quarter of all the pupils enrolled in high schools in the nineteenth century graduated, compounding the difficulty of answering basic questions about the political and economic values taught in the classroom. Most pupils did not study a full course. But that makes informed speculation about political economy and public secondary education all the more interesting.[6]

By the 1880s, enrollments in northern public high schools exceeded those in private schools for the first time. The century witnessed a deluge of printed materials that competed with school-based knowledge. Cheaper production costs, improved marketing and sales, and better transportation led to a surfeit of magazines, religious tracts, books, and other materials that formed a veritable new "information age." An analysis of the main high school textbooks assigned in most institutions before the 1880s, a list culled from the annual reports of dozens of northern towns and cities, shows that, despite this reality, a handful of texts dominated in every subject area. Markets constantly churned out new products, including competing textbooks in the South both before and after the Civil War. At the same time, historian Joseph Moreau explains in his study of history textbooks that older standard bearers continued to sell well in the decades immediately after the Civil War. Districts were loath to purchase new books that parents had to pay for and textbook publishers, having invested in a particular product, "liked to keep a proven title, author, or historical style as long as it would sell."[7]

In the schools, before the 1880s, conformity frequently reigned, both in the assignment of reading materials and teaching practices. Daring approaches to a subject or to teaching were unusual and rarely embraced in northern high schools. The nonclassical curriculum of most secondary schools before the 1880s concentrated on a handful of subjects: science (especially chemistry), mathematics (especially algebra), English, history, geography, and a foreign language (often but not always Latin). All were seen as contributing to mental discipline (to strengthen the varied "faculties" of the mind to ensure intellectual growth) and cultural development (to ensure propriety and sound views on society). But these subjects were also often seen as eminently practical, teaching ways to see the world and one's place within it. A course in Spanish, like other modern subjects, required rigorous study and trained the powers of memory, while also teaching about a language with potential commercial value in trading with neighbors south of the border and overseas. High schools sometimes taught formal courses in civil government and political economy, but usually only in the junior and senior year, when most of the secondary pupils had already left for the workplace. What is fascinating, however, is the core of values related to political economy visible throughout the curriculum. We know little about what was learned, but can try to understand what students were taught.[8]

While it did not exhaust the many purposes of advanced studies or their likely social or intellectual functions, the high school curriculum promoted a core of ideas: the superiority of capitalism and markets, Protestantism, America, and respect for the achievements of hard-working, talented individuals. To make boys into a new sort of Benjamin Franklin, inventive yet moored to familiar values of hard work and propriety, was a clear aim of instruction. How to teach girls the same academic subjects while acknowledging their special talents as teachers and future mothers was also a constant concern. At a time of dramatic social change—when cities (before the Civil War) were growing at their fastest rate in American history, when factories increasingly dotted the land, and social change overall seemed irresistible—middle-class reformers hoped that the new secondary schools would teach the virtues of punctuality, application, and academic achievement to everyone. Like the rest of the system, high schools aimed to preserve what was assumed to be a fluid social order, allowing white children from all social classes to rise and fall based on their individual achievement, the class biases in who actually studied the higher branches notwithstanding. Success at school presumably softened the hard edges of class advantage enjoyed by the favored few, ensuring if not an equal outcome in the race of life, at least a fair chance at respectability and worldly achievement.[9]

The authors of most high school textbooks were born in New England, usually white men who themselves had studied at private academies or other higher schools, including college. Quite a few authors were evangelical Protestants, sometimes ordained ministers, and they were often academy or high school teachers. Some were also college faculty, exemplified by Francis Wayland, president of Brown University and famed author of textbooks on political economy and moral science. Most were Whigs and, after the 1850s, Republicans. During a period of sectional controversies over free labor, slavery, and industrial development that ultimately led to a bloody civil war, these authors typically had a Yankee bias that unmistakably shaped their ideology. Like many educators in the growing public school system that created a widening market for their writings, these authors gloried in the value of textbooks. While the followers of Johann Pestalozzi and Friedrich Froebel, Swiss and German reformers respectively, complained that a reliance upon textbooks deadened the classroom experience for young children, their criticisms and endorsement of more student-friendly pedagogy did not generally transform classrooms, particularly in the secondary schools.[10]

Recall that one famous Connecticut Yankee, William T. Harris, became the superintendent (1868–80) of the St. Louis, Missouri, schools. He brought national prominence to the local schools, which were seen as centers of innovation and academic excellence during this tenure. While Harris early on championed kindergartens, he openly applauded the value of textbooks for offering every child, even in the poorest school district, authoritative knowledge. Without access to the best knowledge available, he asked, how could teachers teach and students learn all that was necessary in the modern world? According to Harris and most educational leaders, the high school, entry to which was the pinnacle of academic achievement in the public schools, should offer a modern curriculum based largely on textbooks. The formal curriculum, many educators assumed, consistently blended the dual aims of practicality and mental discipline into a seamless whole.[11]

In an age of enterprise, science became a core subject in the high school curriculum. Science laboratories in secondary schools were expensive and still rare late in the century, so textbooks largely led students down an often arduous academic path. Occasionally courses were offered in geology, with its obvious connection to expanding extractive industries; so, too, high schools sometimes offered classes in botany, zoology, and natural philosophy (primarily physics). But the key subject in the high school was chemistry. Authors of chemistry textbooks repeatedly claimed that, like other sciences, chemistry not only trained the mind, but also offered a key to understand the dynamic world the young would encounter and need to master after leaving school. Studying the chemistry of cooking, including baking bread, might ensure that those destined for the kitchen also appreciated the utility of science. As a leading textbook author said, chemistry teaches "the processes of human industry, connects its operations with our daily experience, involves the conditions of life and death, and throws light upon the sublime plan by which the Creator manages the world." Chemistry taught a range of useful values—including scientific temperance—as well as the more familiar lessons on the chemical processes at work in the industrial world, thus promoting the cause of economic growth and development. Teaching pupils to avoid alcohol and drugs was one more way in which education contributed to economic productivity.[12]

God was the leading example of industriousness, as His design of the universe seemed to show. "God has no idlers in this world," wrote the popular science author, J. Dorman Steele, who became fairly wealthy from the sales of his chemistry textbook and other school books. Steele was not referring to humankind, which had its share of lazy people. What he meant instead was that "each atom has its use. There is not an extra particle in the universe." God's benevolent hand shaped every aspect of the universe. Steele's chemistry text, rated the

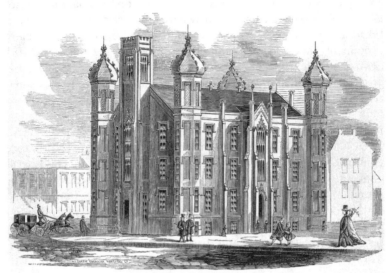

PUBLIC HIGH SCHOOL, ST. LOUIS, MISSOURI.

**Figure 4.1** The Higher Learning in St. Louis
*Source*: American Journal of Education (1873)

best seller in a U.S. Bureau of Education survey in 1880, offered the usual theistic view of the universe. This was common in most science books that generally ignored or dismissed Charles Darwin's ideas on evolution and natural selection after they appeared in the late 1850s; science readers often described humans as part of God's special creation. Like other chemistry texts, Steele's shared a familiar perspective in school reading materials: that scientific knowledge generally enabled people to conquer nature, and that science had its part to play in an expanding capitalist system. Knowing chemistry well had obvious benefits for agrarians seeking more productive farming practices, especially in an age of greater markets for American foodstuff.[13]

As historian Eric Hobsbawm has written more generally concerning the rise of scientific knowledge by the mid-nineteenth century, chemistry in particular taught practical facts with clear industrial applications. Whether in perfecting dyes, understanding food preparation and preservation, or in creating breakthroughs in new corporate industries later in the century, chemistry was useful knowledge. Germany's rise to industrial preeminence in Europe was tangible proof of the linkages of learning, economic growth, and productivity, an object lesson in how the higher learning promoted national greatness. Pupils studying chemistry may have loved it or hated it, or baked bread and lived their lives well without reference to it; but to many prominent educators, the subject was food for the mind and had obvious practical benefits.[14]

Given its abstract qualities, algebra on the other hand struck some observers as fairly useless, but it remained the jewel in the crown within high school mathematics. Before enrolling in algebra, students had to master advanced (or "higher") arithmetic, the texts for which abounded, often filled with written problems about compound interest, money conversion, surveying, building construction, and so on. This was all eminently useful in shaping the intellect and also practical as transportation, communication systems, and jobs for clerks, bookkeepers, and accountants in businesses and banks expanded. Many written problems in the higher mathematics and in algebra offered useful lessons for those laboring in the barnyard or in the urban workplace. They explained how to calculate acreage, crop yields, and other practical information in a class-oriented society. Problems sometimes depicted "gentlemen" dispensing charity to the poor. Pupils were asked to use their math skills to determine how much to give to beggars met along the highway. "A gentleman gave to two beggars 67 cents, giving to the second 13 cents less than to the first. How many cents did each receive?" So asked a textbook in the early 1830s. Whenever laborers appeared in a written problem, they were usually seen as misfits or maladjusted: problems often involved calculating how to dock the pay of the absent or tardy, or those who mishandled goods in the shop or factory. Useful information indeed for the emerging white-collar class, who would work with pen in hand or manage others rather than get sore feet and muscles on the shop floor.[15]

One author at mid-century linked the rise of mathematics with Providential design and republicanism. Here was a school subject that furthered America's mission to rule from sea to shining sea, enabling nation builders to construct better roads, bridges, and machines. Others dispensed with references to the Deity and simply emphasized the obvious: that mathematics was indispensable for those headed "for the farm, the workshop, the profession, or for the most difficult operations of the counting-room and of mercantile and commercial life." The leading author of mathematics textbooks, Joseph Ray, said the subject offered pupils at all levels both "useful knowledge, and the cultivation and discipline of the mental powers." His textbooks sold an estimated 120 million copies by the early 1900s. Only William McGuffey, author of the famous readers and other language texts and a professor of moral philosophy at the University of Virginia, was a more renowned schoolbook author.[16] Mastery of English was intended to give students the capacity to express themselves well, with propriety in written prose and through the spoken tongue. Here too the dominant secondary level textbooks emphasized the importance of individual responsibility. Spelling lessons queried pupils about "A dutifull child" or "an importunate begger" or "A noizy school." Students met drunks, infidels, and lazy people in problems on figures of speech, the use of conjunctions, and the agreement of articles. Lessons on syntax were often lessons in political economy. "Idleness and ignorance is the parent of many vices." "Man's happiness or misery are, in a great measure, put into his own hands." Idlers abounded in English lessons. Franklin's pithy phrases—such as "Life is short, and art is long"—allowed the famous champion of early bourgeois capitalism to come to life, urging students to study what was practical and useful, not ornamental and showy (such as the ancient languages). Lesson after lesson taught older virtues such as punctuality, respect for authority, and duty to teachers, parents, and employers, all so important in the competitive economic world that awaited scholars after they left school.[17]

This mixture of emphasis on mental discipline and practicality was therefore central to the curriculum, reflecting well the values of a broad range of middle-class interests, of business men and professionals who were so active in the political parties that endorsed high schools over the course of the century. In every subject textbooks predominated in instruction, reflecting Whig and Republican views of the world. History and geography classes, for example, provided a rich catalogue of information about the past and about the relationship between climate, economic growth, and national and racial characteristics. Teachers increasingly used more globes, maps, wall charts, and printed chronologies to relieve some of the tedium of overreliance on textbooks. But any student could attest that textbooks remained the *sine qua non* of instruction and everyday classroom experience.[18]

History and geography classes were often exercises in nation building. They had a patriotic aura that assumed America was guided by Providence. Blessed with productive farms, abundant natural resources, a broadened suffrage (for white males), and political freedoms unknown in corrupt, monarchical (and too often Catholic) Europe, America offered ambitious, talented youth a free high school education that stressed individual striving, competition, and achievement. "In the beginning God created the heavens and the earth," but humankind was "condemned to a life of toil and to the forfeiture of immortality" because of its sinful nature. So claimed a popular world history text in 1849, already in its eighth edition. History textbooks typically emphasized how Protestantism freed the world from the shackles of medieval Catholicism, as the Reformation triumphed and led to the progress of Europe, a proud message that Protestant immigrants from Britain carried to the New World. The popular *School History of the United States*, published in 1838, emphasized that America was already one of the most important nations on earth, destined for future greatness. For most authors, the American Revolution was of world-historic importance and the foundation of modern democracy and self-government.[19]

Closely allied ideologically to the ubiquitous texts in world and American history were geography books that similarly espoused a nationalist ethos befitting an age of muscular Christianity and scientific advance. The leading author of geography textbooks in the 1840s and 1850s, S. Augustus Mitchell, reached hundreds of thousands of readers. Knowing geography well was a practical necessity, given the great movements of people traveling, trading, and migrating from one country to another in the nineteenth century. Highlighting the centrality of geography in shaping national character, Mitchell and other geographers praised Europeans for producing the most "intelligent, enterprising, industrious" individuals. Geographers assumed that people from Catholic nations and pagan Africa had lower morals, which led to correspondingly depressed levels of economic growth and development. By the 1860s and 1870s, when the texts of the Swiss-born Arnold Guyot, who taught at Princeton, dominated the textbook market, pupils routinely memorized information about mountain chains, rivers, volcanoes, and other facts about geography, facts that seemed to grow geometrically over the course of the century, thanks to the expansion of knowledge about the physical world. Pupils were also taught moral lessons about the "white man's burden": the need to uplift through Christian means the world's backward peoples. According to the experts, Caucasians were "the most pure, the most perfect type of humanity," a product of living in temperate climates, not the torrid zones that cast nonwhites into a state of barbarism.[20]

While it is impossible to know whether high school pupils experienced the curriculum as a coherent whole, the relative consistency of values that ran throughout the course of study remains striking. Textbooks, the core of classroom instruction, *were* the course of study, and they transmitted a specific world view. Whether studying algebra, chemistry, English, history, or geography, secondary pupils in the

North were exposed to values that reflected the core beliefs of bourgeois Yankee culture. Textbooks extolled the importance of individual merit, personal enterprise, the rights of employers over employees, and the relationship of success at school with future success as adults. While in reality reflections of the values of those who helped champion the establishment of free secondary schools, textbooks offered matter-of-fact views about the nature of economics, politics, and social life that were anything but natural or above debate. Outside of school, adults who belonged to rival political parties or voluntary groups committed to particular reforms debated such issues, often dissenting from the facts presented in school books. At school, however, pupils were encouraged to accept the wisdom and justice of a triumphant economic system and social order and to dismiss critics as dangerous to the republic. Pupils at every turn were enjoined to embrace the ethos of individual responsibility, which explained success and failure. There is little in the historical record to suggest that pupils were encouraged to question values linked with the preservation of a class-stratified society. To most schoolmen, the social order appeared fluid and open to talent.

Since so few pupils actually took formal courses in political or moral economy, their exposure to such courses was not particularly crucial in shaping the dominant values taught in the nineteenth-century high school. Most students left school by age twelve to work and never entered the institution. The majority of secondary students withdrew before the junior year. For those who did stay on for the full course and had access to such courses, the values that permeated the entire curriculum were strongly reinforced, as pupils read more about the beneficence of America's economic system. Courses in political economy and moral science taught the virtues of individual striving and achievement and criticized public aid for the poor and for the casualties of economic expansion. They taught that laziness caused poverty (except for the woes of the insane and sick) and that, in some cases, paupers did not deserve even private charity, lest it produced dependency.

Leading citizens in America became preoccupied with issues of political economy in the 1830s. Political responses to the question of economic growth and development proved contentious, as northern manufacturing interests favored high tariffs approved in 1828 and 1832. However, Southerners bitterly opposed those tariffs for raising the price of agricultural exports. Southern power in Congress ensured that free trade policies and low tariffs prevailed thereafter until the Civil War era. Fully aware that the slave economy had to struggle for survival in a world market increasingly based on free labor, prominent southern political economists concluded that the slave system was doomed, since the prevalence of low wages for free labor would inevitably undercut the higher costs of maintaining slaves. Elite white Southerners nevertheless publicized the moral virtues of slavery, especially its central role in racial domination, attacked northern bourgeois notions of individualism, and favored private over state financed schools. As Elizabeth Fox-Genovese and Eugene D. Genovese have recently written, the "master class" at mid-century usually extolled the benefits of a classical education for elite whites, whether at college or academies, even those restricted to females. In contrast, public high schools were slowly becoming more common in the urban North. They offered a largely non-classical, utilitarian education to middle-class youth, many of whom (the boys, at least) would directly enter a sometimes unsettling commercial and industrial world as part of a new white collar class.[21]

A severe economic downturn began in 1837 that lasted for several years. It brought back unpleasant memories of the panic of 1819 which, incidentally, highlighted the interconnectedness of global trade and global monetary supply. It was in this context that Francis Wayland's *Elements of Political Economy* (1837) gained considerable public notice and became a staple in the upper classes in northern secondary schools. His was a familiar text on the high school and college levels, and it went through many editions. Wayland emphasized that each individual, if healthy, had an obligation to follow certain laws to better himself or herself and the larger society. Doing so inevitably promoted economic growth and prosperity: "*Industry* and *Frugality. Virtue* and *Intelligence.* Possessed of these, no nation, with the ordinary blessing of God, can long be poor. Destitute of either of them, whatever be its natural advantages, no nation can ever long be rich." Such familiar maxims characterized the wit and wisdom of Benjamin Franklin and remained confident sources of guidance as the market system grew and expanded its reach.[22]

"If a man be indolent, the best discipline to which he can be subjected is to suffer the evils of penury," claimed Wayland in his text on moral science in 1835. For only by working hard, applying oneself, listening to employers, showing up at the shop or factory on time, and avoiding drink and other sources of dissipation, claimed the professor and other political moralists, could one hope to benefit from and help strengthen the economic system. Both before and after the Civil War, political economists debated the merits of the tariff versus free trade, but they all united against critics of capitalism. The ubiquitous invisible hand would ensure that self-interest promoted the common good. As Francis Bowen, a prominent Harvard professor and Unitarian, wrote in *American Political Economy* in 1870, "it is true that men are usually selfish in the pursuit of wealth; but it is a wise and benevolent arrangement of Providence, that even those who are thinking only of their own credit and advantage are led, unconsciously but surely, to benefit others." Thus the belief that labor and capital were allies, not enemies–often disputed by radical trade unionists, socialists, and anarchists–was a cardinal faith of the Republican Party and of the books youth read at school.[23]

If the values that animated school reformers and bourgeois political activists found avid expression in school textbooks, what influence did they have on pedagogy? Again, the central role of textbooks in the teaching process was unquestioned, particularly on the secondary level. Textbooks framed acceptable knowledge and offered students facts, names, dates, rules, formulas, and procedures. Equally important, they taught sensibilities and ways of looking at and understanding the larger world. Students were expected to memorize vast amounts of information, from the known periodic table of the elements, to the rules of grammar, to countless facts of American history (especially wars and battles, presidential administrations and discoveries), to its geographical contours, to the countless bits of material found in every sort of school text.

To pass the entrance examination to enter high school, pupils had already learned to mind their manners and discipline their mind. They had already amassed an impressive amount of information and knowledge, so the pedagogy of the high school was a familiar one, following years of classroom socialization. Before their teachers, in class after class, students memorized and recited. The age of the seminar and classroom discussions still lay in the future. If William T. Harris was correct, scholars had nevertheless gained access to some of the world's most authoritative knowledge. What was authoritative, of course, also reflected the dominant values of leading commercial and economic interests and their political advocates. Theorists of child-centered instruction already existed on both sides of the Atlantic, but their impact on theory and practice was fairly non-existent on the high school level. Every time a scholar recited a lesson, it may have also reinforced and deepened respect for authority, for the teacher as well as for the text. Textbooks framed what knowledge was officially of the most worth.

Published lists of high school alumni in most communities late in the nineteenth century indicate that most women students became teachers; many who did not graduate taught in country schools, where the pay was lower than in the cities and turnover high. Most male pupils entered business in white collar jobs. Textbooks–whether dry or exciting, dull to the eye or filled with catchy illustrations–remain a key to understanding the values taught at school. What was taught was not necessarily learned, but textbooks likely set basic parameters on the knowledge and world views found in most classrooms. Serving a small percentage of the adolescent population, high schools helped place students in jobs for which secondary training, and a school credential, were valued by employers. As for the pupils, it is difficult to appraise the effects of the high school on their views of political economy. Many pupils likely internalized the values of competitive individualism long before they entered the high school, which only reinforced what got them there. For dutiful pupils seasoned in the ways of competitive tests and blessed with the family resources to extend their education, high school perhaps only confirmed what they had already learned from their parents, their culture, and eight years of socialization in the lower grades. Textbooks hardly challenged them to question the social order. Perhaps the values of political economy that infused the curriculum seemed transcendent, like the America described in the history books, and not really a product of history and social struggle.[24]

When the free high school secured its place in the social order, it symbolized the widening reach of the public sphere in the education of young people. Without question, the spread of high schools after the Civil War undermined private sector, market alternatives, initially in the North but even in the South by the early twentieth century. The relative place of public versus private schools continues to shape often contentious and sometimes angry debates among citizens, politicians, and policy makers. The nature of that debate, like so many issues of contemporary importance, is illuminated by viewing it in historical perspective.

# Part III

# Private Schools, Past and Present

# Chapter 5

# Changing Conceptions of "Public" and "Private" in American Educational History

Something rather remarkable has occurred in the recent history of American education: a rediscovery of the public benefits of private education. The idea is an old one in the nation's history but has not been seriously entertained by mainstream political leaders or policymakers since the early nineteenth century. When dissenting Protestants, nonsectarian private school leaders, and Roman Catholics in particular protested against the monopolistic nature of public schooling in the mid-nineteenth century, they were loudly criticized and defeated in their efforts to divide the school fund for their competing systems of education. In effect, public schools became a virtual monopoly, and private networks of schooling existed without direct state aid. The public school, and not its private counterpart, became for most Americans the symbol of an indigenous democracy. And, until the final decades of the twentieth century, the majority of citizens and elected officials generally believed that the expansion and proliferation of tax-supported, compulsory public schools best served the common good.

During the past generation, a tidal wave of criticism has engulfed the public schools, leading to a reassessment of private schools and markets in the larger world of education. Concerns over low academic achievement, classroom violence, and the alleged weakening of moral and character education in the public schools, combined with an almost blind faith in the marketplace, have helped reorient popular perceptions of education. In 2002, in a rancorous split decision, the U.S. Supreme Court ruled in favor of a controversial voucher plan in Cleveland, Ohio, where public monies helped subsidize tuition at private religious schools. The long range policy implications of this decision are unclear, but it breached the sometimes high wall separating public funds and private schools.

A diverse range of intellectuals, journalists, religious leaders, lobbying groups, and politicians has increasingly publicized the benefits of private, not public, education. Whereas the eminent common school reformer, Horace Mann, believed that education should not be left to the whims of private enterprise or the capriciousness of parents, marketplace solutions today abound as a panacea for the ills of the schools. Competition in education, it is believed, will produce high academic achievement, strong moral character, and overall excellence in schooling; at the same time, it will force the worst public schools (particularly in the cities) to improve or disappear. Whether private schools and marketplace competition will ensure scholastic excellence remains uncertain, but the idea has recently enjoyed considerable public appeal. Exactly how did the public schools acquire their still dominant place in American education? Why have Americans revived an old notion that private education and the marketplace should play an integral if not more central role in schools? An examination of changing conceptions of "public" and "private" in the American educational experience from the colonial period to the present can help answer these questions.

The creation of public school systems in the nineteenth century—state controlled, compulsory, hierarchical, and in theory standardized—stood in contrast to earlier patterns of education. For no "system" of education per se existed during the colonial and early national periods of American history. Moreover, "the modern conception of public education, the very idea of a clear line of separation between 'private' and 'public,' was unknown before the end of the eighteenth century," as Bernard Bailyn has written. The newly ratified federal Constitution lacked specific provisions for state-controlled education or school systems, which helped contribute to decentralized and local control over formal education after political independence from Britain.[1]

While the notion that education and schooling are synonymous has considerable resonance in the modern Western world, the family served as the basic source of education and socialization in America before the nineteenth century. The dominant nuclear family in the free colonies was both the center of biological reproduction and material production, and it also served as an educational center. If literate, parents (especially the father) normally taught children to read; apprenticeship programs, available for white youth in particular, were family based; and, together with the church, neighborhood, and surrounding community, the family was central to life in colonial America. This was true of the Puritans of New England, of Quakers and other religious groups in the Middle Colonies, and of the more geographically dispersed white settlers of the South. Child rearing ideals and practices, shaped by diverse economic forces and religious sentiments, might differ widely, but the family remained ever dominant.[2]

Schools depended upon local governmental support in the seat of learning in the New World: New England. The laws of seventeenth-century Massachusetts that mandated the creation of schools as population increased were widely ignored and often unenforceable. Whether in New England, the Middle Colonies, or the South—and regional differences would long prevail in schooling and social life generally—schools were an irregular and incidental part of a child's life. Children usually attended schools intermittently and only for a few years; boys often worked on farms in the summer and attended school in the winter session, after the fall harvest. The curriculum, heavily shaped by prevailing religious norms, emphasized basic literacy skills, especially the ability to read Scripture and religious materials. As scholars repeatedly affirm, the American colonies had a diverse ethnic and racial character. The Puritans, however, were nevertheless pivotal in establishing community support for education and schooling, and the earliest and most extensive provision of public education ultimately emerged among their descendants in New England.[3]

Modern distinctions between "public" and "private" in the world of education were noticeably absent in the colonial or even early national era. Many rural and town schools, for example, supplemented modest tax support with donations in kind and tuition from the parents of pupils. In addition, private venture schools emerged in the eighteenth century in many urban areas along the eastern seaboard. These schools were dependent solely on tuition, and teachers offered whatever the market demanded and charged what the market would bear. In a growing metropolis such as New York City or Philadelphia, a private master might open a pay school that offered an array of subjects such as accounting, cartography, or mathematics to meet local demand. Citizens assumed that the teacher was performing a "public" function and offering a "public" education in the sense that anyone who could afford the tuition could presumably attend. An enterprising woman teaching in a dame "school" in her home or a private teacher conducting a writing "school" in a rented room served the "public" by contributing to the welfare of society. The lines separating public and private remained thin.[4]

The creation of a new nation, however, led diverse political leaders to fear for the survival of the republic, which led to a reassessment of traditional ideas about education. In the 1780s and 1790s, national figures including Benjamin Rush and Thomas Jefferson called for finely articulated systems of schools in the several states. Schools, they argued, would teach a diverse, newly independent people (especially the white citizenry) common moral principles and political values, standard English, and basic citizenship skills. Despite the lofty rhetoric about education and nation building in the writings of the Founders, the growth of state-financed schools, completely severed and distinguished from the private sector, did not occur in most northern communities until the mid-nineteenth century. After the 1790s, however, powerful social changes contributed to rising support for a system of public education, especially in the free northern states. The informal, irregular, unsystematic character of educational arrangements in the colonial period ultimately disappeared.[5]

Formal education became more influential in the lives of more children during the nineteenth century, and every state in the Union built a single system of free public schools. Towns and rural communities in the North had built, with a mix of public and private monies, ungraded schools for area children after the mid-eighteenth century, and these became more fully free and remained the basis for mass education. In the cities, where middle- and upper-class children attended tuition schools, voluntary organizations of evangelical Protestants established "free" or charity schools for the urban, especially unchurched poor in the early nineteenth century. After the Civil War, the South (and some places in the North) built separate school systems for whites and African Americans. Across the nation, the family, the press, the church, and other agencies of education and socialization retained their salience in everyday life, but momentous changes swept away familiar social arrangements and laid the basis for a public school system.[6]

Evangelical Protestants played an influential role in the shaping of new patterns of educational control and organization in the nineteenth-century city, highlighting the intimate ties between "private" organizations and the origins of "public" education there. These Protestants were part of the so-called Second Great Awakening that began in the 1790s and was characterized by waves of revivalism and growth in church membership. They formed innumerable voluntary organizations that became central to most reform movements such as temperance, antislavery, and public schooling in the pre–Civil War decades. Carl F. Kaestle's standard history of the rise of the common schools, *Pillars of the Republic*, demonstrates how in city after city, in response to social change and growing fears of poverty and crime, Anglo-Protestant voluntary groups built charity schools for the children of the poor. Once these privately controlled organizations successfully lobbied for more tax support, the basis for the modern public school system was fundamentally laid, however unintentionally. By mid-century, taxpayers in the North assumed the lion's share of financial responsibility for the common (public) schools.[7]

As Kaestle and other historians have written, how this occurred was illuminated well in New York City. There the Free School Society, formed in 1805, represented a range of elite philanthropic Protestants. To help inculcate morality and Protestant ethics in the children of the poor, the Society blended private resources and tax dollars to build what evolved into New York's public school system, open to everyone for free. "Free" education in the cities was long associated with pauper education, a stigma attached to public schools and not easily shaken. Over time, sectarian educational groups were denied any public funds; state aid to Catholic schools, for example, ended in 1825. Local Baptists in the 1820s and Catholics in the 1840s lobbied in vain for a share of property tax revenue.[8]

Activists in the Free School Society (renamed the Public School Society in 1825) thus built a public system that gradually monopolized public taxes. The schools taught a nondenominational version of Protestant Christianity, often called "nonsectarian" by allies but "godless" by Catholics and a minority of dissenting Protestants. The non-Catholic critics who opposed ending church control over education complained that the public schools essentially taught a bland Protestantism. In both rural and urban areas, however, the majority of Protestants in the pre–Civil War decades endorsed this public system of free schools. Before turning to their lessons, children often began their school day by reciting a nondenominational (pan-Protestant) prayer. Teachers sometimes read passages from the King James version of the Bible and children read textbooks filled with slurs on the papacy and Catholic nations.[9]

From the 1830s onwards, the emergence of a school "system" that monopolized tax dollars brought greater clarity to the meaning of "public" and "private." As in the countryside, villages, towns, and cities established school committees, which officially governed the schools previously controlled and operated by the voluntary associations. School board leaders fought to prevent private schools (e.g., academies and many colleges) from receiving public aid. Competition in education still existed, but institutions were denied an equal financial playing field. A public school system that promoted the values of the dominant Anglo-Protestant culture increasingly gathered the majority of children into its embrace. As several historians have noted, critics by mid-century increasingly maligned private schools as un-American, culturally divisive, and contrary to the common good.[10]

Although modern distinctions between "public" and "private" became more common in the North by mid-century, this change was slow and uneven. As in the past, the lines between public and private remained blurry in particular cases for many years. In the early 1800s, though colleges such as Harvard were controlled by private boards, they still received some public monies from the legislature. Dartmouth College enjoyed some public funding after the celebrated Dartmouth case of 1819, which preserved its status as a "private" school. In many cities, philanthropic, interdenominational Protestant voluntary associations operated charity schools for the unchurched poor and received varying levels of tax support. Some northern districts provided private sectarian schools, including Catholic elementary schools, with some tax support, though the practice became rarer over the subsequent few decades and then disappeared.[11]

Secondary education in the North also had a mixed public-private character before the Civil War. Academies (which often included lower grades, too) were ubiquitous and popular institutions. Often established by evangelical Protestants, they frequently served as the predecessors (and rivals) of the new public high school. Academies had existed in the colonial era, but historians note that their dramatic growth began in the 1790s, when concern with women's education accelerated noticeably. Margaret A. Nash has emphasized that the sources of this enthusiasm were diverse, including the value of learning emanating from the Enlightenment and the religious kindling set aflame by the Second Great Awakening that led to increased church membership and denominational sponsorship of schools. By the mid-nineteenth century, academies were found throughout the nation. They numbered in the thousands in the northern states until after the Civil War, and they long retained a commanding presence south of Mason-Dixon. Governed by private boards of trustees, academies survived thanks to a mix of tax support, public land grants, private bequests, and tuition. "States conceived of academies as public institutions," writes Michael B. Katz, and "in the early national period, 'public' implied a performance of broad social functions and the services of a large, heterogeneous, nonexclusive clientele rather than control and ownership by the community or state." Only with the rise of actual state systems of education by the Civil War era did modern notions of "public" and "private" materialize. The establishment of public high schools as part of the common system created serious institutional rivals to academies and seminaries, whose ability to compete declined as public tax support flowed to the new secondary schools.[12]

By the 1840s, champions of public education unleashed a barrage of invective on their competitors. Horace Mann of Massachusetts was one of many reformers in the northern states who popularized the cause of public schools and highlighted the many shortcomings of private alternatives. Private schools, he warned, were hostile to the public interest, favoring the privileged few. He similarly condemned charity schooling for giving free public education—which he wanted available to all (especially white) social classes—a pauper stigma. Everyone should be educated in a single public system. Education, Mann warned in 1848, should not be abandoned "to the hazards of private enterprise, or to parental will, ability, or caprice." Moreover, reflecting the heady nationalism of his times, he feared that "the tendency of the private school system is to assimilate our modes of education to those of England, where churchmen and dissenters—each sect according to its own creed—maintain separate schools, in which children are taught, from their tenderest years to wield the sword of polemics with fatal dexterity . . . ."[13]

Soon a free and "public" education became equated with state-financed education, similar to the way the phrase is used today. One of Mann's contemporaries, George Boutwell of Massachusetts, defined public schooling in an increasingly popular way: "A *public school* I understand to be a school established by the public–supported chiefly or entirely by the public, controlled by the public, and accessible to the public under terms of equality, without special charge for tuition." A contributor to the *American Journal of Education* later provided a more elaborate definition. Public schools, he wrote, were state-sponsored and reached all children in rural and urban areas, providing access to the same academic and moral training, including the norms of good citizenship. Schooling was "public" if it was "established by the State through agencies of its providing, conducted according to the rules of its authorization, supported by funds protected or furnished by its legislation, accessible to the children of all citizens upon terms of equality, and subject to such inspection as the law may institute."[14]

In the post–Civil War decades, Catholic leaders frequently condemned their exclusion from public funding, but Protestant activists ensured that a single "public" system of education enjoyed exclusive access to tax support. The Reconstruction era of the 1870s proved pivotal. Black freedmen joined with Radical Republicans to ensure that the new constitutions of the former Confederate states mandated the establishment of public schools. Several states passed amendments to their state constitutions that prohibited spending any public monies on private schools, a policy aimed directly at the Catholics. (Such laws may continue to frustrate those who want to tap public funds for private schools, unless the U.S. Supreme Court overturns these statutes.) Ulysses S. Grant, Rutherford B. Hayes, and other Republican leaders criticized Catholic demands for tax relief, adding to the era's bitter culture wars. In a few short decades, then, the blurred lines once separating "public" and "private" education came into sharper resolution. Catholics in particular and a minority of dissenting Protestant denominations could establish private schools as an alternative to the public system, but they had to do so without public taxes.[15]

To the defenders of public schools, private education was anathema. Catholics nevertheless built an alternative parochial system that grew impressively in many urban areas, especially in the North. One bigot in a leading educational journal in 1880 accused American Catholics of subservience to the pope, who "has ordered the destruction of our free non-sectarian system of popular education, and the substitution of his own system of church or parochial schools . . . ." Parochial schools in foreign countries, the writer added, were not only divisive, but also spawned antirepublican doctrines, pauperism, and criminality. In 1889, Republican activists in Illinois and Wisconsin passed legislation to regulate private schools, which included prohibition of instruction in any language except English. Catholics and Lutherans joined forces to beat their opponents at the ballot box, but the place of private schools remained contested.[16]

By the late nineteenth century, competing systems of schooling had thus emerged—one labeled public, all others private—and these distinctions long endured. Over the course of the century, the Protestant majority had scored impressive victories for the public system. By mid-century, elected or appointed school boards in the city, not voluntary associations, governed the public schools; free public high schools replaced academies in the North by the 1880s as the main arena of secondary instruction; and the private sector became divided into self-funded religious schools and a small number of expensive and elite independent schools. Catholics constructed the largest network of private schools, and many decades passed before they and other private school advocates found ways to access the public purse. They simply lacked the political leverage in the early twentieth century. For example, Theodore Roosevelt and other Republicans (in contrast to Republican leaders today) applauded the public schools and chastised those who wanted to share the public school fund. Immigration from central and southern Europe swelled between 1890 and World War I, leading to a major increase in the Catholic population. Support for immigrant restriction intensified and finally led to legislation that shut off the spigot in the early 1920s. Catholic schools would nevertheless multiply, leading many native-born citizens to redouble their efforts to favor public over private schools. Public school educators pledged to "Americanize" the children of the foreign-born and make them law-abiding citizens.[17]

Changes were nevertheless underway in the public schools in the early twentieth century, which ultimately weakened some of their public support. These changes formed the backdrop to the rising criticisms of public schools in our own times. They included the growing centralization of administrative authority, professionalization and unionization of teachers, and emphasis on a more secular and vocationally oriented curriculum. Schools, especially in urban areas, assumed a more corporate character, as educators tried to adapt educational institutions to a more ethnically diverse as well as more urban and industrial society. The nineteenth-century public school, whose students were largely in the elementary grades, taught rudimentary literacy and numeracy in an atmosphere shaped by basic Protestant morality. The twentieth-century school had a much more expansive mission, exemplified by the booming enrollments of the high schools, where most of the new vocationally oriented classes appeared. After 1900, superintendents with advanced academic degrees and not lay people on the school board increasingly set policy. School boards were centralized, reduced in size, and elected at large, weakening the participation of local neighborhoods in school governance. These trends spread to rural areas, where school districts were consolidated, superintendents became more powerful, and a more secular curriculum dominated.[18]

Prominent evangelical Protestants in the early twentieth century lamented these secularizing trends. Religious leaders such as Billy Sunday assailed the drift toward vocationalism, which they equated with a materialistic, godless state. In reaction to these developments, they successfully lobbied state legislatures (largely controlled by rural Protestants) to pass laws that required (and thus reaffirmed) morning prayer and Bible reading in the public schools. In the 1920s, they also fought famous battles over the teaching of evolution and usually drove Darwin out of high school biology classes. As a result, most evangelical and fundamentalist Protestants continued to support public over private education, including released time for religious classes, even as they financed more Bible camps, Christian colleges, and Sunday Schools to ensure the survival of their religious beliefs.[19]

Hostility to private education remained potent in the 1920s, when the very survival of parochial schools became an issue in Oregon. Certainly provision of public monies for private education remained unthinkable among the Protestant majority. In an attempt to destroy the parochial school system, Protestant activists in Oregon helped pass legislation requiring all children to attend public schools. Backed by the Ku Klux Klan and other nativist groups, the law was ultimately ruled unconstitutional by the U.S. Supreme Court in a landmark decision, *Pierce v. Society of School Sisters* (1925). As David B. Tyack and other historians note, the Court upheld compulsory school attendance, but affirmed the right of parents to choose between public and private schools. While private (including Catholic and other religious) schools were protected by this ruling, the place of "public" and "private" schools in American society remained unsettled in the decades to come.[20]

Debates over the relative merits of public and private schools resurfaced throughout the twentieth century. Contributors to academic journals and the popular press alike asked whether private schools produced higher academic achievement and whether private education was divisive and elitist. Was the public interest best served by preserving a state monopoly or by expanding the private sector? Few prominent politicians favored direct subsidies to private schools. The only Catholic ever elected president of the United States, John F. Kennedy, had to assure evangelical Protestants during his political campaign in 1960 that he firmly endorsed the separation of church and state and opposed tax support for Catholic schools.[21]

Certain trends had thus occurred in the first half of the twentieth century that opened the public schools to greater critical scrutiny. The rapid expansion of high schools, a more secular curriculum, the centralization of authority in the hands of scientifically trained educational experts, and the rising importance of vocationalism often provoked debates about the role of school in society. Yet it was unclear where these criticisms would lead. The authors of popular jeremiads on the weak standards of the public schools in the early 1950s usually did not demand the dismantling of the system or the funneling of tax monies to Catholic or other competing institutions. A handful of critics called for more market competition in education and tax reforms to aid families with children in private schools. But they were politically isolated and not part of the cultural and intellectual mainstream.

Indeed, the aura of public schooling in the 1960s was still so strong that sociologist Christopher Jencks, who endorsed school vouchers, emphasized that opening the door to greater school choice would not be easy. "Educators," Jencks warned in 1966, "have taught us to use 'public' as a synonym for 'democratic' or just plain 'good,' and to associate 'private' with 'elitist' and 'inequality.' " Decoupling these familiar associations, however, became increasingly common in the decades that followed.[22]

What led more Americans to reappraise conceptions of "public" and "private" in the educational realm after World War II? As is usually true in history, the forces at work were multiple and mutually reinforcing: hostility among conservatives and then among other Americans to rising federal authority in the public schools (particularly in the area of school desegregation), widespread reports of urban school woes, and weakening urban economies. Evangelicals and fundamentalists were particularly incensed by the U.S. Supreme Court ban on state-sponsored prayers in the schools in the early 1960s. Liberalism and secularism, they said, were infecting the entire society. The ascendancy of liberal politics during the era of the Great Society nevertheless proved short-lived. Richard Nixon was elected president in 1968 and 1972, and even the shame of Watergate would not dim the revival of the Republican Party represented in the 1980s in the figure of Ronald Reagan.

Without question, the growing influence of the federal government in the schools and domestic life in general after 1945 generated a conservative reaction that ultimately weakened political support for the public schools. The increased federal role in educational policy making became most dramatic in the 1950s and 1960s and fueled renewed interest in the private sector. Despite some precedents for federal activism in public education—stretching from the early national period, through Reconstruction, to the movement for federal aid for vocational education during World War I—America has been unique among Western nations in its support for decentralized control over its schools. Nothing so stirs public controversy as federal intervention in social life, especially in school policy. After World War II, federal authority expanded so dramatically in certain areas (especially race, civil rights, and religion) that more citizens found its rising power intrusive and subversive of local and state's rights.

As Joel H. Spring explains, federal intervention in school affairs after 1945 was a response to two different developments: the cold war and the emerging civil rights movement. In response to the launching of the Soviet Sputniks, congressional leaders with the support of

President Dwight D. Eisenhower fashioned the National Defense Education Act (1958). This legislation provided financial support for curriculum development in the sciences, mathematics, foreign languages, and to a lesser degree, humanistic subjects deemed essential to the national interest. Some private foundations also joined multisided efforts to strengthen the academic character of the schools to undo the effects of "progressive education" and other forces that had supposedly weakened the fiber of American youth.[23]

Federal involvement in education increased in the 1960s, despite Republican opposition and the growing sense of many Americans that the individual states and not Washington should retain control over public education. Out of Lyndon B. Johnson's "Great Society" reforms came not only an expansion of the power of various federal agencies (such as the Justice Department, to enforce desegregation), but also the Elementary and Secondary Education Act (1965), compensatory education programs such as Head Start, and other initiatives to enhance educational opportunity. Conservatives attacked federal meddling in local affairs and sometimes called for constitutional amendments to allow prayer in the public schools and prohibit court-ordered busing. They were not pleased when President Jimmy Carter, a moderate Democrat, created the new federal Department of Education in 1979.[24]

Few developments so inflamed conservative public opinion, first in the South and then in the North, as the federal government's role in the civil rights movement. This too fueled interest in private education in some quarters. Growing out of prominent efforts by African Americans and white activists for racial justice, the movement was energized by the *Brown v. Board of Education* decision in 1954, which ruled segregated schools unconstitutional. White segregationist academies and private schools sprouted in many parts of the South. In addition, critics believed that the power of the U.S. Department of Health, Education, and Welfare, which had been created in 1953, had increased too rapidly; public school districts that refused to comply with court-ordered desegregation in the 1960s were denied federal funds that had been slowly growing as a percentage of local budgets since World War II. The effort to integrate public schools thus became yet another reason why some citizens looked more favorably on private school alternatives.[25]

If opposition to certain liberal policies of the federal government provoked more criticisms of the public schools, growing support for "private" education also reflected something broader, a remarkable shift in popular attitudes. The accelerating movement away from an agrarian-based social order meant that complaints about rural schools, once commonplace, gave way to intensified scrutiny of their urban counterparts. Since World War II, citizens realized that success at school was more essential to success in the marketplace; employers increasingly used educational credentials to screen job applicants, and deindustrialization eliminated many jobs once held by the less educated. The end of the Great Depression during World War II and the rise of general national prosperity in the late 1950s also nurtured rising expectations about the role of schools in society. The failure to raise academic standards or to increase test scores and graduation rates sufficiently became stock criticisms of city systems in the 1950s, the very time when they were increasingly serving more poor and minority children. Public scrutiny of the schools grew at every turn. It is not surprising that the most important voucher experiments later arose in Milwaukee and Cleveland, in the declining urban industrial heartland.[26]

Yet older concerns about the importance of moral and religious instruction have not dissipated as the economic stakes of school success and failure have risen. By the mid-twentieth century, the state system of education—so widely praised by the vast majority of nineteenth-century Protestants as supportive of a common faith—seemed more hostile and alien to fundamentalist Christians. Protestants once dominated the key educational and administrative posts in local schools, which gradually became more secular, expert controlled, and centralized. In northern cities, Catholic Democrats often ran the political machines that included schools as part of their bailiwick.[27]

Other developments also caused some citizens to revise their beliefs about "public" and "private" schools. After World War II, more public monies indirectly reached more private schools through the creation of various student aid programs. Like other writers, a contributor to the *Nation's Schools* in 1955 concluded that "we do not have clear-cut conceptions of the respective roles of public and private education." The G.I. Bill that was passed in 1944 allowed military veterans to use their grants to pay for higher education, including at church-based colleges and universities; policies such as provision of school lunch, transportation, as well as other new federal programs also benefited both public and private school students and were upheld when challenged in the courts. A writer in *School and Society* in 1957 sensed a more favorable atmosphere regarding public appreciation for private schools. "Many recent discussions of private education," he noted, "have stressed its public character. Indeed, some have recommended that the term 'private' as applied to other than public schools should be abandoned because of historical and sociological connotations of the term." These writers anticipated those who in the decades to come routinely applauded the public benefits of private schools in American society and often urged their expansion through various forms of government funding.[28]

Before 1945, among religious groups Roman Catholics primarily endorsed public aid for private education. But the lobbying base soon widened because of numerous factors. The notion that public support to parochial schools violated church-state separation was weakened in the 1940s by the "child benefit" theory, which posited that indirect public aid to private schools benefited children, not churches. After World War II, federal programs that provided subsidized meals, aid to transportation, and other services allowed private school participation. What had long been mostly a "Catholic" issue—various forms of public aid for private schools—now became a more mainstream national concern. Catholics themselves, many of whom had risen from immigrant families and joined the middle class, were more assimilated into American culture and less threatening to many Protestants. In the 1960s, Lyndon Baines Johnson knew that support for key educational legislation during the "Great Society" depended on two factors: overcoming the resistance of the National Education Association to federal aid to religious schools, and securing the votes of northern Democratic, often Catholic, congressmen. Once their votes were secured, private schools could share in the largesse. Each additional benefit to private school students, of course, only encouraged those who sought other forms of financial relief, from tuition tax credits to vouchers. In addition, by the late 1960s and 1970s, conservatism was recovering from Barry Goldwater's defeat in 1964. Positive views of private schools were also nurtured thanks to growing reactions against the civil rights movement and the widespread belief that public schools generally and inner-city schools in particular were in an edu-cational tailspin. By the 1980s, the Reagan administration gloried in the powers of capitalism and the marketplace, and that attitude hardly dissipated during the Bush-Clinton-Bush era.[29]

The modern champions of public support for private schools after 1945 were a mixed lot. Not all Catholics have supported public aid to their parochial schools, nor have all fundamentalist Protestants. Like many independent schools without sectarian affiliations, numerous church-based schools opposed government aid out of fear that it would lead to intrusive government regulations. An array of school choice and voucher activists had nevertheless arisen by the 1960s and 1970s, including voucher advocates on the left such as Christopher Jencks, free

market economists such as Milton Friedman, traditional Catholic lob-
bies, new allies on the Protestant Christian right and, by the 1980s,
African-American activists disillusioned with inner-city public schools.
Critics said that the public schools had failed, that children needed an
escape hatch, and that choice was desirable as a matter of principle. The
founding fathers of public schools in the nineteenth century had turned
their backs on the marketplace, despite its potent influence in shaping the
national economy. Now an assortment of people across an ideological
spectrum questioned the monopoly of public education.[30]

When Ronald Reagan was first elected president in 1980, the
Republican Party increasingly positioned itself as the leading force for
school choice and alternatives to the public schools. As Timothy
Walch has pointed out, Reagan's endorsement of tuition tax credits
was "half hearted," but it helped solidify his appeal among many
Catholics. The revival of the fortunes of the Republican Party despite
the embarrassment of Watergate and the Carter interregnum drew
sustenance from a wider disillusionment with the economy, military
defeat in Vietnam, and the welfare state. Criticisms of government
were common, and they included numerous salvos against the public
schools, including the famous conservative manifesto, *A Nation at
Risk* (1983), which blamed the schools for most social ills. The inability of the American economy to compete well with the Japanese and
other friendly rivals was laid at the door of the public schools, not
corporations, and private school alternatives and choice became
increasingly fashionable and politically acceptable.[31]

The collapse of the Soviet Union by the late 1980s caused many
Americans to believe that capitalism, choice, and markets were the
wave of the future, not only in newly liberated countries in Eastern
Europe, but also around the globe and, with renewed vigor, at home.
In the 1970s and 1980s, the well-publicized successes of Catholic
schools, with their bare-bones academic curriculum, firm discipline,
and attention to the needs of minorities in the inner cities became the
stuff of newspaper and magazine headlines and scholarly articles and
books. Catholic school enrollments actually peaked in the mid-1960s,
but the commitment of many parochial schools to the inner-city poor
(including many non-Catholic African Americans) understandably
received attention and considerable praise. Good news about public
schools became rarer, as complaints accelerated about low standards
and test scores, undisciplined students, and high drug use among
many pupils. Christian fundamentalist schools and even home schooling grew more popular, and more citizens and elected officials came
to doubt the wisdom of a monopolistic system of public education.[32]

Whether angry about rude students, desegregation, secular humanism, the teaching of evolution, teacher unionism, or just the concept of a state monopoly in an era that extolled markets, Americans by the early twenty-first century may have reached a crossroads in their thinking about the role of "public" and "private" education. Will private schools that receive public aid have to serve all children, including those with special educational needs? Do the public schools best promote the common good, or should the state fund a variety of alternatives?

To defenders of the public schools and those who want a high wall of separation between church and state, the 2002 voucher decision was a major disappointment. Since the great majority of private schools are affiliated with churches or have other religious attachments, liberals continue to argue that taxpayers are subsidizing churches, not children. How many citizens will press for more alternatives to public schools either through sectarian or nonsectarian choices remains unclear. Despite continual complaints about the poor quality of America's public schools, public opinion polls frequently reveal that while citizens overall rate them as mediocre, parents rate their own children's public school higher. This may mean that many citizens are fond of complaining about public services, but not enough to end their traditional support for public education. In well-to-do suburbs as well as more modest communities, the incentive to withdraw from the existing system may be negligible. And many religious denominations, as well as nonsectarian school administrators, remain wary of accepting tax monies for their private schools, fearful of government intrusiveness and regulations that may follow the public purse. Perhaps in the cities, where public school failure seems the highest, school choice by means of vouchers and other familiar alternatives (such as magnet schools and especially charter schools) will become very appealing.

What is clear is that public and private schools reflect the remarkably rich and diverse nature of American culture and political life. Critics of public schools highlight the worst achieving ones, usually in urban areas, where poverty, unemployment, and other social ills compound the problems of the poor. In the suburbs, more frequent complaints include the lack of sufficient advanced college placement courses to ensure greater access to the most prestigious colleges and universities. There are tens of thousands of public schools in America, found in cities, suburbs, small towns, and rural areas, all with some similarities but also many distinctive features and local traditions. Some public high schools, for example, have academic standards that exceed many nonselective colleges; others are chronically under-funded, but still serving the nation's neediest children, who may deserve the most but receive the least. Similarly, private schools in America defy simple generalizations. A comprehensive survey of private schools for the 1999–2000 school year by the National Center for Educational Statistics of the U.S. Department of Education underscored the great diversity of non–public schools. In that year, as in previous decades, about 10 percent of all elementary and secondary pupils attended private schools. More private schools existed in the South (30 percent of the total) than in any other region, and the fewest were in the West (20 percent). Most non–public schools had a religious affiliation, with Roman Catholics representing about 30 percent of all private schools but "almost half of all private school students . . . ." Another 36 percent of all private school students were in other religion-based schools, mostly from a variety of Protestant denominations and sects. Adding further diversity to the mix were nonsectarian and independent schools ranging from progressive and child-centered to extremely competitive and traditional.[33]

Religion-based schools reflected America's pluralistic character. In addition to the Catholic system, there were schools sponsored by the Amish, Baptists, Assembly of God, Church of Christ, Church of God, Mennonites, Pentecostals, Jews, and Black Muslims, to name just a few; Lutherans also supported numerous schools. Within the category of "Christian fundamentalist" and "Christian day schools" came further variety. Most private school pupils were non-Hispanic white. But about a quarter of all Catholic school students were members of a minority group, with Hispanics (11 percent) slightly outnumbering African Americans (8 percent). The national study found that approximately 22 percent of students in conservative Christian (various Protestant evangelical or fundamentalist) schools were also students of color.[34]

The new millennium has brought potentially dramatic changes to the world of public and private education. The popularity of school "choice" and market solutions to education reflects the wider embrace of markets and globalization. Entrepreneurs have created for-profit companies that have been awarded contracts with several urban school districts, promising to raise test scores and make money for stockholders; neither goal has been reached, but it is a sign of the times. The U.S. Supreme Court ruling that allowed the use of public taxes to support attendance at private religious schools in Cleveland may have heralded a sea change in educational policy. President

George W. Bush, thanks to a speech writer's hyperbole, applauded the decision as equal in importance to the *Brown* decision of 1954.[35]

Historians can map the diverse, shifting terrain of "public" and "private" schools over the past few centuries, but the contours of the future are part of an unfolding contemporary drama. It seems like only yesterday—1960—when southern schools were virtually all segregated by race and when state-sponsored prayer was legal everywhere. After Goldwater's resounding defeat in 1964, who could have guessed that the Republican Party could revive so quickly? Who could have predicted that Christian schools would soon become a common feature on the educational landscape?[36]

# Chapter 6

# Soldiers for Christ in the Army of God: The Christian School Movement

In the 1970s and 1980s, America's public schools became the subject of a considerable amount of public scrutiny and criticism. Critics lamented the declining test scores (especially in the Scholastic Aptitude Tests), high levels of drug abuse and school violence, and powerful teacher unions. In 1983, the National Commission on Excellence in Education, sponsored by the U.S. Department of Education, issued its well-publicized report, *A Nation At Risk*, which blamed the schools for the decline of the industrial economy and called for internationally competitive standards. Hundreds of blue-ribbon panels organized by business groups, state governments, and philanthropic organizations soon proposed a variety of reforms to fix what ailed the schools. And, as in the past, private schools offered a refuge for some children whose families retreated from the public system. Christian day schools constituted a small but growing presence within the wider network of private education. They resulted from a diverse movement of Protestant evangelicals and fundamentalists, once the bulwark of the public system in many communities but an increasingly alienated minority in post-1950s America.[1]

"You are the pilgrims of the 1900s," proclaimed a leader of the Christian school movement to an audience in Indianapolis in 1978. Indeed, in small towns and rural areas, in bustling cities and leafy suburban communities, Christian day schools have enjoyed incredible growth since the 1960s. Prior to that time, most Protestant day schools were sponsored by Lutherans, Episcopalians, Seventh-Day Adventists, and other small denominations. By the mid-1980s, however, enrollments at independent Christian day schools, affiliated mainly but not exclusively with independent Baptist churches, soared. They grew to five to six thousand schools with a total enrollment of roughly one million pupils. Christian day schools constituted a tiny proportion of the total private, sectarian school landscape in the nation, being far overshadowed by Catholic schools. Still, their evolution was strong enough to encourage the Rev. Jerry Falwell, leader of Moral Majority, a conservative group of evangelical activists that formed in 1979, to see them as serious rivals to public education and "the hope of this Republic."[2]

This chapter explores the evolution, ideology, main characteristics, and public policy implications of the Christian school movement. Because southern Christian schools that formed in the 1960s were often segregationist havens that were a response to court-ordered racial integration of the public schools, the entire movement was once simply dismissed as a product of regional bigotry, of backwoodsmen and proverbial southern rednecks. But the continued and nationwide popularity of these schools cannot be explained fully by some amorphous white backlash. Without question, Christian day schools constituted a fascinating development in the history of contemporary education. In an age characterized by advanced technology, the spread of global markets, and an expanded federal bureaucracy due to the cold war and Great Society reforms of the 1960s, parents in many conservative Protestant congregations reasserted their faith in Bible-based education and withdrew their children from state-sponsored schooling.[3]

Like the early Pilgrims, Christian school advocates since the 1960s have had a strong sense of religious mission and separatism. This was revealed not only in the writings and sermons of national figures such as Falwell and other evangelists, but also in the thoughts and actions of ordinary citizens at the grassroots level. These activists joined other right-wing populists in criticizing liberal policies from the welfare state to the banning of school prayer. However, unlike populists in the 1890s, they often praised capitalism and held deeply conservative religious values. Josie Zachary, a senior at the Fairfield, Iowa, Baptist church school, exemplified this religious zeal. Like other states in the early 1980s, Iowa was then trying to enforce state controls over fundamentalist schools, but she urged Bible-believing Christians to resist state encroachment. "The Bible," she told a news reporter, "says we're soldiers for Christ in the army of God." Evangelical and fundamentalist Christians had traditionally supported public schools. Now, however, they often saw the state as an enemy in league with liberals and secularists and hostile to God. Only a religious crusade could combat its pernicious influence.[4]

Fundamentalism emerged within evangelical Protestantism in the early decades of the twentieth century. Its followers rejected liberalizing trends within mainstream Protestantism such as the social gospel and the evolutionary view of human origins advanced by Charles Darwin. Appalled by the Russian Revolution, with its call for a worldwide assault on private property and religion, fundamentalists became ardent patriots and outspoken defenders of flag and nation by the 1920s. Many secular writers believed that these conservatives were thoroughly discredited at the Scopes Trial in 1925, where they defended the ban on the teaching of evolution in Tennessee's public schools. Fundamentalists nevertheless made impressive strides between the two world wars. As historians such as Joel A. Carpenter and Edward J. Larson have demonstrated, they created a durable institutional infrastructure of Bible colleges, publishing houses, and voluntary groups dedicated to repelling the advance of modernity. Stirred by the patriotic zeal that combated "godless" communism in the 1950s, southern white fundamentalists reacted strongly against the rising success of the civil rights movement. Groups such as Moral Majority and successor organizations championed traditional family arrangements as they battled against gay rights and the Equal Rights Amendment in the 1970s.[5]

Christian school leaders throughout the nation opposed a variety of liberal causes. The role of race in the history of the movement was ever controversial. When public school desegregation, backed by the Justice Department and federal court orders, arrived in the South in the 1960s, private Christian academies and secular day schools proliferated. Many of these segregationist academies withered, while others flourished and were joined by thousands of new church-based schools by the 1970s. Some Christian school leaders within the burgeoning movement were clearly embarrassed by some of the aggressively racist activists who founded all-white schools and preached racial separatism. They worked hard to overturn the common image of Christian schools as purely segregationist institutions. Indeed, the appeal of fundamentalist education, then as now, went beyond racial issues.[6]

In some respects, the hostility of Christian school leaders toward public education, while extreme, was part of a larger popular dissatisfaction with mass schooling. The sheer expansion of the public school system after mid-century, in which schools became imbedded in every movement for a better society—from racial integration, to defeating the Russians in the cold war, to enhancing academic instruction for the swelling numbers of the college bound, to educating children with special needs—brought it some unwelcome attention.

Scapegoating the schools, which were often asked to solve innumerable social problems as well as to teach academic subjects adequately, became common in the postwar period. The growing alienation of many fundamentalists from the public school system soon constituted a notable moment in the history of evangelical Protestantism.[7]

From the standpoint of history, the anger of many fundamentalist Christians toward state schools by the mid-1960s was remarkable. Since the nineteenth century, Protestants built, instructed in, and shaped the policies and practices of public education in America. When Catholics demanded tax relief for parochial education, Protestants of all persuasions usually railed against them. That some Protestant activists later joined Roman Catholics to lobby for tuition tax credits or school vouchers to support private schools with public monies was a momentous political turnaround. What caused this sea change? In 1967, two writers in *Christianity Today* concluded that transformations in American culture and in the public schools made a "rapid and significant expansion of the Protestant school movement" seem "inevitable."[8]

A wholesale rejection of liberal social welfare policy helped fuel evangelical resurgence and opposition toward public education. Busing for racial integration, for example, was a liberal ideal and not especially popular among white fundamentalists; and court orders to desegregate stimulated private school growth and expansion in the 1960s. At the same time, fundamentalist opposition to state schools was more wide-reaching and never unidimensional. Like other critics of the public schools, activists within the Christian school movement in the 1970s and 1980s complained about declining academic standards, drug abuse among high school pupils, violence among students and toward teachers and other authority figures, politicized teacher unions, and bureaucracy. They were particularly incensed by the 1962 and 1963 decisions by the U.S. Supreme Court, which banned state-sponsored prayers and devotional readings in the public schools. Nor were they pleased when the high court finally reversed the ban on the teaching of evolution in 1968. "The nation was built on God and the Bible," concluded one Baptist minister in Sioux Falls, South Dakota, in 1979. "Public schools are getting away from what the nation is all about."[9]

Fundamentalists certainly came to believe that contemporary public schools did not remotely resemble the schools of their childhood. Indeed, many Christian school activists thought that they had become hostile to "American" values and beyond redemption. In a well-publicized interview in 1982 in an improbable place, *Penthouse*, the Rev. Greg Dixon of Indianapolis, a leader in Moral Majority, argued that the public school system basically "is atheistic, politically it is socialistic, and philosophically it is relativistic." Asked why his congregation formed its own Christian school, a leading Baptist minister in Ohio similarly remarked, "We felt the need was so great because of the moral pollution, drugs, crime, and perverted sex philosophies in the local schools." He said that when "modernism, socialism, and humanism" infected modern public schools, parents could no longer entrust their children to the state. Reacting to criticisms that private schools hurt the public system financially and weakened community support, one Lansing, Michigan, activist, responded that "the private schools aren't destroying the public schools. They're destroying themselves."[10]

Once self-appointed guardians of mass education, fundamentalist Protestants routinely attacked public schools for undermining traditional values such as hard work, respect for authority, unquestioned patriotism, and faith in God. The Rev. James E. Lowden, Jr., Executive Director of the Alabama Christian Education Association, testified before a 1979 Congressional hearing on tax exemptions for Christian schools and made statements that would have shocked earlier generations of evangelical Protestants. "I stand before you today," he argued, "and say that I believe that, given the philosophy of public school education today, it is a sin for a true believer in the Lordship of Jesus Christ to send their [sic] children to a public school." More extreme statements, though hardly common in Christian school circles, surfaced in Louisville, Kentucky, in 1975, when an activist said, "we want public schools abolished. We believe public schools are immoral . . . . The public schools breed criminals. They teach [children] they're animals, that they evolved from animals. Christianity has been replaced by humanism in the public schools. It's disgusting."[11]

According to many Christian school enthusiasts, "secular humanism" had overwhelmed the public schools. Children, they said, read secular textbooks taught by secular teachers who preached that man, not God, was the center of the universe. So claimed national leaders such as the Revs. Tim LaHaye and Jerry Falwell and the countless allies at the grassroots who formed the backbone of the Christian school revival. As John Ward, principal of the Calvary Christian Academy in Montgomery, Alabama, insisted, "public schools as a whole have a humanistic philosophy that does not include God." One activist from Peoria, Illinois, even proclaimed that a "pagan philosophy" ruled the typical school. "A curriculum has to be based on a philosophy," said one fundamentalist from Nebraska in 1981, "and the public schools are now based on humanism." A fellow Nebraskan added more fuel to the rhetorical flames by saying that humanism has "turned our public schools into a jungle in which any kind of animal can do anything it wants."[12]

The notion that schools were once heavily Protestant and God-centered but became humanistic if not atheistic pervaded the ideology of the Christian school movement. Fundamentalist Christians were well aware that their forbears formed the vanguard of the public school movement in the nineteenth century and that the church was traditionally a powerful force in educational life. They sometimes pointed to the elimination of school prayer as symbolic of a left turn in American political life, heralding the collapse of Protestant, Christian values before a rising bureaucratic state and secular culture. Others pointed more vaguely to the pernicious influence of "progressive education" and John Dewey as the cause of low standards and cultural relativism in the schools. But virtually all Christian school activists viewed modern public education as hostile to religion. As a result, many fundamentalist churches attracted to private schooling claimed only to be reviving past educational ideals and practices, not subverting the social order. Appeals to history were common. As one Christian leader from Oregon commented, "[I]n colonial times, that's the way it was—the church was the schoolhouse as well as the church." Since modern Christian schools were usually bound to local churches, he added, "[W]e've come full circle." In 1973 Carl F. Henry wrote in *Christianity Today* that "until the twentieth century, most American education presupposed a supernatural God as its ultimate explanatory principle and as the cohesive and integrative factor in learning."[13]

Whereas nineteenth-century Protestants believed that state-controlled education reinforced mainstream religious and moral values, Christian school reformers regarded modern schools as godless, atheistic, immoral, and out-of-step with decent religious values. Avoiding racial integration in the public schools certainly attracted some parents to private alternatives. But the decision to drop out of public education was more complicated than the issue of desegregation. When asked in 1975 why parents patronized Christian schools, one church school administrator in Indianapolis thought that "they express a need felt for an old-fashioned school that teaches basic things and from a Christ-centered point of view." Old-fashioned schools—by custom in many parts of the North, and by law in the South before 1954—were not racially integrated, of course, and the Indianapolis schools were then engaged in civil rights battles that ultimately led to busing for desegregation between certain townships and the central city. Still, parents in Indianapolis and elsewhere commonly spoke of the multiple attractions of a Bible-based school closely tied to parents, a local congregation (or group of churches), and a cohesive community of believers. This was not conducive to breaking down racial divisions, but more was at work than racial bigotry. Indeed, many fundamentalists simply regarded state-controlled public education—even in lily-white communities where neither busing nor racial integration was an issue—as inimical to their children's education, chances for success on earth, and eternal salvation.[14]

By the mid-1980s, as Catholic school enrollments continued to decline, the Christian school movement became the nation's fastest growing segment of private education, squarely opposed to modernizing and liberal trends. Fundamentalist ministers—whether Baptist, Assembly of God, Church of God, or from smaller denominations—believed that America had reached a turning point in its educational history. Like many secular critics, they stereotyped public schools as centers of moral confusion and indicted them for low academic standards. And, given their sense of what worked best in history, before the twentieth century spawned powerful secularizing trends, they wanted to restore parents to a central place in children's education and schooling. To Christian school activists, educational and religious training, seen as conceptually distinct by many citizens, was actually mutually reinforcing and even synonymous. Since state-sponsored schools undermined sound morals and academic standards, they opposed state regulation of their rapidly expanding network of schools. "As the twig is bent, the tree inclineth," said the Bible. And born-again Christians revived the age-old question of who should control children's education: parents or the state? Their answer was clear. Throughout the nation, Christian fundamentalists who favored private education argued that only parental control over schooling could protect youth from a secular, godless social order. The Bible, they believed, insisted upon parental responsibility for the education of youth, whose salvation was at stake.[15]

Christian conservatives repeatedly underscored the significance of parents in the educational process. While public schools, in their eyes, had grown too bureaucratic, centralized, and professionalized, Christian schools encouraged parental input. "We feel God gives parents the right to choose the kind of education they want their children to have," claimed the Rev. Ivan White, principal of the Billings Baptist Temple School in Montana. He would have assuredly agreed with the South Carolina fundamentalist school official who told listeners in 1979: "You own nothing as important as the children God has entrusted into your care. God holds mothers and fathers responsible for their children. He does not hold the church responsible, he does not hold government responsible." Many fundamentalists concurred. Asked why he sacrificed his money to provide his children with a Christian education, one father from Syracuse, New York, had a ready reply: "They're not sacrifices. It's more an investment in our children, an investment that will have eternal value. When I stand before God, I'll wish I had spent more."[16]

Parental involvement was common in the daily life of Christian schools. The very existence of the schools depended on the willingness of parents to pay tuition or congregations to raise tithes to fund their alternative schools, and fundamentalist ministers tried to unite church, home, and school as closely as possible. To help create a community of like-minded families, Christian schools often required proof that at least one parent of a prospective pupil was born again. Given the biblical imperative of parental control over children's education, fundamentalists believed that accusations that they were simply closet segregationists overlooked the complex historical origins of Christian schools. They vigorously argued that control—not race—was their central concern. In an age when markets were increasingly ascendant and politically further strengthened with the collapse of the Soviet Union, school "choice" soon became an ideal among nonfundamentalists as well; by the 1990s, it would become a many-splendored thing, embraced by parents who had supported the public schools and those who favored home schooling that largely grew out of the Christian school movement.[17]

The president of Religious Roundtable, a prominent conservative organization, typically emphasized that political control was at the heart of the culture wars wracking the schools. Listen to his testimony before a Congressional committee studying the issue of tuition tax credits for private schools in 1982. Since the Bible demanded the proper training of children, "the question is, who should do that training? the state? the NEA? the ACLU? the Utopians? the Behaviorists? or the parents?" Like activists elsewhere, a Christian school advocate from Kanawha County, West Virginia, said the choices were clear. Kanawha County was the site of public school bombings in the early 1970s when working-class fundamentalists clashed with school officials over the adoption of sex education and textbooks deemed too secular and humanistic. Many analysts reduced the complex struggle to a story of hayseeds banning books. In reality, according to this private school activist, "[T]he real issue here is not busing, or integration, or dirty textbooks. The issue is: who is going to control the education of your child. Is it going to be the state—or the parents. The battle is over freedom of choice, something Americans have cherished for 200 years."[18]

Because of the primacy placed on parental control and the separatist tradition of Baptist reformers in particular, state regulation quickly emerged as a lightning rod in policy disputes. Many states were very lenient about the operation of private schools and only required the enforcement of fire and safety codes. But some states had more activist departments of public instruction with more stringent regulations, especially in the areas of teacher certification and accreditation. Catholics, Lutherans, and Seventh-Day Adventists had often accepted minimal state standards and accommodated themselves to them. And so these groups did not usually join Protestant fundamentalists in the mid-1980s in lawsuits or boycotts against state regulation. Baptists, however, had supported the separation of church and state since the colonial period, and many activists proudly invoked that history.[19]

Employees of state departments of public instruction regarded strong regulation as a safer guarantee of quality education. To fundamentalists, however, it was an imposition and unwarranted. Seeing schools as extensions of families and their church ministry, they viewed church and state as distinct spheres. The church and school, many said, were distinct yet constituted two sides of the same coin. The state lacked any constitutional or moral right to interfere; it only threatened their autonomy and separation from the secular system. "The state of Alabama is not interested in registering my Sunday school, and I don't think they should register my Monday school," argued W. R. Whiddon, president of the Alabama Association of Christian Education in 1981. As one Indiana activist similarly asserted, "[W]e don't think of our school as being anything separate from our church . . . . We have Sunday school, Monday school, Tuesday school, Wednesday school, and so on. To us, it's all the same." Standing in a cold drizzle in Louisville, Nebraska, in 1981, where he joined a local Christian school's nationally publicized fight against state accreditation, Jerry Falwell warned his listeners that "to submit to certification is to submit to licensure and the right of the state to license a church and its Christian ministry. We believe the church and church school are all the church."[20]

By the mid-1980s, Christian fundamentalists had successfully countered movements for increased state control in Ohio, Kentucky, Indiana, North Carolina, and Idaho, while they were less successful in Nebraska. There the defiance of one school that refused to submit to state accreditation led to a three-month prison term for a fundamentalist minister, who became a martyr within the movement. When a local judge reluctantly padlocked the door to his church, since "school" was being held within the building in defiance of a court order, it exacerbated the fears and hostility of many conservative Protestants toward public regulation. Consequently, in state after state, Christian fundamentalists staged impressive protests and lobbied to turn back legislation deemed harmful to their schools. Many Christian school associations united their members against state certification, refused to supply basic data on enrollment to state officials, and like earlier radicals on the left, who also emphasized community control and parental rights, turned their philosophy of separatism into political resistance.[21]

Accreditation and licensure of fundamentalist schools, their sponsors believed, ultimately came from God. The state, seen as contaminated by an unresponsive, bloated, secular bureaucracy, was the enemy, a quasi-socialistic monolith that endangered their freedom. "We feel we're accredited by the Lord," one Baptist preacher in Illinois insisted in 1977. Texas evangelist Lester Roloff joined hundreds of fundamentalists in Iowa a few years later to denounce what they viewed as state harassment of Christian day schools. God's rule superceded the state's, he thundered to a receptive audience. "The Bible is our book of standards, rules, and regulations . . . ." An Iowa minister similarly asserted that the states seemed preoccupied with minimum standards (such legislation for public schools had proliferated by the late 1970s). Christian schools, in contrast, got their marching orders from above. "We have maximum standards."[22]

Some fundamentalist schools accepted a degree of state regulation, which they felt did not compromise their religious principles. A Christian school in Lake Oswego, Oregon, was one of many that required teachers to have state certificates. But this was a minority position. Most fundamentalists, especially from independent-minded Baptist churches, resisted state interference and reminded people of the old tale of what happens when the camel's nose is allowed under the tent. In Kentucky, where the state association of Christian schools warded off attempts at increased state control, one prominent leader raised a perennial issue: "If the state tells us what kind of textbook to have, what do we have? A glorified public school." Allies also concurred with the sentiments expressed by a minister from Albany, New York, who had founded a school and warned about working "under state education auspices and curriculum and finances. We fear state control."[23]

When policemen padlocked the Baptist church of the Rev. Edward Sileven in Louisville, Nebraska, it confirmed the worst fears of the faithful. Rodney Clapp, writing about the controversy in 1982 in *Christianity Today*, explained how Sileven and his congregation viewed the situation: "With their private, religious school, they believe they have built a thought-tight submarine, uncontaminated by the secular humanism they think floods public schools. Now that the school is built, they believe seeking state licensure would make as much sense as drilling holes in the submarine: state licensing opens the way to state control, and control means slavery to humanism." In this insular world of Christian education, bound together into a community of believers linking parents and children with the church and the school, the state remained unwelcome.[24]

The outcome in Nebraska—the conviction of a minister and padlocking of a church—was hardly the typical state response in the formative decades of the Christian school movement. Christian legal associations since then continue to fight what are regarded as intrusive state initiatives and regulations, and they early on scored important victories in the courts, particularly in Kentucky and Ohio. Rallies and political lobbying squashed efforts to tighten state controls elsewhere. By the mid-1980s, many states, including Alaska, Kansas, and Oklahoma, had few regulations governing private schools. Sometimes representing themselves as a persecuted minority, Christian school reformers actually enjoyed considerable freedom and quite a few legal victories, a testimony to their savvy use of boycotts, rallies, and lawyers to defend their First Amendment freedoms.[25]

From this perspective, even the well-known rulings by the U.S. Supreme Court on Bob Jones University and the Goldsboro, South Carolina, Christian schools, which upheld the denial of tax exemptions for schools because of racial discrimination, were not, as some conservatives feared, part of a godless plot by the state. Since the 1960s, hundreds of "Christian" schools in the South opened to avoid racial integration, yet only about one hundred of them by the late 1970s had lost their tax-exempt status. When the Internal Revenue Service (IRS) tried under newly proposed guidelines in 1978 to require racial integration at Christian schools, only the U.S. Department of Health, Education, and Welfare in Washington and a few civil rights groups endorsed the plan. Major nonfundamentalist religious groups also attacked the IRS proposal, and many fundamentalists testified at public hearings that true racists were a minority of their movement and an embarrassment to it. The principle of church-state separation— leaving church-based schools free from quotas or other forms of interventionist policies—was more important than trying to punish a few racists by punishing everyone.[26]

By the late 1970s, then, far from being an anomaly, Christian schools were becoming a small but permanent and growing part of the educational landscape. Their champions saw their schools as a response not to a single source such as race but to wholesale changes in the larger society and its schools. The new schools were a direct challenge to what they (and leftist critics in the academy) called the public school monopoly. With the spread of public criticism of modern schools, the revival of the Republican Party by the 1980s, and ongoing assaults on liberal school reforms emanating from the 1960s, self-styled soldiers for Christ had built, brick by brick, alternatives to the established school system.[27]

In the early 1970s, popular books appeared on the rise of free schools, open classrooms, and sundry left-leaning alternatives to conventional pedagogical practices. These schools often declined in significance as the left-liberal culture evaporated in the political and cultural malaise of the Nixon-Carter years. In contrast, the Christian school movement rode the waves of the new conservative revival, of which fundamentalism remained an essential part. With the godless state, there could be no compromise, one Christian activist from Maryland told the *Washington Post*: "We will not keep abandoning the ship to the cancerous liberal element that wants to contaminate everything." Like others, he believed that fundamentalists in the past had wrongly stood by as the schools were taken over by secular, humanistic values and the teachings of John Dewey. No one who entered a new Christian school would have doubted that the fundamentalist schools, in every way, differed from the public system.[28]

The character of Christian day schools, while diverse, had some unifying characteristics. And the contrast with the public system was often very dramatic. "I pledge allegiance to the Christian flag and to the Savior, for whose kingdom it stands. Our Savior, crucified, risen and coming again, with life and liberty for all who believe." With these or similar words, piously pronounced, many children began their school day in the thousands of independent Christian day schools that had opened since the 1960s. Saluting first the Christian flag and then the American flag, children thus set a moral tone at the beginning of each school day. Early writings about the origins of these private sectarian schools focused on racial issues and state regulation. In time, however, more research yielded knowledge about the inner life of these schools. Who sent their children to Christian schools? Who taught in these schools? What curricula, formal and hidden, were taught? How did these schools offer an alternative to the typical public school?[29]

In terms of their physical size, Christian day schools by the 1980s tended to be small. This was hardly surprising, since these institutions drew upon a local population of born-again Christians from a particular church or congregations nearby. Parents alienated by the red tape of many public school systems, angered by recurrent teacher strikes over pay and working conditions, and convinced that school officials cared about their input only when bond issues needed approval, naturally preferred small-scale institutions in which their voice counted. Throughout the twentieth century, public school administrators and most prominent reformers had fought for larger schools, made possible as more districts consolidated. Economies of scale resulted, but so did alienation among many students and their families from the public schools. Christian schools varied in size, ranging from those that enrolled a handful of children to those with a few thousand. Paul Kienel of the Association of Christian Schools International determined in 1979 that, of the 1,042 institutions represented by his organization, the average school enrolled 218 pupils. Other estimates placed the number at half that size. Many schools, of course, only accommodated as many pupils as could fit in the church basement or in a small building adjoining the sponsoring church. Since most were elementary schools, it saved the costs associated with secondary education.[30]

Since they frequently operated on a tight budget, Christian schools usually kept expenditures on facilities to a minimum. A few schools were magnificently furnished and compared well with an elaborate public school complex; more typically, school facilities were modest. Many schools were in church halls and basements. Studies conducted by different Christian school associations indicated that 80 to 95 percent of all independent Christian schools were church-sponsored; the remainder were parent-sponsored, without ties to any particular religious institution. In the majority of church-sponsored schools, "almost without exception, the pastor of the church is the superintendent of the school." This helped reduce expenses. Thus, the typical school was usually small, modest, and church-affiliated, whether located in rural Kentucky or urban Ohio.[31]

Exactly who sent their children to the nation's five to six thousand Christian schools that dotted the land by the mid-1980s? The paucity of records, guaranteed by a movement of the independent-minded who resent outside meddling, makes definitive answers elusive. These schools often refused to share the most barebones information with state officials. In 1981, the executive director of the Council for Private Education referred to Christian school parents as "lower-middle-class." A writer in Virginia claimed that Norfolk's schools appealed "primarily to solidly middle-class families." A credible study of North Carolina's fundamentalist schools found "working and lower-class families" and parents of "modest means" generally patronizing these schools. Addressing a Senate committee on the issue of tuition tax credits, Jerry Falwell described Christian school parents as "rank and file Americans, middle income and down."[32]

To send children to any private school required surplus capital, and clearly the majority of families that supported Christian schools had attained middling social class standing or were struggling to rise up from respectable working-class ranks. The very wealthy and the very poor did not seem common in these schools. Within an admittedly diverse network of schools, numerous schools were largely working class. But David Nevin and Robert E. Bills, in their study of Christian schools in 1976, concluded that most parents attracted to these private schools were from the middle ranks of society. "Most of the students come from unbroken homes and live in houses that stand half-paid-for in undistinguished suburbs with a second car or a pickup outside or a small boat in the yard. Many of these families have moved from relative poverty to relative comfort by very hard work and are not yet secure in their standing." Most commentators ultimately concluded that families attracted to independent day schools were middle to lower-middle class.[33]

Just as the social backgrounds of parents varied from church to church, so did the expenses related to school attendance. Some churches required their members to tithe to defray the expenses of operating a school and to lessen the burden of tuition on needy parents. Tuition varied greatly, even within a single geographical area. One study of the schools in Cleveland, Ohio, for example, revealed in 1981 that tuition varied from $650 to $2,000 per year, depending on the institution and level of instruction. Many schools had sliding tuition scales to enable poorer children to attend at reduced rates; other schools could not extend that opportunity to the disadvantaged. The very existence of special financial packages for lower-income students, of course, illuminated the broad middle-class character of most of these schools. As in most spheres of consumer society, money mattered.[34]

By the 1980s, Christian schools also mostly enrolled white pupils. There were certainly racially mixed schools, but the small percentage of African Americans heightened impressions of their Jim Crow nature. Since churches were usually not racially integrated, schools reflected the social makeup of local congregations. African Americans in the South frequently had their own well-established institutions, including a range of Baptist and African Methodist Episcopal (AME) churches. But with some important exceptions, such as the rising number of blacks in inner-city Catholic schools at the time, historically their allegiance had been to the public schools. Unlike ethnic Catholics or Lutherans, for example, African Americans did not create their own separate school systems, though they were forced to attend segregated public schools by law or custom throughout much of the country before the civil rights era. The dream of the post–war civil rights movement, before the rise of racial separatism and reaction against liberalism at the polls by 1968, had been integration in the public sphere. Many African Americans who remembered well that early southern academies had undermined the cause of racial integration understandably remained offended by their existence.[35]

Because of these factors, even well-intentioned Christian school leaders in the 1970s and 1980s were often unable to draw African Americans into their institutions. In contrast to the lingering perception of the racist origins of the movement, many principled fundamentalists refused to accept white parents and their children who were trying to avoid racial integration in the public schools but did not share the educational philosophy of their schools. Church administrators sometimes placed ceilings on enrollments when local public schools faced court-ordered busing; others were frustrated by their inability to change the movement's image as a haven for white flight. W. Wayne Allen, of the Briarcrest School System in Memphis, Tennessee, operated a network of institutions with 3,800 pupils. In 1979 he told a House Committee studying the tax-exempt status of private schools that nothing seemed to lure African Americans into the system. He tried to build alliances with black ministers, and he advertised in newspapers and other media. The reputation of Christian schools as racist would take a long time, if ever, to wither in many communities.[36]

Given the politically conservative people behind the Christian school movement, it is not surprising that teachers employed in fundamentalist institutions differed noticeably from their public school counterparts. Although public school teachers were traditionally screened for their moral and sometimes political, as well as academic, qualifications, the religious and moral background of prospective employees was of particular importance in these schools. Often suspicious of those educated in secular public or private colleges or universities, fundamentalist school administrators preferred teachers trained at Bible colleges and other religiously oriented schools; many former public school teachers who shared the precepts of Christian schools also found their way into the alternative system. Many independent schools hired teachers who lacked state certification, and the schools themselves frequently lacked state accreditation.

"Certification means nothing to us at all," claimed Dewayne Payne, administrator of the East Park Christian School in Anchorage, Alaska. "Certification is just something the state does." Many Christian schools employed teachers trained at state colleges and universities, but this was hardly seen as a prerequisite for employment and was sometimes viewed with suspicion. Instead of hiring a teacher trained in a school of education with a "secular" or "humanistic" orientation, Christian school spokespersons noted their interest in a different type of BA: a Born-Again Degree. Moreover, teachers were usually scrutinized for evidence of sound moral character and religious conviction. "We do not hire a teacher who smokes, drinks, curses, or goes to public dances," asserted the Rev. Floyd H. Jones, an administrator of the First Christian Assembly in Memphis. The Thrifthaven School, located in the same city, had an application form in the early 1970s that asked: "Are you now . . . or have you ever been a Communist? A homosexual or pervert of any kind?" Hostility to gay and lesbian culture remained common in the movement, and public schools were frequently accused of favoring alternative lifestyles as long as they were not Christian.[37]

With a national surplus of college-educated teachers and a revival of popular interest in private schools, Christian schools operated without the costs associated with high teacher salaries, fringe benefits, or retirement plans. Insiders remarked that "the pay isn't great, but the retirement benefits are out of this world." In this material world, however, fundamentalist teachers received low salaries, lacked job security, and yet filled an essential, vital role in the schools. Since many private schools, including Catholic schools, often struggled mightily to remain economically solvent, these teachers not only formed a central link between home, church, and school, but also enabled many schools to survive stagflation—high unemployment and high inflation—during the late 1970s.[38]

Christian school teachers, therefore, often differed from public school counterparts in their preparation for their work, their religious commitments, and their financial rewards. But even more so than public school teachers, they were greatly affected by modern efforts to create a uniform, teacher-proof curriculum. Across the twentieth century, educational reformers devised numerous ways to shape if not control teacher behavior, including the scientific rating of teaching, comparisons of student-standardized test scores to judge teacher competence, the use of teaching machines, and the behavioral objectives craze of the 1970s. Christian schools, too, often tried to deskill teaching. Because many fundamentalist schools ran on a tight budget, some favored a curriculum that was not overly dependent on a large or well-trained teaching staff. Teaching the basics was also a high priority. Many small schools taught children of all ages in a single room, reminiscent of the old one-room schoolhouse, and they used curriculum packages such as Accelerated Christian Education (ACE). The program was affordable, efficient, and popular.[39]

Begun in 1970, ACE was adopted in a few thousand schools by 1981. The majority of schools did not use ACE but purchased textbooks from a few major Christian publishing houses. But all Christian schools—whether they used the prepackaged materials or textbooks—offered an instruction that differed significantly from the typical public school. The ACE curriculum consisted of four broad areas of instruction: mathematics, language arts, social studies, and science. Children plowed through workbooks for each grade level, took tests at the end of particular lessons, and moved forward at their own individual pace. For most schools using ACE, therefore, social promotion was nonexistent. Teachers were available to help answer questions as students worked on their own most of the day, perhaps in their own study carrels, and the curriculum was heavily oriented toward reading and individual mastery of materials. Heavily laced with religious teaching and reflecting conservative social, political, and economic viewpoints, ACE fit the overall ideological orientation of the schools well. Like some other critics, the principal of the Portland, Oregon, Christian High School complained that "the kids get sick of sitting for a whole year in their cubicles doing their booklets. It's deadly." On the other hand, such curricular materials kept costs low and schools afloat.[40]

Since its emergence in the early twentieth century in reaction to modernist trends in society and in mainstream Protestantism, fundamentalists have emphasized that the Bible is literally the word of God and should mold one's life on earth. Prayer and Bible reading were crucial in fundamentalist schooling, and teachers and ministers viewed academic and religious training as closely related if not identical. This followed logically from the oft-held claim that Sunday school and Monday school were indistinguishable.[41]

Christian school activists regarded the Bible as the most important text children would ever encounter. As one Colorado minister asserted in 1981, "[A] Christian education is created around God's word—the Bible. It is a commandment of Scripture to teach the word of God to our children and that involves a Christian school." Christian schools that often taught a nondenominational, ecumenical

Protestantism that differed from traditional parochial schools. "Their goal is to make more Catholics or Lutherans," one Nebraskan believed. "Ours is to teach the Bible." Since knowledge of God was the beginning of wisdom, Christian schools tried to create an academic and religious climate to help save children's souls. "We want our boys and girls to be saved and go to heaven," a Nashville, Tennessee, school principal asserted, and the hope was that the Bible and religious training led to that outcome.[42]

Whether or not they utilized prepackaged curriculum materials or employed teachers as monitors or aides or in traditional roles, Christian schools linked formal instruction to the Bible. Children always learn (or fail to learn) more than is explicitly taught, but in these schools they were in an environment in which adults believed that "if you're not taught the Bible, there's nothing to teach. The Lord gave us math, science. He gave us all our subjects." "Our study materials are loaded with Scripture—and the Bible is our main textbook," said a spokesperson from the Charles City Baptist School in Iowa in 1980. Over and over again, fundamentalists active in the movement highlighted the inseparability of religion and education. "No education has any foundation other than the Lord Jesus Christ," announced the principal of the Temple Christian School in Newark, Delaware. "We teach all subjects in relation to the Creator, who in his mind created mathematics, syntax, social studies—history is his story."[43]

Not every Christian school teacher and administrator believed that all subjects were easily taught from a fundamentalist perspective. Trudy Hathaway, principal of the Faith Heritage School in Syracuse, New York, explained the problem: "Some subjects are harder to relate to the Bible than others. Science is easier, math is harder. Social studies—we teach them to be responsible as Christian citizens. English— He wants us to speak clearly, to understand and to get our ideas across." School people generally saw God's design in every academic subject. History, everyone could agree, was God's unfolding plan, a time-honored Christian view. Also, observed one fundamentalist, "[I]t's not just happenstance that numbers fit together as they do." For "[I]n mathematics, we see reflected the order of God's universe. Two plus two equals four. It's that way yesterday, today, and tomorrow." When a conflict arose between a textbook and Biblical teaching, some fundamentalists quickly disposed of the problem. "If the Bible and a textbook differ, we know the textbook is wrong, and we teach children that."[44]

Through the conscious molding of a Bible-based curriculum, Christian school administrators and teachers created a genuinely alternative form of education. Academic subjects—math, history, and literature—were imbued with a religious orientation clearly absent in the public schools. Subjects such as science—especially the study of evolution—created special but not insurmountable problems in some Christian schools. "Evolution is not taught here," one Iowan explained, and his stance was hardly unusual. Many schools either did not teach evolution or simply taught that Genesis was correct and Darwin wrong: "We believe and we teach that man was created by God, and not derived from a monkey or any other source." A few schools apparently taught pupils that God created the world but that evolution also shaped human destiny, in accordance with a divine plan. By the 1980s, many taught creation science, which rejected Darwinian theories of evolution and emphasized "scientific" research that was presumably compatible with Genesis.[45]

Even science classes, therefore, reflected the religious values that permeated Christian schools. And when one looked beyond the formal curriculum to the overall climate of fundamentalist classrooms, one discovered an attempt to recapture a lost or mythical educational past, when all children presumably respected authority, had faith in God and nation, and became God-fearing and literate adults. Children learned much more than the materials contained in their ACE workbooks, for example, as they pored over them at their school desks or cubicles. Like pupils in more conventional Christian classrooms, they were taught about power and authority, propriety and decorum. If, as with public school children, they failed to learn these lessons well, it was not due to the lack of effort on the part of their teachers.

Like all schools, Christian academies taught values as well as academic subjects. Christian school activists regularly criticized the public schools for their liberal student dress and behavior codes, more casual attitudes about teacher authority, and presumed ethical decline due to the rise of a permissive culture in the 1960s. In 1981, a minister from Atlanta writing in *Christianity Today* conveniently summed up the fundamentalist position by asserting that "parents could once assume that when they sent their children to school, the traditional Judeo-Christian values they held would at least be respected by the schools, if not reinforced. But no longer can parents make that assumption." A high school senior in the Midwest, who similarly stereotyped the public system, made the identical point when she compared public school and Christian school discipline. "Here they teach us character and to have morals. In the public schools, they just let you go."[46]

Respect for authority, an aim that never disappeared from the public schools, became a central concern of fundamentalist education.

Dress codes and rules for personal behavior were standard in the typical Christian day school. For example, students (especially in ACE schools) frequently wore uniforms, appropriately often available in red, white, and blue. "If kids dress sharp, they're going to act sharp," said one Wichita, Kansas, private school activist. Pupils were expected to learn early in life that obedience and patriotism were closely bound at school and later in adult life. "If they [the students] don't salute the flag, they're out the door," said one partisan from Illinois in 1977. Taking this one step further, the principal of the North Coast Christian School in Seaside, Oregon, soon after told the *Portland Oregonian*, "I would like to be able to say that every boy who leaves this school would be willing to die for his country." Those who so openly expressed hostility toward the state for liberal social policies as openly proclaimed a manly patriotism and love of country.[47]

Obedience to authority was reinforced in countless ways during the school day. Children working in their cubicles on ACE materials, for example, raised Christian or American flags when they had a question for the teacher. Students at the Dade Christian School in Miami, Florida, were required to take an oath: "As a student of Dade Christian School, I will not cheat, swear, smoke, gamble, dance, drink alcoholic beverages, and will act in a very orderly and respectful manner." Moreover, students promised "not to draw, wear, or display in any way the 'peace' symbol" that many school leaders associated with liberal, even anarchist, views. One Christian school in Providence, Rhode Island, dispensed demerits for humming or singing without permission, and another prohibited children from getting closer than six inches from each other "to keep teenagers from necking and young children from fighting." These were not isolated examples but indicative of Christian school practices. Because students needed time to adjust to the traditional dress codes and discipline, the Kent Christian School in Delaware placed entering new students on six-week probationary status.[48]

To challenge authority (except for godless actions by the state) was a sin in the eyes of many Christian fundamentalists. A pamphlet for the Capital City Baptist School in Lansing, Michigan, stated: "The challenge to the authority of a parent or teacher is a challenge to God's authority." A Baptist preacher from Montgomery, Alabama, claimed that "we will not put up with any disobedience, disrespect to teachers or anything else. We try to build character as well as stress academics." For that reason, parents whose children attended fundamentalist schools often had to sanction the use of corporal punishment. One inventive pedagogue etched the words "Board of

Education" on the school paddle. "The Lord God made the butt for sitting on and for spanking," said a fundamentalist from Texas, and one national leader allegedly claimed that a genuine spanking leaves "marks" on the child. That attitude led to some lawsuits on child battery when teachers or principals used excessive force in some situations. These were extreme cases, and fundamentalist parents seemed to endorse corporal punishment when reasonably dispensed and with just cause.[49]

Emphasizing respect for God, parents, and nation, Christian schools during their formative decades tried to reconstruct an educational environment that many evangelicals and fundamentalists believed once existed in most public schools. Unfortunately, in their opinion, creeping secularism and liberalism undermined the state system and undermined its true mission: to produce students who were patriotic, mindful of authority, and decidedly Christian. Unlike public schools, which after World War II were legally and morally bound to admit and educate children from every background, no matter what the mental disability or other handicap, Christian schools, like all forms of private education, had much greater control over their student body. They chose who to admit and expelled those who violated their rules or were disruptive and troublesome. Christian school pupils caught smoking, drinking, or dancing were routinely expelled from many schools without a second chance, another example of substantive differences between the public and private sector. Strict dress codes virtually disappeared from many public schools in the 1970s but were ubiquitous in Christian academies. Teachers and administrators argued that short hair on boys and modest dress for girls reflected respect for authority and helped turn youth into productive, honest, and patriotic adults.[50]

In the larger and well-equipped Christian schools, especially on the secondary level, pupils participated in an array of school activities similar to those available in the secular system. Students joined the school chorus, marching band, academic study clubs, and a variety of service organizations, sometimes engaging in charitable projects to aid the poor and disadvantaged. As in public high schools, men's and women's team sports attracted eager participants and even more fans. Yearbooks applauded the heroics of the best players, highlighting the glory of victory, fair play, fortitude in the face of defeat, and school spirit—all familiar tropes in American athletics. Critics from the 1960s and afterwards nevertheless continued to criticize Christian schools for isolating their pupils from the modern world. All private schools, whether secular or sectarian, have historically been selective in who they attract, appeal to, and invite into their hallowed halls. But the charge of isolation from the larger world either infuriated or amused Christian school partisans. After all, their expressed desire was to shield children from the evils they perceived in the public schools. School activities aimed to reinforce Christian values, not imitate the

**Figure 6.1**   Some First Grade Pupils in a Christian School: Florida, 1988
Courtesy: Jeffrey Loveland

**Figure 6.2**  Karl Shoemaker and Teammates; Florida Christian School, 1988

Courtesy: Jeffrey Loveland and Karl Shoemaker

secular culture. As Christian teachers and administrators saw it, their overall aim was to protect their children from the low expectations of the public schools, the drug culture, secular textbooks, and a human-centered curriculum. A Christian school leader in North Carolina, recognizing the selective quality of pupils in religiously based schools, argued that "if anyone is isolated from ideas, it is the public schools. They are deprived of the Christian philosophy. They are a captive audience in the atheistic-humanistic culture."[51]

Oriented toward the Bible, determined to link spiritual training with sound basic academics, and led by individuals who were not afraid to contest state power, Christian schools testified to the diversity of educational life in post–World War II America. Americans will never agree upon a best way to educate everyone, and in a nation with deep religious roots, watered every generation by new waves of religious enthusiasm, fundamentalists came to espouse values that liberal academics and other critics denounced as racist, blindly patriotic, and narrow-minded. It did not deter these populists on the right. Some pressed for tuition tax credits during the Reagan years; others became strong advocates of voucher plans to enhance Christian education. However unique the historical circumstances surrounding their movement, they were part of a larger movement that questioned the hegemony of a state system of schools. Even nonfundamentalists unhappy with the system became attracted to school "choice" in the 1980s and 1990s, often but not always seeking alternatives within the public schools.

Throughout the 1970s and 1980s, the issue of state aid to fundamentalist institutions rightly troubled many fundamentalist activists. Increasingly a number of private school leaders, encouraged by the first Reagan administration, became attracted to the cause of tuition tax credits, to provide financial relief to parents who sent their children to non–public schools. But many remained skeptical of the state and worried about the intrusiveness that might follow any kind of public aid. When tuition tax credits were discussed in congressional hearings in the nation's capitol, groups such as the Alabama Christian Education Association and the North Carolina Association of Christian Schools adamantly opposed state aid. At the grassroots level, many individuals remembered that state control, to their thinking, had ruined mass education in the first place. As the principal of the Salem Academy in Oregon put it, "[W]e don't want some of that humanism imposed on us."[52]

These individuals found it inconsistent and possibly dangerous to refuse state regulation of their institutions, based on First Amendment rights, and then to lobby for various forms of direct and indirect public aid. They thought Christian educators were being hypocritical, and they opposed what appealed to others in the movement. A Pentecostal minister from Kentucky said it well in 1978 when he warned private school leaders about state entanglement: "We don't want any state money . . . . We don't want their nose in our business all the time." Similarly, a Baptist minister from Buffalo, New York, ridiculed the idea of tuition tax credits. "We feel Christian education should not be subsidized from other people's pocketbooks. Besides, anytime there is a subsidy, it opens the door to interference."[53]

Despite these warnings, some Christian school associations and fundamentalist leaders actively endorsed various schemes for state aid. When the Packwood-Moynihan tuition tax credit proposal was debated in 1978, *Christianity Today* observed that the bill had a range of supporters, including "many evangelicals who support private schools." Jerry Falwell and other evangelists, representing groups that historically opposed state aid and favored church-state separation, had done an "about-face." While Catholics, Lutherans, and traditional parochial schools had often fought in the past for various forms of state aid, the magazine continued, the "strongest support" for the bill "may be coming from backers of fundamentalist schools."[54]

There was no small measure of historical irony in the rise of evangelical and fundamentalist support for public aid to sectarian schools. When the U.S. Supreme Court upheld such support in its landmark decision in 2002, it heralded a break from the past. Recall that Protestants had been crucial in the creation of America's public school system and had vehemently rejected aiding religious schools. What was once a predominantly Catholic issue, however, now enjoyed wider support among former rivals than ever before existed in the nation's history. Not so long ago, when John F. Kennedy ran for president in 1960, he had to assure southern Protestants that he would not extend aid to parochial schools. But the court decision also followed a generation of changing public opinion about the place of schools in the social order. Altered perceptions of the public schools, hardly limited to fundamentalist Christians, had helped erode some age-old divisions between Catholics and Protestants as school choice and the expansion of private schools gained greater legitimacy. Christian school enrollments continued to grow in the 1990s and early twenty-first century. A minority within the massive Southern Baptist Convention even lobbied in 2004 for a resolution that would require all of its members to withdraw their children from public schools.[55]

In a little over a generation, Christian day schools and academies arose to become a common presence in the nation. At first most visible in the South, where they were scorned by liberals for undermining efforts at public school desegregation, Christian schools spread to every state, to big cities and small towns, suburbs and rural retreats. At the dawn of the millennium, about 22 percent of their pupils were from minority groups. Wherever these schools appeared, parents and religious leaders tried to recreate a world they believe once existed, one based on moral absolutes and certainty, safe havens of academic excellence and moral and religious probity. These schools would fuse religion into the curriculum and set their tone, thus enabling the young to become productive, God-fearing, patriotic adults. Youth could then become soldiers for Christ in the army of God.[56]

Christian day schools are examples of the plural worlds of values and institutions that have long characterized American culture. During the past few decades, these schools have educated millions of children whose parents dissented from the public system. Like most citizens, the advocates of Christian schools drew upon history to help understand their society and their response to modernity. They were convinced that the story of American public education was one of cultural and educational decline, of institutions that had fallen from a higher to a lower state. Fundamentalist (as well as secular) critics have put those who defended public schools on the defensive over the past half century, an era marked by sweeping change that accentuated the importance of schools in the modern world. Citizens disagreed about whether public schools effectively shaped both the personal and common good, and whether they were capable of reform and redemption. History also provides some perspective on how to think about those issues.

# Part IV

# The Fate of the Public Schools

# Chapter 7

# Public Schools and the Common Good

In the early twentieth century, numerous educational reformers had an expansive vision of the purposes of public education. Some lobbied for additional high schools to meet the exploding demand among adolescents for more secondary education; others as a result of this growth sought more vocational education programs for the less academically talented; and still other activists called for public funding for new social programs and services for children, from playgrounds to free breakfasts and lunches, especially for the urban poor. Another popular reform was the opening of schools in the evenings as neighborhood social centers. As part of this trend, schools served as polling centers on election day. Once contested reforms, these innovations remain a familiar and uncontroversial feature of local school systems.

In the mid-1980s, these reforms had a special professional and personal appeal. I taught at Indiana University in Bloomington and had recently completed a history of school innovation in the Progressive Era. Moreover, every election day, I voted at the local elementary school. At one particular school board election, I found myself standing in line next to a dean from the university's college of arts and science. Always friendly to me and confident in his opinions, he proceeded, despite our proximity to the voting booth, to tell me who deserved my support. A friend later persuaded me to volunteer as a "sheriff" for the Democratic Party to enforce the rules on election decorum, including the removal of campaign buttons and political signs too near the polls. But on the day in question the dean was lobbying for candidates who favored more programs for gifted pupils. That so many academicians and professionals whose children already attended the best public schools wanted more perquisites puzzled me, as did their occasional assurances that their children were, truly, above average. Children in some Bloomington neighborhoods lived in Appalachian-style poverty and attended the least prestigious schools, so I assumed that the already gifted would thrive without my electoral help.[1]

The one-sided conversation with the dean reminded me that the "chattering classes" (as the English call them) may support the schools but always want more for their own. Schools are always a site of competition for real and symbolic social advantages. And the last decades of the twentieth century were a good time to reflect upon the history of public education, since complaints about the system were ubiquitous and historical perspective sometimes missing. By the early 1980s, Republicans were increasingly ascendant on the national level and regularly heaped scorn on the schools, praised markets and private school alternatives, and thought public institutions deserved less, not more, support. President Ronald Reagan famously called government the problem, not the solution to problems.

All of this gave rise to a number of questions. What had been the role of public schools in contributing to the common good? Should schools, as part of the public sphere, try to offer a common course of study and common social experiences to everyone? What allowed the already advantaged to reap the most benefits from the system? The answers to these questions seemed buried in the past, which was worth exploring to learn how Americans had arrived at the present historical juncture. Choices and decisions made in the past are not binding on the future, but the legacies of various reform movements over the course of the twentieth century weakened the prospects of promoting the common good in contemporary schools. Understanding history helps to explain why.

Common, free schools, offering the best education found in private academies and seminaries, available to all children is a dream that had inspired the most idealistic northerners during the generation of Horace Mann. The secretary of the State Board of Education in his native Massachusetts from 1837 to 1848, Mann, along with countless northern reformers, assumed that a common curriculum and widely acceptable values could be defined and promoted through a single system of tax-supported education. Common schools remained the ideal but not always the reality. Most notably, African Americans faced educational exclusion or segregation in most of the northern states; nearly all working-class children had to work and never reached high school, and girls, though the majority in most secondary schools, similarly experienced discriminatory treatment (yet often thrived academically compared with boys). Still, the most prescient and thoughtful defenders of the rising public system, which ultimately enrolled the vast majority of white pupils, complained about how racism and poverty shackled children's lives. Abolitionists, feminists, and socialists frequently demanded more access to schools for the downtrodden and recommended more common treatment, not less, to address the inequalities in their midst.[2]

First in the North in the 1830s and 1840s and then more slowly in the South (after the Civil War), a diverse network of reformers led concerted campaigns to undermine the private sector and advance a common culture of knowledge and values in the schools. Private schools seemed exclusionary and thus socially divisive, while public schools promised to teach values fundamental to public order and to the survival of the republic, where laws and not men, said the textbooks, ultimately ruled. As the editor of the *Common School Assistant* wrote in 1839, all pupils would ideally be taught "in the same house, the same class, and out of the same book, and by the same teacher," which would shore up morality and ensure greater opportunity for everyone. Recall that "free schools" in cities traditionally served pauper children, including the churchless poor. As Mann wrote, however, Americans did not need a system of schools that "was necessarily cheap, ordinary, inferior, or which was intended for one class of the community; but such an education as was common in the highest sense, as the air and light were common; because it was not only the cheapest but the best, not only accessible to all, but, as a general rule, enjoyed by all."[3]

Then, as now, the suggestion that schools should transmit a common culture or body of ideas stirred up numerous critics. Private school masters and teachers resented the loss of income and parental choice that accompanied the rise of public schools, which monopolized tax dollars in the northern states by mid-century. Mann, like many common school leaders, had actually received some of his formal education at an academy, at a time when private school distinctions were less prominent or politically significant. Many former academy and private school teachers ultimately joined the public system as teachers and principals and sent their own children to the local free schools. On the other hand, the very notion of a common system of public education ignited intense controversies in other quarters, particularly among some outspoken religious leaders. Catholic bishops, for example, urged the faithful to build parochial schools and in the 1840s demanded, without success, tax relief. In the decades that followed, Catholics reliably complained about the sometimes open, sometimes thinly veiled Protestant values that often permeated the public schools, exemplified by morning prayers and readings from the King James Bible.[4]

In a careful study of educational practices in New York state, historian Benjamin Justice has revised our understanding of the place of religion in local schools in the nineteenth century. Scholars of church-state-school relations have often emphasized the centrality of conflict, exemplified by notable disagreements between Catholics and evangelical Protestants on policies such as school prayer, Bible reading, and the division of the school fund. National magazines and prominent journalists publicized these dramatic encounters, forming the impression that conflict was ever present in the nation's schools. In contrast, Justice shows that in New York state, school districts often resolved many disputes amicably, reaching consensus on which religious practices were permissible and frequently excluding practices that offended religious minorities. Local control allowed democratic processes to prevail in many communities in the Empire State, as parents and school officials worked out their differences peacefully and responsibly.[5]

The power of compromise can be seen in the various editions of the famous McGuffey Readers. William Holmes McGuffey was not only a college professor, but also was licensed as a Presbyterian minister whose popular series of readers and textbooks set a common standard in the public schools. To ensure the widest readership, McGuffey softened the sectarian tone of his books in successive editions, which satisfied the Protestant majority and ensured economic and pedagogical success. There were always some dissenting Protestants and Catholics who called the public system godless and overly secular. Compromise meant watering down sectarian beliefs to a more homogeneous Protestantism, but it helped the common system survive in a land of cultural and religious diversity.[6]

Building a common system was always fraught with difficulties and contradictions. Since the early republic, countless writers had emphasized the importance of establishing public schools. As early as 1779, Thomas Jefferson called for public funding for a network of schools for white children, including elementary education for boys and girls. To ensure social mobility among the poor and a more fluid social order, he envisioned a system that would identify the most talented boys at each level and advance them to a higher level, forming what he called a "natural aristocracy" of leadership drawn from the best and brightest students. Over the next generation, legislators in his native Virginia simply ignored his educational proposals, but some of the Founding Fathers and other national figures embraced the notion that schools should reward individual merit and play an elevated role in society. This was not lost upon Horace Mann's generation.[7] As historians Carl F. Kaestle and Maris A. Vinovskis have demonstrated, school attendance rates were already impressive in the North by the time of the "common school revival" in the 1820s and 1830s. Mann's generation labored to limit tax support to a single public system, undermine or eliminate private alternatives, and build a state-level bureaucracy to upgrade the schools. Compared to Jefferson, Mann had more expansive rhetoric about the benefits of state-sponsored schooling. Schools, he and his allies argued, promised something for everyone: literacy and numeracy, the inculcation of the values of personal responsibility, ambition, obedience to authority, and moral training through the teaching of nondenominational Protestantism. This would produce a literate work force and a strong economy. Such an eclectic rationale for a public school system, wrote historian Merle Curti, included guaranteeing everything from opportunity and mobility for the poor to security and safety for the rich.[8]

Mann and like-minded reformers wanted schools to unite a very diverse citizenry whose ethnic, racial, and class divisions lurked just beneath the surface, and exploded with fury in the 1860s. Yet the growth of the system continued. In the North, most white children attended elementary school for at least a few years, and the public sector expanded with each passing decade. Public, tax-supported schools also appeared in the South during Reconstruction due especially to the labors of freedmen and women, whose children were ultimately forced into underfunded Jim Crow schools as Democrats violently seized control of state governments in the region. In the northern schools, however, a common set of textbooks and values undergirded public education. Everywhere children sat in classrooms facing portraits of Washington and Lincoln: clear symbols of patriotism, valor, and nationalism. (In the South, Robert E. Lee adorned the segregated white schools.) Everywhere children studied similar subjects that promoted basic literacy, numeracy, and at a minimum knowledge about geography and history, all taught in a patriotic vein. Ploughboys and poor girls alike temporarily left cornfields and the family wash for the lofty worlds of Shakespeare and Wordsworth, whose words graced the ubiquitous McGuffey readers. Whether in homogenous one-room schools in the countryside or immigrant-filled graded classrooms in the city, children were taught (even if they did not always learn) common values: self discipline, delayed gratification, and deference to their elders and to their often young and inexperienced female teachers.[9]

To share in a common culture: this was seen by the most idealistic educational reformers in the nineteenth century as a democratic right and the hope of the republic. While offensive to some Catholics and sectarian Protestants, the schools emphasized an ecumenical Protestantism to ensure the widest participation in the system. Foreign languages were added to the curriculum in some northern cities, reflecting the political clout of immigrants. Adding German also drew German-speaking youth out of private academies and into the system. Late in the century, schools typically maintained their focus on English language instruction, cultural assimilation, and social cohesion. Indeed, if growth is the principal measure of success, the public system triumphed impressively. Responding to the demands of reformers across the political spectrum, the schools soon added a range of social services and new curricula, expanding their mission and accentuating their importance in the nation's welfare.[10]

Beginning in the 1890s, America entered a new age of reform commonly known as the Progressive Era (ca. 1890–1920). It was a period personified on the national level by such figures as John Dewey, Jane Addams, Theodore Roosevelt, and Woodrow Wilson. Imbued with a sense of hopefulness and confidence in human progress, many lesser-known people on the local level became identified with various reform causes, including the democratization of education and the schools. Contemporaries thus had good reasons to believe that public education would receive heightened attention and perhaps extend the promise of American life to more young people. Would schools mostly advance the wants of the few or the aspirations of the many? How this question was answered would shape the basic contours of modern American education.

The economic depression of the 1890s was the worst yet experienced in American history, and the human misery it spawned gave rise to a range of reform movements, many of which focused on the young. Exposés of poverty and its effects on children's life chances and academic performance were common by the turn of the century. Citizens also worried about whether the nation could adequately assimilate and educate immigrants from central and southern Europe who arrived by the millions, seeking work in the industrial North. As waves of displaced rural folk and the immigrant newcomers transformed the economy, private charities and public services faced unprecedented demands. Numerous voluntary associations, often led by women, called for the adoption of more social services in the urban schools, from summer enrichment classes, to playgrounds, to the overall wider use of schools. Moderate socialists such as Robert

Hunter and other citizens lobbied for free school meals for the poor, and progressive trade unionists often rallied behind the cause. Along with other social justice liberals, Jane Addams, the famous settlement house leader in Chicago, urged teachers in the schools—whose main job included teaching English and integrating students into the "melting pot"—to better appreciate the cultural "gifts" of the immigrant newcomers. And while Jim Crow still ruled the South and racial discrimination remained all too common in the North, white and black activists in 1909 formed the National Association for the Advancement of Colored People, which began its long struggle for civil rights and school desegregation. For the public schools, the essential question was whether they would teach commonality and cultural assimilation to enhance opportunities, or emphasize human and cultural differences to promote inequality.[11]

In the early 1900s, philosophers such as John Dewey expanded upon what Jefferson, Mann, and other writers earlier said about the place of public schools in the social order. No one reflected more thoughtfully about the place of schools in local communities and the intimate relationship between democracy and education than Dewey. Democracy, Dewey believed, was impossible in a modern industrial world unless all children had access to common knowledge, values, and understandings. The methods by which children were taught—a time-revered emphasis on rote memorization and recitation of knowledge learned from textbooks—was mind-numbing but, Dewey argued, schools were integral to accessing and transmitting knowledge in the modern world. The scientific and technological innovations of the past half century, which underpinned the industrial revolution, destroyed traditional crafts and time-honored ways of living. It was also a small step from Darwin's theory of evolution and natural selection to conclude that institutions, like everything in the natural world, either adapted to change or faced extinction or decline. Dewey feared that unless children were exposed to the recent explosion of knowledge and taught how to think creatively and independently, they would be ill prepared to cope with modern civilization, a world of factories and cities, and constant change. Without effective schools, democracy would wither.[12]

In the decades that followed, various conservatives, including fundamentalist Christians, frequently blamed Dewey for any number of unwanted changes perceived in modern schools. He was held responsible for the secularization of the schools, declining standards, and an amorphous humanism that presumably displaced God from the classroom. In truth, as historian Herbert M. Kliebard explains, Dewey's

impact on the schools is difficult to pinpoint. Dewey had a host of
followers within liberal circles and especially among professors of education. But he was first and foremost a philosopher, not an in-the-
trenches school reformer. When appointed to a professorial post at the
University of Chicago in the 1890s, he established an experimental
school that largely served the children of fellow faculty members in
Hyde Park. The "Lab School" became world famous, but it was his
only real connection to on-the-ground school reform. Off to
Columbia University in 1904, Dewey wrote a number of landmark
books on education (and many other subjects) over the next forty
years. His criticisms of traditional teaching methods, emphasis on the
importance of scientific experimentation and the scientific method,
and endorsement of critical thinking rather than on religious instruction and inculcation of absolute truths, made him popular among
liberals and the bête noire of many conservatives.[13]

Dewey's writings were very critical of the unsettling consequences
of industrial capitalism, and he wanted schools to become the center
of a democratic community. Numerous left-liberal thinkers and
school reformers in the early 1900s became attracted to "progressive
education," an amalgam of sentiments whose basic premise was
more freedom for the child and more "child-centered" instruction.
These individuals frequently cited Dewey as a major source of inspiration. Had he not criticized traditional pedagogy and built a famous
laboratory school? Did he not promote evolutionary perspectives and
eschew a fixed curriculum that would endure for all times? Yes, but as
he made clear in *Experience and Education* (1938) and elsewhere,
Dewey found many of his erstwhile followers, who often patronized
private schools, misguided. They sometimes embraced saccharin views
of the child and lacked clear instructional aims. The fact that he long
inspired them fueled the popular notion of his profound impact on
modern schooling. Documenting his influence upon public schools,
however, is much more difficult.[14]

Public intellectuals such as Dewey certainly elevated the quality of
debates on education and democracy among a national audience, and
contemporaries such as Lucy Sprague Mitchell—founder of the
progressive Bank Street College of Education—among many others
helped popularize novel views on children and teaching. In different
times and places, reformers who did not seem to read or, if they did,
understand his writings, invoked Dewey's name to support any
number of innovations: child-centered education, the elimination of
textbooks and elevation of "hands-on" learning, narrow vocationalism, and so forth. That he never championed these reforms seemed

irrelevant to his fans and detractors. Even today's "progressive educators" are shocked to hear that Dewey believed that much child-centered instruction was mere pabulum.[15] Dewey was never a dominant or powerful voice in mainstream school reform movements during the Progressive Era. Others with much less regard for democracy and community were far more influential in shaping the modern school system. Even child-centered progressive educators, as Dewey pointed out, focused most of their efforts on private, not public schools, the latter being in the grip of didactic teaching methods and rote learning in the 1920s as before. Child-centered progressives had little influence upon what was happening in the public schools that the masses of children attended.

During the Progressive Era, there were certainly prominent examples of efforts to humanize the schools, exemplified in the expanding array of social services, vacation schools, playgrounds, and use of the schools as social centers. But other reforms were underway that undermined democratic participation and substantially weakened the ideal of the common school.

The Progressive Era was an age in which many college-educated, equally reform-minded people and more conservative business elites together successfully eliminated neighborhood representation by leading campaigns to consolidate and centralize town and city school boards. As David B. Tyack and numerous scholars have demonstrated, these reformers elevated the role of expertise and hierarchy in the schools, particularly the office of superintendent, opposition to which encouraged teachers to form their first labor unions. Influential lay people and educators often promoted more nonacademic curricula for increasing numbers of children in the form of vocational education programs. The phrase "common school" became archaic in the wake of these dramatic changes.[16]

Ability grouping, evident in some urban schools in the late nineteenth century, soon became a familiar classroom practice. Generally overrepresentative of the poor, the slower tracks of pupils were separated from the higher-status academic tracks in which the middle and upper classes predominated. Instead of having access to teachers' aides and other support to lift them closer to the higher achievers, children in the lowest ability groups generally received more didactic instruction and conventional discipline. There was usually little movement between ability groups, and the slower pupils, once behind, rarely caught up. Social promotion also became more common after World War I, and the ability groups of the elementary grades became the feeders for the differentiated curricula found in more secondary schools.[17]

The ideal of a common school and a common educational experience for everyone, always easier to honor in theory than in practice, retreated amid these changes. Academic instruction became more closely associated with children from better-off families, though never exclusively so. Professionals and elites who favored the adoption of vocational education for other people's children nevertheless did everything possible to keep their own out of such tracks and programs. Unlike Germany, where tighter connections between industry, the state, and the schools raised the level of technical training, vocational education in the United States remained low status, often serving as a holding tank for poor underachievers and troublesome youth. William T. Harris's earlier concerns about the weakening of a common curriculum for all pupils thus proved to be prescient. Along with labor groups in Chicago, Dewey opposed efforts among local businessmen to establish separate vocational and academic high schools. Naively or not, he believed that schools should not physically separate the student body, but provide everyone with the critical intelligence to help in the reconstruction and democratization of industrial society. But fundamental organizational and curricular changes, when reinforced by new educational theories that emphasized human differences, tended to confirm and reinforce the social inequalities of different groups of children.[18]

In an era of rapid social and industrial change, the common school ideal lost its resonance as liberal academicians, conservative businessmen, and a range of educational leaders remade schools in the image of the new bureaucratic order. Technological inventions displaced many youngsters from the workforce before World War I, and child laborers were replaced by the steady supply of adult immigrants seeking industrial jobs. All this meant that more working-class children spent more years of their lives in school. As children from diverse backgrounds entered school for longer periods, a small number of the most talented and ambitious poor students had greater opportunity to attend high school and improve their life prospects. But scientific developments that increasingly shaped educational policy effectively undermined the broadest access to high-quality instruction. Intelligence tests—initially promoted in Europe to help individuals by diagnosing learning problems—were a major innovation of the Progressive Era, and they helped sort, classify, and stream children of the working classes into the least academic curricula. Often attracted to eugenic theories that emphasized the inherent inferiority of particular ethnic and racial groups, many of the inventors and popularizers of the tests were no friends of democracy or to the idea of equal access to common schools. Test results, said many, demonstrated the inherent inequality of children.[19]

Historians studying the early twentieth century have thus discovered an apparent paradox: an age in which child-centered, positive affirmations of the child flourished as did concerted efforts to undermine equality in the schools. Children were placed into ability groups and tracks on the basis of grades, IQ tests, and achievement scores and such classification would long remain an impediment to equal education. Jim Crow also solidified in the South, and racial tensions sometimes turned into riots after African Americans moved to the North. Having been displaced from farms, they were attracted to jobs made available as European immigration slowed during World War I and was virtually ended by immigrant restriction laws in the mid-1920s. In addition, advocates of vocational education and scientific testing always ensured that their own children attended the best available schools, public or private. Those who patronized private schools also

**Figure 7.1** Jim Crow in the Midwest: First and Second Grade in New Albany, Indiana, 1908

*Source*: Twenty-Fourth Biennial Report of the State Superintendent of Public Instruction (Indianapolis, 1908)

Courtesy: Wisconsin Historical Society Image ID Whi-42582

often made sure that these schools had not only innovative pedagogy, but also solid academic courses. Leading social scientists and researchers who worked at the University of Chicago, Teachers College, Columbia, or other centers of academic influence saw little contradiction between calling for a less academic education for the working classes and enrolling their own children in the choicest schools. Lucy Sprague Mitchell of Bank Street, known for yelling at neighborhood children who strayed onto her lawn, typically sent her children to private school, continuing a family tradition. Academic liberals were nevertheless eager to experiment with the education and life chances of public school children, helping them adjust to the emerging corporate state.[20]

Most liberal academics were comfortable with the dominant school reforms of the period. They were hostile toward political machines and working-class politics and supported the drive to consolidate power in the hands of professionals within the schools. They applauded the new, long-lasting reforms that entered most school systems: testing, ability grouping, tracking, and vocational education. As the decades passed, school districts consolidated, and smaller schools were replaced by larger ones, making the expansion of diversified curricula easier. Appropriately enough, schools sometimes resembled industrial plants, the organizational models most prized by administrators in the urban North. These were among the really substantive changes that transformed the schools in the formative decades of the twentieth century.[21]

Without a doubt, the child increasingly became the object of "scientific" study in the early twentieth century. Even though some of Mitchell's children, it turns out, felt like "guinea pigs," public and private research universities increasingly promoted the scientific study of the child. Recall that the Progressive Era witnessed the creation of university departments of education and research bureaus in major cities and state departments of public instruction. Higher education provided the expertise to evaluate, examine, and disseminate new research on children, from studies on health to academic performance. Somehow the research results never led many educators to promote a common, high-quality academic curriculum for everyone. The research also never seemed to support such measures as reducing school bureaucracy or diminishing ethnic and racial stereotypes once the test results were posted.[22]

Meeting the needs of children, a commonly invoked objective in the early twentieth century, became a scientific and moral imperative and promised social efficiency and order. Child-centered reformers and theorists, often liberal or otherwise left-of-center politically, usually emphasized in their own more romantic ways that children were different, that they needed different curricula, pedagogy, and experiences at school. It was impossible to argue with the self-evident truth that all people are individuals, and different. Some pupils also had severe disabilities that made learning a high-quality academic curriculum impossible. But for most children, the question remained: were the differences a matter of degree, or of kind? Turn-of-the-century reformers involved in the testing movement concluded that individual differences were profound and innate; a common course of study for the majority of children was therefore economically wasteful, socially harmful, and contrary to scientific evidence. These academics, it should be emphasized, frequently thought of themselves as liberal-minded activists, opposed to tradition. And tradition, at its idealistic best, held that everyone should have access to as much common learning as possible.

Liberals active in school reform wanted to separate the poor for their own academic good. Testing and sorting—revived in our times as a central tool of educational improvement—placed disproportionate numbers of working-class children in nonacademic tracks to "meet their needs." This became a mantra in the early decades of the century. Prominent educators from the leading universities, armed with the results from IQ and other tests, publicized the incontrovertible truths about human inequality. Scientific study showed that only a select few could profit from serious academic instruction; there was no point in educating everyone for the top of the occupational ladder. Pupils varied in their intelligence, ambition, and probable life destiny, and school attendance, researchers said, actually exacerbated those differences. As a scholar from the University of Wisconsin wrote in the *Elementary School Journal* in 1914, "[T]he concept of the normal child is a rather useless fiction." Responding to the dramatic growth of high schools that increasingly enrolled more working-class youth, the long-time editor of the *High School Journal* shared the common view in 1935 that an academic curriculum was inappropriate for the new waves of pupils, given their "great range of individual abilities, interests, aptitudes, and outlooks. . . ." Textbooks in teacher training courses claimed that it made little sense to educate future truck drivers, domestics, and the college-bound in similar academic subjects.[23]

Many of the original advocates of scientific testing believed in eugenics, which was not incompatible with political radicalism, as Margaret Sanger, M. Carey Thomas, and other elite feminists demonstrated. John Dewey, Walter Lippmann, and other liberals condemned the excesses of scientific testing and exposed their ethnocentrist, racist, and class biases. Assaults on eugenics also multiplied in reaction to the rise of fascism in the 1920s and 1930s. But the popularity of testing and evaluation, shorn of their most pernicious ethnocultural prejudices, lived on as schools became ever important in the second half of the twentieth century. As credentials became more central to adult success, tests in various forms determined school achievement, college access, and educational worth.[24]

The fate of the common good after World War II remained bound by the lasting scientific reforms of the Progressive Era and reflected familiar battles over the purpose of public education. How should schools respond to human differences? Should schools strive for greater inclusion? Public schools were often in the center of many struggles for democracy and social justice—promoting racial desegregation following *Brown v. Board of Education* (1954), raising school achievement among the poor through Great Society programs, and expanding opportunities for children with special educational needs. Democracy nevertheless created its opposite. By the late 1960s, elite liberals, often describing those unlike themselves as "culturally disadvantaged," often pressed for more freedom for the child and a softening of standards. A weakening economy in the 1970s then fueled a resurgent political conservatism that led many people to believe that the schools were somehow responsible for the nation's economic woes, which included high levels of inflation and unemployment.[25]

By the early 1980s, neither conservative nor liberal critics of the schools seemed particularly concerned about promoting the common or public good in the schools. Few voices could be heard calling for a demanding academic curriculum for everyone. Conservatives, enamored with limiting government spending on social welfare but not on the military, complained about high taxes and low academic standards and wanted more tax breaks for the rich and a better supply of workers for the service economy. But they hardly endorsed full and equal funding for education or the elimination of vocational programs, still common in many schools, even though so-called practical courses were usually academically anemic and did not lead to decent jobs. Liberal educationists at the university (whose own children were often groomed for elite private colleges) almost universally attacked the suggestion that everyone should learn a common body of knowledge, never mind "cultural literacy." Radical revisionist historians, to the left of liberalism, said schools had always been complicit in keeping the social order unequal. The appeal of educational "choice" came from the left and right of the political spectrum, and it fit well the market ethos of the times. It meant many things to many people—magnet schools, alternative high schools within the public school system, Christian academies for those dropping out and, by the end of the century, charter schools.[26]

The Democratic Party lost its once commanding leadership in shaping debates about educational policy. Moreover, as my little incident near the voting booth revealed, the liberal Democratic elite supported the schools, but always ensured that children from their own social class were favored anyway; conservative Republicans in turn wanted to privatize every sector of society, widening the economic gap between rich and poor and assailing the public sphere whenever possible. As the Democratic Leadership Council, led by the then Governor Bill Clinton of Arkansas, helped tilt Democrats to the right in the late 1980s and early 1990s, both major parties seemed indistinguishable on many issues, from support for standardized testing to ongoing criticisms of teachers and pupils. In Washington, Democrats followed Republican leadership and endorsed national educational goals, including making America number one in math and science, which won bipartisan support, at least rhetorically. There were certainly differences between the two parties. Democrats were less likely to endorse tuition tax credits or vouchers, which would have alienated part of their political base: teachers' unions. But the distance between them had narrowed as the Democratic Party tried to become more nationally competitive. Criticizing the public schools and calling for their "reform" became the norm no matter who sat in the White House.[27]

Many things stood in the way of reviving the notion that the schools might or should offer each child a high-quality common curriculum and teach a common value system. While there was some raising of standards in the 1980s due to the restoration of some required courses in lieu of electives, overall the improvements were minor, and the achievement levels of minority groups and the poor did not improve as dramatically as reformers desired. Moreover, school funding among districts remained very unequal as the nation approached the millennium. Inner cities, which after World War II became increasingly poor and nonwhite, struggled to attract the best teachers and sometimes seemed on the verge of social meltdown. Suburbs varied in wealth and status, but they were largely white and more prosperous, with the capacity to fund their schools well. Those with the most economic resources had the most access to a college preparatory education. Civil rights groups battled successfully in the courts in many states to equalize funding, but legislatures frequently dragged their feet to ensure another round of lawsuits.[28]

As if access to the best local schools was not enough, middle- and upper-class (and usually white) families found other ways to ensure a competitive advantage. Advanced placement courses, first created in the early 1950s, remained scarce in urban high schools, which struggled to provide enough up-to-date textbooks and optimal learning environments for pupils. Poor children, frequently but not always nonwhite, formed the majority of pupils both in special education and vocational education. Despite the achievements of the civil rights movement, equalizing access to high-quality education proved elusive. In the cities, conservatives as well as liberal middle- and upper-class parents regularly sent their children to private schools. At the end of the twentieth century, establishing a more democratic school system focused on equality and the common good seemed doubtful.[29]

Horace Mann and his generation had dreamed of an inclusive, tax-supported school system that assimilated the foreign born, allowed talent from all social classes to rise, and taught a common curriculum and similar values. This ideal was undermined by key scientific and organizational reforms of the Progressive Era and by the waning of the modern civil rights movement. On college campuses late in the century, academic liberals who administered teacher-training programs disparaged the idea of the melting pot, seeing it as a form of cultural genocide and a cover for the bourgeois norms of the white middle classes. Bilingualism and multiculturalism were the favored reforms, mostly rejected by the resurgent Republican Party, which increasingly called for more choice programs, voucher initiatives, charter schools, and alternatives to the public schools. When they called for higher standards and more accountability in the public schools, conservatives usually ignored the problems of childhood poverty or the lack of sufficient resources for many schools. A few theorists in the academy periodically endorsed a core curriculum in the liberal arts, but they were usually dismissed by colleagues as misguided or politically dangerous.[30]

When President George W. Bush, with help from the nation's most visible liberal Democrat, Senator Ted Kennedy of Massachusetts, sponsored "No Child Left Behind" (2001), it brought renewed emphasis to standardized tests. Testing in its different expressions had an old, sometimes unseemly history, but its appeal had never been limited to "conservatives." While commonly associated with modern-day Republicans, testing was avidly supported by leading liberals after World War II. During congressional hearings on the establishment of Great Society programs to boost the academic achievement of the poor, Bobby Kennedy, not Strom Thurmond, insisted on mandatory evaluations to see if the programs worked. Major advocates of national testing in the 1960s included Francis Keppel, former Harvard dean of education and the U.S. Commissioner of Education during the Kennedy and early Johnson administrations, and Ralph Tyler, who had headed a team of researchers in the 1930s that studied and praised progressive teaching practices in selective secondary schools. Tyler was a significant force in national testing and in the establishment of the National Assessment of Educational Progress (NAEP), begun in 1969. Critics suspect that the Bush administration made testing central to "No Child Left Behind" to help undermine public schools and elevate the private sector. They may be correct, but testing has long enjoyed favor on both sides of the political aisle.[31]

During the 2004 presidential campaign, George W. Bush promised to extend the federal requirements on testing, now limited to elementary and middle schools, upward to the high school during his second term. The inner city and rural poor have never outperformed wealthier families, and the test results will probably confirm that history can repeat itself. Those who reduce education to test results, important as they are, rarely take the full measure of a school. Schools offer many children positive benefits. In poor neighborhoods, the local school is often safer than the surrounding city streets. In a nation without universal health coverage and with millions of poor children, schools often provide subsidized or free meals at breakfast and lunch, provide psychological counseling and guidance, and other social services. Despite the obstacles, some very poor youth continue to rise, as Jefferson predicted. And many teachers still teach pupils right from wrong, the importance of punctuality and hard work, and the skills and sensibilities that can lead to adult success.[32]

Schools have long served multiple purposes, many of them nonacademic. This has only obscured what should be a prime aim of any modern educational system: providing the wherewithal for the vast majority of pupils to be intellectually engaged by an academically respectable curriculum. Is this a pipedream in a class-stratified though often expansive and vibrant economy? Schools were long able to keep standards high for the few, and lower for the many, since an industrial economy allowed many poorly educated people to sustain themselves and their families. That economic world has disappeared, as low-end, low-pay jobs without health insurance and adequate pension plans for workers have proliferated. And Americans have long turned to the schools to meet various social ends, from providing entertainment on the gridiron on Friday night to feeding hungry children. I am reminded of the multiple roles schools play in society and their contributions to the common welfare every time I now vote at our neighborhood elementary school in Madison, Wisconsin. The school is ironically enough named for a nineteenth-century romantic who briefly and unsuccessfully tried his hand at teaching: Henry David Thoreau.[33]

# Chapter 8

# Why Americans Love to Reform the Public Schools

Americans from all walks of life espouse the cause of school reform. The past generation has witnessed the rise of education governors and education presidents. The CEOs of major corporations, big-city mayors, private sector entrepreneurs, inner-city parents, the heads of teacher unions, and every politician under the sun have often found the mantra of school reform irresistible. Public Broadcasting System documentaries, B-movies starring heroic teachers (sometimes armed with clubs) battling ignorance and the streets, and editorials in local newspapers about this or that educational crisis have kept the problems and promise of public schools visible, though the public's attention span is often about as long lived as morning glories.

Over the last century, schools have become multipurpose institutions, which is why they are so easy to criticize and forever in need of reform. Schools are expected to feed the hungry, discipline the wayward, identify and encourage the talented, treat everyone alike while not forgetting that everyone is an individual, raise test scores but also feelings of self-worth, ensure winning sports teams without demeaning academics, improve standards but also graduation rates, provide for the differing learning styles and capacities of the young while administering common tests, and counter the crass materialism of the larger society while providing the young with the skills and sensibilities to thrive in it as future workers. No other institution in American society carries this weight on its shoulders. No other institution is so public, familiar, and exposed to such scrutiny. The current penchant of equating a school's worth with its test scores makes sense in a sports-saturated world of winners and losers, but does it really reflect society's full range of expectations for the schools?[1]

The bewildering, often contradictory range of expectations ensures that some people are perpetually unhappy with public education. And therefore school reform remains a very hardy perennial. In good times and bad, teachers enjoy relatively low status as professionals and are routinely ridiculed in the press yet ironically always have tall orders to fill from the public's wish list: to strengthen children's character, morals, manners, work ethic, civic consciousness, racial and multicultural sensitivities, and anything else needing improvement. Nothing in the preceding sentence deals directly with academic achievement. Unlike test results, these familiar goals may be important, but difficult to measure and quantify and to know when one has reached them. Moreover, this begs the question of why teachers, so often accused of teaching the basics so poorly, should be entrusted with other grave responsibilities.[2]

Future historians will have their hands full trying to explain why the public and countless policymakers in the past half century regarded every social, economic, and political ill as an educational problem. Why were schools, as in previous generations, supposed to compensate for the deficiencies of parents, religious leaders, or the actions of high-placed government officials? When Sputnik was launched in the late 1950s, critics especially found the schools wanting, even though scientists working in the defense establishment and politicians in Washington received some condemnation. Similarly, when Japan's economy boomed in the early 1980s and America's sputtered, many people principally blamed the schools, not Detroit. The nation was at risk because of a lousy school system, said the Reagan administration. When the economy improved, teachers hardly shared in the credit; indeed, criticisms of the schools continued unabated.[3]

After Japan's economy precipitously declined, American admirers of its schools were notable for their silence. This should have lessened the number of seat-of-the-pants' judgments about school quality and cause-and-effect relationships between schools and the economy. But the schools still enjoyed a largely negative press and remained an endless field of dreams for assorted reformers. Accountability in all its permutations lost none of its appeal. By the late 1980s, national education goals, targeted for the year 2000, attracted bipartisan support including that of a young governor from Arkansas, Bill Clinton. Both the Clinton presidency and Goals 2000 are now history. Today the Bush administration has directed the schools to leave no child behind, or at least untested, even in cash-strapped, poor districts, some of which spend much less per capita on the instruction of their pupils than affluent neighbors. Obviously, those who think only Democrats endorse unfunded mandates have not been paying attention. Over the last generation, Republicans have mainly kept school reform prominent, with Democrats trailing behind.[4]

For all the easy talk about educational improvement, reformers closer to the trenches than to a pundit's mighty pen have long despaired at effecting comprehensive changes in the schools. All institutions may be complicated places, but it is hard to change the inner life of the typical school. That has not stopped anyone from trying, or at least from writing or talking about it. Various reformers typically aim their sights on different problems—bureaucracy, poorly trained teachers, low reading scores, low graduation rates, uninspired pedagogy, an outmoded or impractical curriculum, poor achievement in math and science, and everything else eighteen-year-olds do not know well. The job of improvement is rarely comprehensive, despite occasional rhetorical spin, and victory (as in any war on sometimes multiple, elusive targets) proves nearly impossible. Schools affect so many different aspects of the lives of children and youth that the playing field for constructive change has neither clear boundaries nor universally accepted ground rules.

A many-splendored thing, school reforms sometimes resemble, at least superficially, those of yesteryear. The discovery that poor children start life with educational and social disadvantages caused some reformers in the nineteenth century to champion kindergartens; a century later, Head Start, while hardly a new version of the child's garden, shared similar assumptions about poverty and the need for early intervention. Some reforms seem timeless. That schools can teach vocational skills, especially to those who are not prize scholars, remains popular even though study after study reveals little economic payoff for the academically challenged. Still other reforms try to eliminate earlier ones. For many decades, for example, the educational establishment shared the time-tested view that what was good for General Motors was good for education; it nearly unanimously championed the consolidation of school districts and the construction of big schools. Small was not beautiful. Bigger schools promised to save money through economies of scale; bigness also allowed the spread of more courses and electives. But critics in the 1960s and 1970s said that large impersonal schools bred anomie and spawned curricular chaos. Another reform, perhaps—such as "schools within schools"— would help save the day. Other reformers applauded the concept of multiage classrooms, once the mainstay of one-room schools, which took over a century for reformers to eliminate. One generation's improvement had become another's source of complaint.[5]

Why do Americans love to reform the schools? My answer has three parts. First, there is an old and persistent cultural strain in American history, derived from many sources, that seeks human perfection and sees education and schooling as essential to that perfectibility. That goal is high enough to guarantee that most people will not cross the finish line. And this means that numerous citizens at any point in time bemoan the quality of the public schools, which cannot simultaneously achieve laudable but mutually contradictory goals, such as high standards and equality. Second, many Americans believe that our nation is uniquely respectful of the individual and, as a corollary to that belief, has a remarkably fluid social order. Individuals are so highly regarded that they are held personally responsible for their school performance. In the modern world, schools decisively help determine which individuals will or will not attend college, who will rise into the professions or sink into the service economy. When schools cannot produce success for everyone, citizens often blame teachers, not the more powerful folks in charge of the economy. Third, as alluded to earlier, over the past two centuries America's public schools have assumed so many responsibilities for the care, discipline, and education of the young that they inevitably disappoint many people. The current mania for standardized testing hardly means that schools have shed their many social functions, many unrelated directly to academic achievement. The dream of perfection, the supreme faith in the individual and social mobility through appropriate schooling, and the unexamined assumption that schools should cure whatever ails the nation make educational reform a constant concern in American society.

One primal factor, then, in America's fascination with school reform is an enduring popular faith in social improvement and human perfectibility, despite abundant contrary evidence about the behavior of real people. Some of the most famous original white settlers in America grappled with the ancient problem of free will and the question of human improvement. Readers may recall from history class that the Puritans settled in the Massachusetts Bay colony in the 1630s and 1640s. The nation's leading satirist of the 1920s, H. L. Mencken, defined "puritanism" as "the haunting fear that someone, somewhere, may be happy." Living in the age of Freud, Mencken blamed the Puritans for every contemporary repressive movement, from the Ku Klux Klan to prohibition. They are also often stereotyped as dour individuals, though their penchant for hanging witches in Salem and Quakers in Boston has not helped their reputation. Fundamentally, however, the Puritans who came to America, unlike those who stayed in England, were reformers, not revolutionaries. They did not behead kings but they did found schools, despite their insistence that parents and the ministry were essential in children's education. They hardly intended to build a comprehensive or inclusive system of education in any modern sense, yet they certainly shaped cultural attitudes about the young and about schools that still resonate.[6]

The Puritans were part of the larger Protestant Reformation that began in the German states in the early sixteenth century, thanks to the labors of Martin Luther. As part of a multipronged assault on the authority of the Church of Rome, Protestant reformers throughout Europe stressed the importance of individual conscience in matters of faith. Access to the word of God and divine wisdom, they said, should derive not from the teaching of priests but through individual access to the Bible. That required a widening of literacy and greater emphasis on education in general and schools in particular. Arising in the late 1500s during Elizabeth's reign, the English Puritans shared this larger Protestant faith in the individual and in the importance of literacy; they wanted to purge the Anglican Church, set up by Elizabeth's father Henry VIII, of its popish trappings. By the 1620s, however, as the economy soured and religious repression by the Stuarts intensified, they concluded that New rather than Old England might be a better place to build a model society and reform their world.[7]

One of their leaders, John Winthrop, reminded his brethren that the Puritans did not wish to break away from England but serve as an example to it. In what became a famous sermon delivered to the faithful as they departed for New England, Winthrop urged the establishment of a "city upon a hill," a beacon of Christian light so powerful that it would illuminate and reform their sinful homeland. This idea of creating a model commonwealth was shared by some rivals such as the Quakers of the Middle Colonies. Like other Protestant reformers, Puritan leaders held a high standard for personal probity and achievement, and their theology and everyday experience taught them that humans, especially the young, were morally frail and imperfect. Many of these little sinners were destined to fail on earth and suffer an eternal winter below.[8]

By the second generation of settlement, the Puritans were loudly bemoaning the failures of their society: the young, they claimed, were using too much foul language, and young men grew their hair too long and were insolent and disrespectful of their elders. In numerous sermons and published tracts, ministers denounced these evil tendencies, including the horrible reality that many second and third generation Puritans increasingly failed to have a born-again experience, or religious conversion. Technically, they were not Christians. The American Jeremiad—named for the gloomy prophet of the Old Testament—was born. Cultural decline, it seemed, was the order of the day. For many, saintly perfection was an unattainable ideal, though Puritan striving helped counter this declension and led some to worldly success, which became a visible sign of the elect. According to Max Weber, this strain of Protestantism nurtured the famous work ethic that became the midwife of early capitalism and a more secular culture.[9]

By setting the standard high for right living, economic success, and intellectual achievement (which included founding Harvard College in 1636), the Puritans encouraged a level of attainment beyond the reach of many. Standardized tests to measure academic success lay far in the future, and no one had yet devised national educational goals or timetables, but the Puritan dream of a city upon a hill was the first of many utopian aspirations of what was possible in America. Realizing that parents and churches alone could not lead the young toward literacy and decency, the Puritans (like Luther and his followers in Germany) established tax-supported elementary and grammar schools. These schools helped make New England one of the most literate parts of the world around the time of the American Revolution.[10]

The Puritans not only contributed to the notion of community responsibility for establishing schools, but also provided later generations, even those that grew more secular, with a ritualized way of thinking about society and young people. They frequently reminded listeners of the failings of the young, whose behavior vividly contrasted with the achievements of their elders. As the *New England Primer* taught generations of children in the colonial era, "In Adam's Fall, we sinn'd all." But the young seemed to sin and falter the most. Periodic waves of evangelical revivalism in the centuries that followed reminded many citizens of the sins of society, and the measurable results of schooling later showed how far up the achievement ladder the young still needed to climb. Most never reached the top, though a mediocre report card seemed less onerous than a long stretch in hell.[11]

The heavily Protestant culture of early American society has strongly helped influence how citizens view their schools. The idea of America as a "city on a hill" recurs in political oratory. Adults who have never heard of the *New England Primer* or a Puritan jeremiad often claim that the younger generation is for whatever reasons less hardworking, achievement-oriented, and disciplined. Test scores seem to fall more than rise, bad manners are too common, teen crimes more vicious. And the schools—the embodiment of hope followed by despair—seem unable to restore an imagined past of high achievement befitting a nation presumably founded on lofty ideals. The humorist Garrison Keillor understandably gets a laugh whenever he describes all the children of Lake Wobegone as "above average," which only occurs in real exams if enough people cheat or if the books are cooked.[12]

The second animating force that generates enthusiasm for school reform is the idea that society should respect and help each worthy individual, who has unparalleled opportunities to rise in the social order. These twinned ideals also have a relatively old lineage in America. Over a century after the first Puritans arrived in the New World, Thomas Jefferson—a southern aristocrat and revolutionary—presented seminal ideas about the individual, schools, and the social order in his only book, *Notes on the State of Virginia*, written in 1781 and first published in France. Recall that Jefferson endorsed free elementary schools for all white children, including girls, funded by the state; the most talented boys would progress upward to grammar schools and a smaller number afterwards to the state university. Individual geniuses, he said in the indelicate language of the day, would "be raked from the rubbish," or common lot. The class system, closed in Europe, was permeable in America.[13]

Like other Founding Fathers, Jefferson in his many writings often contrasted the values of the new republic with the corruptions of Europe, where birth determined everything. In America, he said, the abundance of land, access to schools, and willingness to work hard would allow talent to rise. The success of Benjamin Franklin, born into a poor family of Puritans who rose to wealth and international prominence, was recounted in innumerable schoolbooks in the coming century, the most famous example of what the virtues of Poor Richard yielded. As Jefferson and countless writers noted in the early national period, schools and other educational institutions would also popularize learning, nurturing the intelligence necessary for political leaders and voters alike to sustain the new republic. In contrast to Europe, individuals could enjoy greater economic mobility and political freedom and share in the pursuit of happiness.[14]

Critics then as now exposed the hypocrisy of Jefferson's meritocratic schemes, since girls (except for access to primary classes) and especially slaves and free blacks were denied opportunities initially touted for white males. These revisionist views have not gone unchallenged. In a recent history of the American Revolution, Gordon S. Wood places the Founders in their own eighteenth-century context and urges readers not to judge them by today's standards. After all, the revolutionaries lived in a world of monarchs and class systems with intricate and mutually reinforcing forms of political dependency.

Ideals such as democracy, individual freedom, and human equality that became enshrined in documents such as the Declaration of Independence and the Constitution were revolutionary in their day, and they ultimately provided oppressed groups with the tools to fight for human rights and social justice. Scholars such as Joseph Ellis similarly acknowledge that the Founders were not demigods but flawed individuals living in another age. They were unwilling to end slavery, which they knew was immoral and surely contradicted the natural rights of man, which the Revolution claimed to secure. Knowing that the South would secede if abolition triumphed, the Founders preserved the fragile republic, at the expense of black slaves.[15]

Jefferson's views on state-assisted schooling were advanced and enlightened in his day. They contradicted the traditional belief that education largely confirmed one's place in the social order; not surprisingly, his plans for schools never came to fruition in his lifetime. Virginia's legislators repeatedly ignored his endorsement of a state system of schools, even for white children. But Jeffersonian ideals influenced those who guided the creation of free public schools during the nineteenth century, first in the antebellum North and then, after the Civil War, in the former slave states. As historian Jennings L. Wagoner, Jr., emphasizes, Jefferson was the original "education president," always emphasizing the integral bonds that united literacy and learning with freedom, opportunity, and the training of leaders and citizens. Jefferson's support for the concept of a fluid social order and belief that talent inheres in all social classes remains a guiding ideology of many Americans. Every time pupils compete for the best grades it reinforces the notion that individuals strongly determine their own destiny and that schools are central to the struggle for economic survival and preferment.[16]

Whether such claims are true and desirable or honored more in theory than in practice has long been debated. But that is beside the point. The ideals are commonly espoused if never fully realized. The Puritans and other Protestants emphasized the central role of the individual in learning, principally at first to read the Bible, and Jefferson—an architect of the radical notion of the separation of church and state—reinforced this emphasis upon the individual by saying that schoolchildren with the most individual talent would excel in school and might later advance in society. The blending of two basic ideas—that human striving toward perfection was the ideal, and that the individual through educational means became responsible for the survival of the republic and perpetuation of an open social system—was, for those who built public school systems in the nineteenth century, an intoxicating drink.

The establishment of state-funded public school systems in New England in the pre–Civil War era reflected an evangelical faith in the power of schools, literacy, and broadly acknowledged Christian values. The greatest school reformer of the age, and a person met in different contexts in this book, was Horace Mann, born in 1796. Raised in a Puritan household in Massachusetts and later a convert to a more liberal Unitarianism, Mann popularized the utopian possibilities of schooling. Schools, he said, would help assimilate the millions of immigrants arriving from Germany and Ireland, teaching them American values, Christian (Protestant) morals, and the values of Poor Richard. As his rhetoric reached fever pitch, he promised that schools could end poverty, crime, and social strife. The prospects of human perfection, social harmony, and the safety of the republic were soon tied up with the fate of the emerging public school system.[17]

In an editorial in the *Common School Journal* in 1841, Mann editorialized that both Protestant Sunday schools and common schools were "*the great leveling institutions of this age*. What is the secret of aristocracy? It is that *knowledge* is *power*." While a Whig and not a Jacksonian Democrat (the political descendants of Jefferson's Republicans), Mann applauded the Jeffersonian view that schools existed to diffuse knowledge and reward excellence and should teach rich and poor alike in a common system. In a famous report in 1848, Mann described the schools as "the great equalizer of the conditions of men—the balance-wheel of the social machinery." Helping the poor, protecting the rich, ensuring a stable social order: was there anything schools could not do?[18]

We may seem far removed from the worlds of Thomas Jefferson and Horace Mann, but American faith in the ability of schools to address innumerable social, economic, and political ills seems unshakeable. Indeed, the third reason why Americans love to reform their schools is that they are unable to imagine that many everyday problems lack a clear educational source and educational solution. That is, since at least the mid-nineteenth century, virtually every social group, including those once excluded from the system, has appealed to the schools to address the shortcomings of families, churches, and the workplace.

Historically, public schools have never made the life of the mind, or mastery of academic subjects, their central or only mission. Consider the multiple roles that have accrued to schools over time. In the 1880s, the typical white child in the northern states, the most favored region, received only a few years of schooling, mostly in ungraded, one-room buildings. By the early twentieth century, however, even high school enrollments were booming; secondary enrollments doubled every decade between 1890 and 1930, and the South, too, began investing more heavily in (albeit racially segregated) high schools. Everywhere the role of schooling overall expanded so dramatically that leading school officials wondered if there was a central purpose to modern education.[19]

The growing social functions of the schools certainly worried some educators, many of whom nevertheless realized that society often sloughed off responsibilities better suited to parents, churches, employers, or other institutions. When children's morals were in question, wrote the well-known educationist at the University of Michigan, B. A. Hinsdale, in 1896, citizens seemed to turn naturally to the schools. He pointed to the experiences of children in America's large cities. "[W]here else do tens of thousands of them learn such valuable lessons in punctuality, regularity, obedience, industry, cleanliness, decency of appearance and behavior, regard for the rights and feelings of others, and respect for law and order as in the public schools?"[20]

Over the course of the twentieth century, schools assumed a multitude of new responsibilities. Schools would increasingly be called upon to feed the hungry and malnourished. Since private corporations lacked any strong system of apprenticeships, Americans would periodically demand better vocational programs to aid young people in the transition from school to work. School curricula diversified to try to find something every individual would enjoy or succeed at. The nonacademic features of the schools noticeably expanded, catching the attention of many foreign visitors and blurring the purposes of modern education. Historian Lawrence A. Cremin noted in 1965 that, despite the hullabaloo over the academic failures of the schools in the wake of Sputnik, enrollments rose not in the hard sciences but in driver's education! The fact that there were too many deaths on the nation's highways was now a concern of the schools. "It is a curious solution," Cremin remarked, "requiring courses instead of seat belts, but typically American." Even today, while academic subjects leave many students cold, student activities from service learning to Bible study continue to engage some student interest. Competitive sports—hockey in Minnesota, basketball in Indiana, and football in Texas—draw more adults to sports arenas than to Parent Teacher Organization meetings statewide. So many different things transpire in school simultaneously that it necessarily lacks a coherent purpose or rationale.[21]

Parents want schools to help improve the life chances of their children, to ensure social order and stability, and to teach responsibility, hard work, delayed gratification, and any other values deemed in short supply in the larger society. Social ills in other nations might lead to revolution, but Americans often respond by establishing a new course or curriculum or program. Where in Europe, for example, can one find a secondary school that on any given day not only teaches calculus but also driver's education, that sponsors the computer club as well as a student rally before the big game, and provides job counseling and has tryouts for the cheerleading squad? In recent decades, federal laws have also required greater educational access for children whose disabilities had once routinely barred them.[22]

Federal legislation such as "No Child Left Behind" mandates increasingly heavy doses of standardized testing to measure student progress in academic subjects. But this hardly limits what Americans routinely want from their schools. According to a 1990 Gallup poll, 90 percent wanted schools to offer drug abuse education, 84 percent alcohol abuse education, and over 70 percent sex education and information about AIDS. Well over half wanted instruction on environmental issues as well as in "character education." Nearly half thought schools should teach parenting skills. Another poll found that over 90 percent wanted schools to teach honesty, the golden rule, democracy, tolerance, patriotism, and "caring for friends and family members." The vast majority of those polled in 1993 wanted schools to provide free meals, eye and ear exams, and inoculations against communicable illnesses; some adults even wanted condoms distributed to whoever requested them.[23]

The multiple purposes of modern public schools ensure that they are forever, from some one's point of view, doing a poor job, and in need of reform. Families and churches have hardly retreated as influential forces in the lives of children and youth, but the growth and reach of public schools in the twentieth century was nothing short of phenomenal. In the last two generations, expectations have grown dramatically. Rising expectations that emanated from the civil rights movement and the Great Society led many citizens to demand better and more equal treatment for their children to enable them to share in the American dream. As educational credentials have risen in importance, the price of failure in the classroom has correspondingly accelerated, intensifying anxieties among parents and the public about the prospects of the young. To secure high academic standards for everyone is nevertheless to dream of something that has never existed in our society. What the larger society cannot seem to create—a more just democracy and economically fairer world—has often been laid as a problem at the schoolhouse door. Can schools solve fundamental problems of economic and social injustice that they did not principally create?[24]

When the schools fail to attain the highest standards, or the young seem far from perfect compared to their elders, the old lament of declension, shorn of its religious roots, sprouts anew. When the economy falters and good jobs become scarce, public complaints about the failures of teachers and the schools intensify. That schools try to serve so many competing interests testifies to a broad public faith in the possibilities of social and individual improvement. But it guarantees that the current fascination with standardized test scores on academic subjects will only scratch the surface of what Americans routinely expect of the schools. In 1999, a total of 71 percent of those polled by Gallup favored "reforming the existing public school system" over scuttling it, somewhat surprising given the widespread criticisms of schools during the last few decades. It mattered not that the pollsters did not define "reform." Like the pursuit of happiness, reform is elusive yet never loses its popular appeal.[25]

Jefferson's famous claim in the Declaration of Independence that citizens had natural rights to life, liberty, and the pursuit of happiness remains part of a hallowed American tradition. Like any ideal, his words are still easier to extol than define or act upon to everyone's satisfaction. Like other revolutionary thinkers of his day, Jefferson knew that tradition often stood in the way of progress and that education in its broadest sense offered the best path to human enlightenment. One could not be ignorant and hope to be civilized and free. In a letter written in 1816, he insisted:

> Laws and institutions must go hand in hand with the progress of the human mind. As that becomes more developed, more enlightened, as new discoveries are made, new truths disclosed, and manners and opinions change with the change of circumstances, institutions must advance also, and keep pace with the times. We might as well require a man to wear still the coat which fitted him as a boy, as [to expect] civilized society to remain ever under the regimen of their barbarous ancestors.[26]

Enlightened people no longer speak of their ancestors as barbarous, and the idea of progress is not universally shared in our postmodern world. But Jefferson's claims nicely capture the central argument of this book. What is history has ever been contested, and changing interpretations of history, education, and the schools remain the norm, not the exception. The issues that concern us today shape the questions we ask about earlier moments in history. We can only study a fragment of past human experiences, most of which have vanished without a trace. We strive to understand the past in its own context while guided by the multiple needs that historical understanding has always tried to serve. "All historians," Arthur Schlesinger Jr. recently noted, "are prisoners of their own experience and servitors to their own prepossessions. We are all entrapped in the egocentric predicament. We bring to history the preconceptions of our personality and the preoccupations of our age. We cannot seize on ultimate and absolute truths."[27]

And yet most historians, including Schlesinger, agree that their labors remain different from that of the novelist or poet. While each generation of historians will continue to ask questions that matter in the here-and-now, the perennial challenge is to retain one's humility about the parameters of human knowledge, to avoid confusing the past and present, and to apply the most rigorous means available to understand people and events in another time and place. Whether written by amateurs or professionals, history will always try to fulfill the deep human need to know what came before, to document what human beings have been capable of. Written history will continue to amuse or infuriate, confuse or enlighten, and serve many ends. As Thomas Jefferson realized, education, too, will always assume different forms, from the public systems he advocated to the private alternatives common during his lifetime and which for some families still remain so vital. No generation writes history once and for all, and each generation draws on the past, however selectively, to help chart its future course.

# Notes

## Introduction

1. James G. Percival, "An Ode to Music," in *Poems* (New York, 1823), 278.
2. Thomas Bullfinch, *Bullfinch's Mythology: The Age of Fable* (Philadelphia, ©1987), 22. This book was originally published in 1855.
3. John Lewis Gaddis, *The Landscape of History: How Historians Map the Past* (New York, 2002), 6, 146–51.

## Chapter 1  On the Nature and Purpose of History

This chapter has been adapted from William J. Reese, "Bearing Witness: On the Nature and Purpose of History," in *A History of School Mathematics*, ed. George M. A. Stanic and Jeremy Kilpatrick (Reston, VA: National Council of Teachers of Mathematics, 2003): 1: 3–39. It is reprinted with permission by the National Council of Teachers of Mathematics. All rights reserved.

1. Charles William Fornara, *The Nature of History in Ancient Greece and Rome* (Berkeley, 1983), chapter 1. On the multiple uses of history, see Allan Nevins, *The Gateway to History* (New York, 1938), chapters 1–2; and Ernst Breisach, *Historiography: Ancient, Medieval & Modern* (Chicago, 1983), 2.
2. Donald R. Kelley, *Faces of History: Historical Inquiry from Herodotus to Herder* (New Haven, CT, 1998), 2.
3. Herodotus, *The Histories* (London, ©1972), 41; Paul K. Conkin and Roland Stromberg, *The Heritage and Challenge of History* (New York, 1971), 11–12; M. I. Finley, *The Portable Greek Historians* (London, ©1959), 7; and R. G. Collingwood, *The Idea of History* (London, ©1946), 17–19. Arnaldo Momigliano, in *The Classical Foundations of Modern Historiography* (Berkeley, 1990), 40, points out that even Herodotus's admirers doubted the reliability of his history. Kelley emphasizes that Herodotus anticipated the rise of "cultural history" (of growing interest by the eighteenth century) through his interest in "all

aspects of human interest," not simply war and politics. See *Faces of History*, 3, 19–28. In *Herodotus in Context: Ethnography, Science, and the Art of Persuasion* (Cambridge, UK, 2000), Rosalind Thomas recreates the larger intellectual world in which Herodotus lived.

4. Joseph Gavorse, ed., *The Complete Writings of Thucydides, The Peloponnesian War* (New York, ©1934), 3, 13–15; Donald R. Kelley, *Versions of History from Antiquity to the Enlightenment* (New Haven, CT, 1991), 28–29; Kelley, *Faces of History*, 28–35; Beverley Southgate, *History: What and Why? Ancient, Modern, and Postmodern Perspectives* (London, 1996), chapter 2; and Richard E. Neustadt and Ernest R. May, *Thinking in Time: The Uses of History for Decision-Makers* (New York, 1986), 233. For scholarly debates about views on time among the ancients, see Herbert J. Muller, *The Uses of the Past: Profiles of Former Societies* (New York, ©1952), 68–69; Arnaldo Momigliano, *Essays in Ancient and Modern Historiography* (Middletown, CT, 1977), 184–86, 197; and Gerald A. Press, *The Development of the Idea of History in Antiquity* (Kingston and Montreal, 1982), 9–10, 125. As David Rohrbacher explains in *The Historians of Late Antiquity* (London, 2002), 159, speeches were commonly included in classical historiography, though they were obviously not "verbatim" but "approximations of what was actually said."

5. G. R. Elton, *The Practice of History* (London, 1967), 12; and Kelley, *Versions of History*, 36–37.

6. M. I. Finley, *The Use and Abuse of History* (London, 1971), 12–15.

7. Kelley, *Versions of History*, 62; and Fornara, *The Nature of History*, 135–36.

8. Ronald Mellor, *The Roman Historians* (London, 1999), 4, 10, 193; and Kelley, *Versions of History*, 77–78.

9. Kelley, *Versions of History*, 128; Kelley, *Faces of History*, 85–89; and Page Smith, *The Historian and History* (New York, ©1960), 17. On historiography in the medieval period, see Conkin and Stromberg, *The Heritage and Challenge*, chapter 3.

10. Kelley, *Versions of History*, 147–48; Kelley, *Faces of History*, 89–92, 95–96; and Peter Brown, *Augustine of Hippo: A Biography* (Berkeley, 1969), chapter 9.

11. Charles Homer Haskins, *The Renaissance of the Twelfth Century* (New York, 1927), chapter 8; Harry Elmer Barnes, *A History of Historical Writing* (Norman, OK, 1937), 64–88; Breisach, *Historiography*, 98, 101, 128; Kelley, *Faces of History*, chapter 5; and Brian Croke and Alanna M. Emmett, "Historiography in Late Antiquity: An Overview," in *History and Historians in Late Antiquity*, ed. Brian Croke and Alanna M. Emmett (Sydney, 1983), 9, who wrote that by the seventh century the various historiographical genres were largely set for the medieval period and "converged in a common goal, to tell the story of salvation and to demonstrate the ways of God

to men both now and since time immemorial." See also Dominic Janes, "The World and Its Past as Christian Allegory in the Early Middle Ages," in *The Uses of the Past in the Early Middle Ages*, ed. Yitzhak Hen and Matthew Innes (Cambridge, UK, 2000), 102–13.

12. Barnes, *A History*, 97; Haskins, *Renaissance*, 224, 228–29; Donald J. Wilcox, "The Sense of Time in Western Historical Narratives from Eusebius to Machiavelli," in *Classical Rhetoric and Medieval Historiography*, ed. Ernst Breisach (Kalamazoo, MI, 1985), 172; and Gillian Evans, "St. Anselm and Sacred History," in *The Writing of History in the Middle Ages: Essays Presented to Richard William Southern*, ed. R. H. C. Davis and J. M. Wallace-Hadrill (Oxford, UK, 1981), 199.

13. Barnes, *A History*, 99–100; Breisach, *Historiography*, 160; E. B. Fryde, *Humanism and Renaissance Historiography* (London, 1983), 4, 7–9, 55; Herschel Baker, *The Race of Time: Three Lectures on Renaissance Historiography* (Toronto, 1967), 35–36, 40, 45–46, 60–64, 76–77; Donald R. Kelley, *Renaissance Humanism* (Boston, MA, 1991), 25, 94–102; Fornara, *The Nature of History*, 195; Patrick Collinson, "Truth, Lies, and Fiction in Sixteenth-Century Protestant Historiography," in *The Historical Imagination in Early Modern Britain: History, Rhetoric, and Fiction, 1500–1800*, ed. Donald R. Kelley and David Harris Sacks (Cambridge, UK, 1997), 37–68; Conkin and Stromberg, *The Heritage and Challenge*, 31–32; and Joyce Appleby, Lynn Hunt, and Margaret Jacob, *Telling the Truth About History* (New York, 1994), 60.

14. Kelley, *Versions of History*, 446; Fritz Stern, ed., *The Varieties of History: From Voltaire to the Present* (Cleveland, OH, ©1954), 35–45; Theodore S. Hamerow, *Reflections on History and Historians* (Madison, WI, 1987), 227–28; David Carrithers, "Montesquieu's Philosophy of History," *Journal of the History of Ideas* 47 (January–March 1986): 61; and Martine Watson Brownley, "Gibbon's Artistic and Historical Scope in the *Decline and Fall*," *Journal of the History of Ideas* 42 (October–December 1981): 629–42. For a succinct analysis of the incorporation of pagan classics into Christian theology, read Richard E. Rubenstein, *Aristotle's Children: How Christians, Muslims, and Jews Rediscovered Ancient Wisdom and Illuminated the Middle Ages* (New York, 2003).

15. Henry F. May, *The Enlightenment in America* (Oxford, UK, 1976); and Appleby, Hunt, and Jacob, *Telling the Truth*, chapters 1–2. There has been an efflorescence of scholarship recently on the Scottish Enlightenment; see, for example, Arthur Herman, *How the Scots Invented the Modern World: The True Story of How Western Europe's Poorest Nation Created Our World & Everything in It* (New York, 2001).

16. Hayden White, *Metahistory: The Historical Imagination in Nineteenth-Century Europe* (Baltimore, MD, 1973), 136.

17. Georg G. Iggers, *Historiography in the Twentieth Century: From Scientific Objectivity to the Postmodern Challenge* (Hanover, NH, 1997), chapter 1; Breisach, *Historiography*, 293; Appleby, Hunt, and Jacob, *Telling the Truth*, chapter 2; and J. H. Plumb, "The Historian's Dilemma," in his edited volume, *Crisis in the Humanities* (Baltimore, MD, 1964), 26–27.

18. Peter Novick, *That Noble Dream: The "Objectivity Question" and the American Historical Profession* (Cambridge, UK, 1988), 28; and Iggers, *Historiography*, 24.

19. Jurgen Herbst, *The German Historical School in American Scholarship: A Study in the Transfer of Culture* (Ithaca, NY, 1965); Laurence R. Veysey, *The Emergence of the American University* (Chicago, 1965); and John Higham, *History: Professional Scholarship in America* (New York, 1965), 9–10.

20. Bonnie G. Smith, *The Gender of History: Men, Women, and Historical Practice* (Cambridge, MA, 1998), especially chapter 5. On the American scene, read Julie Des Jardins, *Women & the Historical Enterprise: Gender, Race, and the Politics of Memory, 1880–1945* (Chapel Hill, NC, 2003).

21. Novick, *That Noble Dream*, 33; and Higham, *History*, 11–12.

22. Novick, *That Noble Dream*, 1–2.

23. Pieter Geyl, *Use and Abuse of History* (New Haven, CT, 1955), 33–34, 52–56; Iggers, *Historiography*, 31–35; Appleby, Hunt, and Jacobs, *Telling the Truth*, 73–74; and William J. Reese, *The Origins of the American High School* (New Haven, CT, 1995), 117–18.

24. Conkin and Stromberg, *The Heritage and Challenge*, 79; Novick, *That Noble Dream*, chapter 5; Smith, *Gender and History*, 146–53; and Richard Hofstadter, *The Progressive Historians: Turner, Beard, Parrington* (New York, 1968), 41–43. For a different perspective on the Progressives, read Ernst A. Breisach, *American Progressive History: An Experiment in Modernization* (Chicago, 1993).

25. Hofstadter, *The Progressive Historians*; Appleby, Hunt, and Jacobs, *Telling the Truth*, chapter 4; Higham, *History*, part III, chapters 3–4; and Novick, *That Noble Dream*, chapter 4. On the evils of presentism, see Bernard Bailyn, *On the Teaching and Writing of History* (Hanover, NH, 1994), 42.

26. James Harvey Robinson, *The New History: Essays Illustrating the Modern Historical Outlook* (New York, ©1965), 1; and Kevin Mattson, "The Challenges of Democracy: James Harvey Robinson, the New History, and Adult Education for Citizenship," *Journal of the Gilded Age and Progressive Era* 2 (January 2003): 48–79. Ellen Fitzpatrick has laid to rest the common misconception that the "new" history proposed during the Progressive Era did not materialize until

the 1960s. See *History's Memory: Writing America's Past 1880–1980* (Cambridge, MA, 2002).

27. Robinson, *The New History*, 47–48, 54, 135.
28. Robert William Fogel and G. R. Elton, *Which Road to the Past? Two Views of History* (New Haven, CT, 1983), 11–23.
29. Becker's paper, delivered in 1926, was not published until 1955; see Carl L. Becker, "What Are Historical Facts?" *The Western Political Quarterly* 8 (September 1955): 327–29, 332.
30. The 1931 address was reprinted in Carl L. Becker, *Everyman His Own Historian: Essays on History and Politics* (New York, 1935), with quotations from 243, 254; and Carl L. Becker, *The Heavenly City of the Eighteenth-Century Philosophers* (New Haven, CT, 1932), 44, 88.
31. Novick, *That Noble Dream*, 104; and Hamerow, *Reflections*, 232–33.
32. Charles A. Beard, "Written History as an Act of Faith," *American Historical Review* 39 (January 1934): 219–20, 226. As John Lewis Gaddis notes in *The Landscape of History: How Historians Map the Past* (New York, 2002), historians actually had much in common with scientists not confined to the laboratory, for example, geologists.
33. Herbert Butterfield, *The Whig Interpretation of History* (New York, 1931); C. T. McIntire, *Herbert Butterfield: Historian as Dissenter* (New Haven, CT, 2004), ix–xi, 56–77, on the English context; and Collingwood, *The Idea of History*, 251–52. Collingwood emphasized that history was a science of a special sort. In *What is History?* (New York, 1961), 50–51, Edward Hallett Carr, in his critique of objectivity, noted that Butterfield, who had attacked the Whiggish, presentist view that history was an unfolding tale of greater liberty, applauded the tradition of liberty during World War II!
34. Marc Bloch, *The Historian's Craft* (New York, ©1953), 14–26; Geyl, *Use and Abuse*, 61; and Plumb, "Historian's Dilemma," 43.
35. On the 1960s, see John Higham, *Writing American History: Essays on Modern Scholarship* (Bloomington, IN, 1970), chapter 9; on the 1950s, Higham, *History*, Part III, chapter 6; and Bernard Sternsher, *Consensus, Conflict, and American Historians* (Bloomington, IN, 1975). For examples of trends in social history, see the essays in Part II of Michael Kammen, ed., *The Past before Us* (Ithaca, NY, 1980); and Olivier Zunz, ed., *Reliving the Past: The Worlds of Social History* (Chapel Hill, NC, 1985). See also Thomas S. Kuhn, *The Structure of Scientific Revolutions* (Chicago, 1962), which was interpreted by many critics as proof that even science was not particularly objective. In *History's Memory*, chapter 5, Fitzpatrick reminds readers that many excellent histories appeared in the late 1940s and 1950s that did not reflect the values of "consensus" history.
36. On the French contribution, see Traian Stoianovich, *French Historical Method: The Annales Paradigm* (Ithaca, NY, 1976); and Peter Burke, *The French Historical Revolution: The Annales School* (Stanford, 1990).

37. Conkin and Stromberg, *The Heritage and Challenge of History*, 90–91. Also see Terrence J. McDonald, "What We Talk about When We Talk about History: The Conversations of History and Sociology," in *The Historic Turn in the Human Sciences*, ed. Terrence J. McDonald (Ann Arbor, MI, 1996), 112–13. For the traditional statement on why historians should avoid theories drawn from other disciplines, see the previously cited books by G. R. Elton.

38. Carr, *What is History?*, 10.

39. Elton, *The Practice of History*, 84–85, 87. Elton was born in Tubingin but educated at the University of London and spent his professional career in England. For a sense of the great range of historical studies available today, see the essays in David Cannadine, ed., *What is History Now?* (New York, 2002).

40. I am relying heavily on Kenneth Cmiel's outstanding essay, "Poststructural Theory," in *Encyclopedia of American Social History*, ed. Mary Kupiec Cayton, Elliot Gorn, and Peter W. Williams (New York, 1992): vol. 1, 425–33. Also read Robert F. Berkhofer, Jr., *Beyond the Great Story: History as Text and Discourse* (Cambridge, MA, 1995); and Keith Jenkins, ed., *The Postmodern History Reader* (New York, 1997). Commenting on the impact of postmodernism on historical scholarship on the early Middle Ages, Matthew Innes writes that the idea that all there is, is discourse, with no "reality external to . . . discourse, has had no real takers in early medieval studies." But he goes on to say that it has enlivened debates about sources, texts, and the reconstruction of historical context in the field. See Innes, "Introduction: Using the Past, Interpreting the Present, Influencing the Future," in *The Uses of the Past*, ed. Hen and Innes, 3–4. A few years earlier, Gabrielle M. Spiegel offered a most optimistic view of the impact in *The Past as Text: The Theory and Practice of Medieval Historiography* (Baltimore, MD, 1997), chapter 4, especially page 77. Gary McCulloch and William Richardson, in *Historical Research in Educational Settings* (Buckingham, UK, 2000), 33, notes how many historians ignore theory and have not usually embraced postmodern views.

41. Geoff Eley, "Is All the World a Text? From Social History to the History of Society Two Decades Later," in *The Historic Turn*, 207; G. R. Elton, *Return to Essentials: Some Reflections on the Present State of Historical Study* (Cambridge, UK, 1991), 31; and White, *Metahistory*, 13, 283, 332.

42. Hayden White, *Tropics of Discourse: Essays in Cultural Criticism* (Baltimore, MD, 1978), 41. Sol Cohen explores the implications of postmodernism for historians of education in several chapters of *Challenging Orthodoxies: Toward a New Cultural History of Education* (New York, 1999). Richard T. Vann notes the impact of White on literary scholars, outside the field of history, in "The Reception of Hayden White," *History and Theory* 37 (May 1998): 148–49, 156.

43. In addition to the books previously cited on social history, good introductions to modern historical scholarship include the following: James B. Gardner and George Rollie Adams, eds., *Ordinary People and Everyday Life: Perspectives on the New Social History* (Nashville, TN, 1983); and Eric Foner, ed., *The New American History* (Philadelphia, PA, 1990). On the problem of overspecialization in the historical profession, read Thomas Bender, "Whole and Parts: The Need for Synthesis in American History," *Journal of American History* 73 (June 1986): 120–36, which generated lively debates with other scholars in subsequent issues of this journal.

44. Keith Jenkins, *Re-Thinking History* (London, 1991), 5, 13, 32.

45. Keith Jenkins, *On "What is History?" From Carr and Elton to Rorty and White* (London, 1995), 7, 20, 178–79.

46. Southgate, *History*, 85; Elton, *Return to Essentials*, 41, passim; Lawrence Stone, "History and Post-Modernism," *Past and Present* 131 (May 1991): 217–18; and, for the quotations in the text, Lawrence Stone, "History and Post-Modernism," *Past and Present* 135 (May 1992): 190–191, 193. For a lively assessment and attack on the linguistic turn and other new approaches in social history, read Bryan D. Palmer's *Descent into Discourse: The Reification of Language and the Writing of Social History* (Philadelphia, PA, 1990); and Richard J. Evans, *In Defence of History* (London, 1997), a brilliant interpretation of the history of historical scholarship and critique of postmodernist excesses. In response to this sort of hostile reception of postmodern scholarship, also read Patrick Joyce, "The Return of History: Postmodernism and the Politics of Academic History," *Past and Present* 158 (February 1998): 207–35.

47. Bailyn, *On the Teaching and Writing of History*, 75.

48. Ernst Breisach, *On the Future of History: The Postmodernist Challenge and Its Aftermath* (Chicago, 2003), 200–01; Appleby, Hunt, and Jacobs, *Telling the Truth*, 7, 12, 196, 235, 247–51, 275; and Iggers, *Historiography*, 12–13, 132–33, 145. On page 13, Iggers notes, "The contradictions of resolving history into purely imaginative literature become apparent in Hayden White's admission that from a moral perspective it is unacceptable to deny the reality of the Holocaust, yet it is impossible in a historical narrative to establish objectively that it happened." On the debate over the relationship between relativism, postmodernism, and historical understanding, read Patrick Finney, "Ethics, Historical Relativism, and Holocaust Denial," *Rethinking History* 2 (Autumn 1998), 359–69. Richard Aldrich notes in his Inaugural Lecture at the University of London's Institute of Education, *The End of History and the Beginning of Education* (London, 1997) that, contrary to the views of Hayden White, most historians continue to discover more evidence than they invent and that the differences between history and literature remain evident.

Also see Roy Lowe, "Postmodernity and Historians of Education: A View from Britain," *Paedagogica Historica* 15 (1996): 307–23. As Gaddis noted in *Landscape*, 9–10, 33–34, 136, most practicing historians did not welcome another lecture on the "the relative character on historical judgements," since scholars generally knew that no human being could claim to capture the past in its entirety or find or intuit the whole truth and nothing but the truth about what went before. Like cartographers drawing maps, he argued, historians write about the past from a certain vantage point, field of vision, and perspective, trying to represent and approximate reality with the best intellectual tools at their disposal.

49. Dorothy Ross, "The New and Newer Histories: Social Theory and Historiography in an American Key," in *Imagined Histories: American Historians Interpret the Past*, ed. Anthony Molho and Gordon S. Wood (Princeton, NJ, 1998), 99–100. On the quotation from Cicero, see Kelley, *Versions of History*, 77–78.

## Chapter 2    What History Teaches about the Impact of Educational Research on Practice

This chapter has been adapted from William J. Reese, "What History Teaches about the Impact of Educational Research upon Practice," *Review of Educational Research* 24 (Spring 1999): 1–20.

1. Michael Kammen, *Mystic Chords of Memory: The Transformation of Tradition in American Culture* (New York, 1991), 351–58 (quotations from page 352). On the overall popularity of history among the public, read Kenneth T. Jackson, "The Power of History: The Weakness of the Profession," *Journal of American History* 88 (March 2002): 1301–2.

2. Charles A. Asbury, "Why Educational Research Is of Limited Use to the Community," *Journal of Negro Education* 45 (Winter 1976–77): 21; Maureen T. Hallinan, "Bridging the Gap between Research and Practice," *Sociology of Education* (1996, special issue): 131; and *Forty-Ninth Annual Report of the Board of Commissioners of Public Schools, to the Mayor and City Council of Baltimore, for the Year Ending October 31, 1877* (Baltimore, MD, 1877), 3.

3. Ellen Condliffe Lagemann, "Contested Terrain: A History of Education Research in the United States, 1890–1990," *Educational Researcher* 26 (December 1997): 5–17; Peter Novick, *That Noble Dream: The "Objectivity Question" and the American Historical Profession* (Cambridge, UK, 1988); and Ellen Condliffe Lagemann, "The Plural Worlds of Educational Research," *History of Education Quarterly* 29 (Summer 1989): 183–214. From the 1980s to the

present, standardized testing—producing a record of measurable, quantifiable outcomes—has risen to ever greater importance in federal policy. Ironically, many graduate students in schools of education lack advanced training in statistics and quantitative research methods.

4. Ellen Condliffe Lagemann, *An Elusive Science: The Troubling History of Education Research* (Chicago, 2000), which demonstrates that while education research has long been diverse and pluralistic, quantitative methods early and long have defined the main paradigm in educational study. Also read David B. Tyack, *The One Best System: A History of American Urban Education* (Cambridge, MA, 1974); and Wayne E. Fuller, *The Old Country School: The Story of Rural Education in the Middle West* (Chicago, 1982).

5. Lagemann, "Contested Terrain," 6.

6. J. Cayce Morrison, "The Role of Research in Educational Reconstruction," in *The Forty-Fourth Yearbook of the National Society for the Study of Education*, ed. Nelson B. Henry (Chicago, 1945), 238.

7. Morrison, "Role of Research," 240, 243. In *The Making of the Modern University: Intellectual Transformation and the Modernization of Morality* (Chicago, 1996), 185, Julie A. Reuben highlights the widespread belief among social scientists of the Progressive Era that statistics offered objective measures of reality and helped to "confer authority" to fledgling social science disciplines.

8. Lawrence A. Cremin, *The Transformation of the School: Progressivism in American Education* (New York, 1961), 3–8, 110–15; Lagemann, "Plural Worlds"; Paul Davis Chapman, *Schools as Sorters: Lewis M. Terman, Applied Psychology, and the Intelligence Testing Movement, 1890–1930* (New York, 1988); JoAnne Brown, *The Definition of a Profession: The Authority of Metaphor in the History of Intelligence Testing, 1890–1930* (Princeton, NJ, 1992); and Michael M. Sokol, ed., *Psychological Testing and American Society* (New Brunswick, NJ, 1987).

9. Martin Bulmer, Kevin Bales, and Kathryn Kish Sklar, "The Social Survey in Historical Perspective," in *The Social Survey in Historical Perspective 1880–1940*, ed. Martin Bulmer, Kevin Bales, and Kathryn Kish Sklar (Cambridge, UK, 1991), 1–48; Hollis L. Caswell, *City School Surveys: An Interpretation and Appraisal* (New York, 1929), 5; and Morrison, "Role of Research," 238–65. Also see Allen F. Davis, *Spearheads for Reform: The Social Settlements and the Progressive Movement, 1890–1914* (New York: 1967), 30, 85. Theodore M. Porter, *Trust in Numbers: The Pursuit of Objectivity in Science and Public Life* (Princeton, NJ, 1995), 200, explains that statistical inference was especially popular among weaker disciplines, such as psychology, which was the leading discipline within the field of education.

10. Morrison, "Role of Research," 239, 242, 243. On how educational psychologists, as opposed to other reformers of the Progressive Era, interpreted the concept of "individual differences," read Robert L. Church,

"Educational Psychology and Social Reform in the Progressive Era," *History of Education Quarterly* 11 (Winter 1971–72): 400.

11. Hamilton Cravens, *Before Head Start: The Iowa Station & America's Children* (Chapel Hill, NC, 1993); and Morrison,"Role of Research," 253, 256.

12. Morrison, "Role of Research," 245; and Abraham Flexner, *Universities: American, English, German* (New York, 1930), 127. Bruce A. Kimball notes that around 1910 a "conventional scepticism" about education research shifted "to a deep antipathy" in *The "True Professional Ideal" in America: A History* (Cambridge, MA, 1992), 227–28. Kimball also shows that hostility to schools of education was less deep seated in Midwestern public universities (which admitted women, the mainstay of teaching training programs) than at their older east coast, private school counterparts.

13. David B. Tyack and Elisabeth Hansot, *Managers of Virtue: Public School Leadership in America, 1820–1980* (New York, 1982), 105–28; and Lagemann, "Contested Terrain."

14. Thomas L. Haskell, *The Emergence of Professional Social Science: The American Social Science Association and the Nineteenth-Century Crisis of Authority* (Urbana, IL, 1977), 25; Roger L. Geiger, *To Advance Knowledge: The Growth of American Research Universities, 1900–1940* (New York, 1986), 20–39; Tyack and Hansot, *Managers of Virtue,* 129–52; and Novick, *That Noble Dream.*

15. Caswell, *City School Surveys,* 3–4, 21.

16. Ibid., 5, 96–97; and Tyack, *One Best System,* 191–94.

17. On the status wars and their influences upon the field of education, see Geraldine Jonçich Clifford and James W. Guthrie, *Ed School: A Brief for Professional Education* (Chicago, 1988).

18. On Judd, read Lagemann, *An Elusive Science,* 66–70.

19. Charles H. Judd, "The Contributions of School Surveys," in *The Thirty-Seventh Yearbook of the National Society for the Study of Education,* ed. Guy Montrose Whipple (Bloomington, IL, 1938): 2: 9, 12; Robert M. W. Travers, *How Research Has Changed American Schools: A History from 1840 to the Present* (Kalamazoo, MI, 1983), chapter 1; Carl F. Kaestle, *Pillars of the Republic: Common Schools and American Society, 1780–1860* (New York, 1983), 187; and Tyack and Hansot, *Managers of Virtue,* 160–67.

20. Douglas E. Scates, "Organized Research in Education: National, State, City, and University Bureaus of Research," *Review of Educational Research* 9 (December 1939): 576, 590; and Douglas E. Scates, "School Surveys," in *Encyclopedia of Educational Research,* ed. Walter S. Monroe (New York, 1950), 1126–33.

21. Scates, "School Surveys"; Bangnee Alfred Liu, *Educational Research in Major American Cities* (New York, 1945), chapter 7; and Morrison, "Role of Research," 265.

22. Maris A. Vinovskis, "The Changing Role of the Federal Government in Educational Research and Statistics," *History of Education Quarterly* 36 (Summer 1996): 119–20; and Harold H. Abelson, "The Role of Educational Research in a Democracy," *Journal of Educational Sociology* 21 (April 1948): 455–56.

23. Vinovskis, "The Changing Role," 454–461; and H. Stuart Hughes, *History as Art and as Science: Twin Vistas from the Past* (New York, 1964), 93. For a masterful study of the politics of science education after World War II, see John L. Rudolph, *Scientists in the Classroom: The Cold War Reconstruction of American Science Education* (New York, 2002).

24. Travers, *How Research Has Changed American Schools*; Diane Ravitch and Maris A. Vinovskis, eds., *Learning from the Past: What History Teaches Us about School Reform* (Baltimore, MD, 1995); Barbara Finkelstein, *Governing the Young: Teacher Behavior in Popular Primary Schools in the Nineteenth-Century United States* (New York, 1989); and Kate Rousmaniere, Kate Dehli, and Ning De Coninck-Smith, eds., *Discipline, Moral Regulation, and Schooling: A Social History* (New York, 1997). The "What Works Clearinghouse" is easily accessible on the Web site of the U.S. Department of Education in Washington, DC.

25. Judd, "Contributions of School Surveys," 18.

26. Joyce Appleby, Lynn Hunt, and Margaret Jacob, *Telling the Truth about History* (New York, 1994); and Beverley Southgate, *History: What & Why? Ancient, Modern, and Postmodern Perspectives* (London, 1996).

27. Geraldine Jonçich, *The Sane Positivist: A Biography of Edward L. Thorndike* (Middletown, CT, 1968); and Geraldine Jonçich Clifford, "A History of the Impact of Research on Teaching," in *Second Handbook of Research on Teaching*, ed. Robert M. W. Travers (Chicago, 1973), 3–4.

28. Clifford, "History of the Impact of Research," 5, 21–22.

29. Ibid., 19, 23.

30. William R. Johnson, "Empowering Practitioners: Holmes, Carnegie, and the Lessons of History," *History of Education Quarterly* 27 (Summer 1987): 229.

31. Carol H. Weiss and Margaret Vickers, "Research, Impact on Educational Policy," in *Encyclopedia of Educational Research*, ed. Marvin C. Alkin (New York, 1992), 3: 1093, 1098; Robert L. Linn, "Achievement Testing," in ibid., 1: 3; Nancy L. Karweit, "Retention Policy," in ibid., 3: 1117; and Willis D. Hawley, "School Desegregation," in ibid., 4: 1133.

32. Larry Cuban, *How Teachers Taught: Constancy and Change in American Classrooms, 1880–1990* (New York, 1993).

33. Ibid., xvii–xix.

34. Tyack, *One Best System*; David B. Tyack and Larry Cuban, *Tinkering toward Utopia: A Century of Public School Reform* (Cambridge, MA, 1995); Herbert M. Kliebard, *Schooled to Work: Vocationalism and the*

*American Curriculum, 1876–1946* (New York, 1999); Maurice R. Berube, *American School Reform: Progressive, Equity, and Excellence Movements* (Westport, CT, 1994); William J. Reese, *Power and the Promise of School Reform: Grass-Roots Movements during the Progressive Era* (New York, 1986); William J. Reese, *America's Public Schools: From the Common School to "No Child Left Behind"* (Baltimore, MD, 2005); Sokol, *Psychological Testing*; Henry L. Minton, *Lewis M. Terman: Pioneer in Psychological Testing* (New York, 1988); Margo Horn, *Before It's Too Late: The Child Guidance Movement in the United States, 1922–1945* (Philadelphia, PA, 1988); and Arthur G. Wirth, *Education in the Technological Society: The Vocational-Liberal Studies Controversy in the Early Twentieth Century* (Scranton, PA, 1971). One particularly impressive study, by Barry M. Franklin, analyzed the complicated role of psychological, medical, and educational research in special educational programs in the early twentieth century; see *From "Backwardness" to "At Risk": Childhood Learning Difficulties and the Contradictions of School Reform* (Albany, NY, 1994).

35. Tyack and Cuban, *Tinkering toward Utopia*; and Selwyn W. Troen, *The Public and the Schools: Shaping the St. Louis System, 1838–1920* (Columbia, MO, 1995), chapter 5.

36. Lagemann, "Plural Worlds" and "Contested Terrain" as well as *An Elusive Science*. Lagemann's book appeared soon after I published an earlier version of this chapter in the *Review of Educational Research*; while its focus is not on the impact of research on practice, it is now the standard work on the nature of educational research.

37. See Carl F. Kaestle and Marshall S. Smith, "The Federal Role in Elementary and Secondary Education, 1940–1980," *Harvard Educational Review* 52 (November 1982): 388–408; Maris Vinovskis, *Revitalizing Federal Education Research and Development: Improving the R & D Centers, Regional Educational Laboratories, and the "New" OERI* (Ann Arbor, MI, 2001); Finkelstein, *Governing the Young*; Rousmaniere et al., *Discipline, Moral Regulation, and Schooling*; and Ravitch and Vinovskis, *Learning from the Past*.

## Chapter 3   Public Education in St. Louis

This chapter has been adapted from William J. Reese, "Public Education in Nineteenth-Century St. Louis," in *St. Louis in the Century of Henry Shaw: A View Beyond the Garden Wall* (Columbia, MO, University of Missouri Press, 2003), ed. Eric Sandweiss, 167–87.

1. The standard history of the common schools is by Carl F. Kaestle, *Pillars of the Republic: Common Schools and American Society, 1780–1860* (New York, 1983), and it provides numerous references to

the secondary literature on public education. On Mann, see Jonathan Messerli, *Horace Mann: A Biography* (New York, 1972).

2. Kaestle, *Pillars*, chapters 2–3; and William J. Reese, *The Origins of the American High School* (New Haven, CT, 1995), 21–27. Patricia Albjerg Graham, in *Schooling America: How the Public Schools Meet the Nation's Changing Needs* (New York, 2005), 28, argues that urban public schools (especially outside of immigrant neighborhood schools) still had a decent reputation as late as 1920.

3. *Fourth Annual Report of the President, Superintendent and Secretary, To the Board of St. Louis Public Schools, For the Year Ending July 1, 1858* (St. Louis, 1858), 47; Selwyn K. Troen, *The Public and the Schools: Shaping the St. Louis System, 1838–1920* (Columbia, MO, 1975), 34; and *Forty-Sixth Annual Report of the Board of Education of the City of St. Louis, Mo., For the Year Ending June 30, 1900* (St. Louis, MO, 1901), 47–48, 110, 153.

4. Elinor Mondale Gersman, "The Development of Public Education for Blacks in Nineteenth-Century St. Louis," *Journal of Negro Education* 41 (Winter 1972–74): 35–47. The most important history of the St. Louis schools is by Troen, *The Public and the Schools*. For additional commentary on the St. Louis schools in the nineteenth century, also see William J. Reese, *America's Public Schools: From the Common School to "No Child Left Behind"* (Baltimore, MD, 2005).

5. On Harris, see Kurt F. Leidecker, *Yankee Teacher: The Life of William T. Harris* (New York, 1946); Neil McCluskey, *Public Schools and Moral Education: The Influence of Horace Mann, William Torrey Harris, and John Dewey* (New York, 1958); and Herbert M. Kliebard, *The Struggle for the American Curriculum, 1893–1958* (New York, 1995).

6. *Eleventh Annual Report of the Board of Directors of the St. Louis Public Schools, For the Year Ending August 1, 1866* (St. Louis, MO, 1866), 43.

7. *Eleventh Annual Report*, 38, 42; *Twenty-Seventh Annual Report of the Board of President and Directors of the St. Louis Public Schools, for the Year Ending August 1, 1881* (St. Louis, MO, 1882), 36, 39; Troen, *Public and the Schools*, 15–17, 22–27; and Reese, *Origins*, 90.

8. *First Annual Report of the General Superintendent of the St. Louis Public Schools, For the Year Ending July 1, 1854* (St. Louis, MO, 1854), 13.

9. These multiple goals for the schools, described in the *First Annual Report*, were commonly invoked in local reports throughout the remainder of the century. Complaints about the dull teaching in the schools were ubiquitous.

10. *Fifteenth Annual Report of the Board of Directors of the St. Louis Public Schools, For the Year Ending August 1, 1869* (St. Louis, MO, 1870), 110. For a more complete assessment of Harris, see William J. Reese, "The Philosopher-King of St. Louis," in *Curriculum & Consequence: Herbert M. Kliebard and the Promise of Schooling*, ed. Barry M. Franklin

(New York, 2000), chapter 7; and William J. Reese, "Public Schools and the Elusive Search for the Common Good," in *Reconstructing the Common Good in Education*, ed. Larry Cuban and Dorothy Shipps (Stanford, CA, 2000), 25–31.

11. Kliebard, *Struggle*, 15, 32–34, 55–56.
12. Quoted in Leidecker, *Yankee Teacher*, 262; and Troen, *Public and the Schools*, 61–65. Harris's conservatism was the theme of a leading critic, Merle Curti, *The Social Ideas of American Educators* (Totowa, New Jersey, ©1935).
13. *Fifteenth Annual Report*, 27.
14. Troen, *Public and the Schools*, chapter 5.
15. Barbara Beatty, *Preschool Education in America: The Culture of Young Children from the Colonial Era to the Present* (New Haven, CT, 1995), 46, 71, 52–53, 64–67; and Barbara Beatty, "Susan Elizabeth Blow," in *Historical Dictionary of American Education*, ed. Richard J. Altenbaugh (Westport, CT, 1999), 48–49. For Harris's views on progressive writers on education, see Reese, "The Philosopher-King," 170–75.
16. Beatty, *Preschool Education*, 65–67. Also invaluable are the lengthy commentaries by Harris and Blow in the annual reports to the school board in the 1870s.
17. There is a voluminous literature on Froebel and his ideas; see at least Norman Brosterman, *Inventing Kindergarten* (New York, 1997), chapter 1.
18. See Harris's comments in the *Seventeenth Annual Report of the Board of Directors of the St. Louis Public Schools, For the Year Ending August 1, 1871* (St. Louis, 1872), 37–38; and in the *Nineteenth Annual Report of the Board of Directors of the St. Louis Public Schools, For the Year Ending August 1, 1873* (St. Louis, 1874), 18–19.
19. *Twenty-Fifth Annual Report of the Board of Directors of the St. Louis Public Schools, For the Year Ending August 1, 1879* (St. Louis, 1880), 136; and Troen, *Public and the Schools*, 108.
20. Troen, *Public and the Schools*, 112–114; and *Thirty-Ninth Annual Report of the Board of President and Directors of the St. Louis Public Schools, For the Year Ending June 30, 1893* (St. Louis, 1894), 89.
21. *Forty-Second Annual Report of the Board of President and Directors of the St. Louis Public Schools, For the Year Ending June 30, 1896* (St. Louis, 1897), 98, 111.
22. The standard study of the rise of the "new education" and progressivism is by Lawrence A. Cremin, *The Transformation of the School: Progressivism in American Education, 1876–1957* (New York, 1961). Cf. Reese, *America's Public Schools*, chapter 3.
23. *Forty-First Annual Report of the Board of President and Directors of the St. Louis Public Schools, For the Year Ending June 30, 1895* (St. Louis, 1897), 47.

24. For Harris's views on vocational education, see Reese, "Philosopher-King," 165.
25. On the quarrels between Woodward and Harris, see Herbert M. Kliebard, *Schooled To Work: Vocationalism and the American Curriculum, 1876–1946* (New York, 1999), 6–12. The 1873 essay was reprinted in 1879 in the first edition of Calvin M. Woodward, *The Manual Training School* (New York, ©1969), 274.
26. In addition to Kliebard, *Schooled to Work*, see Charles M. Dye, "Calvin Woodward, Manual Training, and the Saint Louis Public Schools," *Missouri Historical Society Bulletin* 31 (January 1975): 111–35; and Peter Sola, "Calvin Milton Woodward," in *Historical Dictionary*, 390.
27. Calvin M. Woodward, untitled essay, *Journal of Education* 22 (December 22, 1885): 411, where he praised two leading European romantic educators, Johann Pestalozzi and Friedrich Froebel.
28. *Twenty-Eighth Annual Report of the Board of President and Directors of the St. Louis Public Schools, For the Year Ending August 1, 1882* (St. Louis, 1883), 106.
29. Dye, "Calvin Woodward," 111–35.
30. *Forty-Sixth Annual Report*, 27.
31. Dye, "Calvin Woodward," 116; and Troen, *Public and the Schools*, 157, 166–67.
32. See Troen, *Public and the Schools*, chapter 4; Gary R. Kremer, "James Milton Turner and the Reconstruction Struggle for Black Education," *Gateway Heritage* 11 (Spring 1991): 67–75; and Gersman, "Development of Public Education," 35–47.

## Chapter 4   Political Economy and the High School

This chapter has been adapted from William J. Reese, "American High School Political Economy in the Nineteenth Century," *History of Education* 27: 3 (1998). 255–66. The journal website is http://www.tandf.co.uk.

1. For a comprehensive account of the themes in this chapter, see William J. Reese, *The Origins of the American High School* (New Haven, CT, 1995).
2. Charles Sellers, *The Market Revolution: Jacksonian America, 1815–1846* (New York, 1991); Reese, *Origins*, 11–15; and *The System of Education Pursued at the Free Schools of Boston* (Boston, MA, 1823), 6, 16, 23. On the backgrounds of the school commissioners who advocated the English high school, see Loraine McMichael Webster, "American Educational Innovators: A Sub-Committee of the Boston School Committee in 1820," (Ed.D. dissertation, Arizona State University, 1970).
3. Bruce Laurie, *Artisans Into Workers: Labor in Nineteenth-Century America* (New York, 1989); Theodore Sizer, ed., *The Age of the Academies* (New York, 1964); and Henry Barnard, *School*

*Architecture; or Contributions to the Improvement of School-Houses in the United States* (New York, 1848), 99, 101.

4. Reese, *Origins*, 142–61.

5. Daniel Walker Howe, *The Political Culture of the American Whigs* (Chicago, 1979); and Eric Foner, *Free Soil, Free Labor, Free Men: The Ideology of the Republican Party Before the Civil War* (New York, 1970), provide indispensable portraits of political parties and their stance on policy matters in the nineteenth century.

6. On dropout rates, see Reese, *Origins*, 236–55. Also see Joseph Moreau's excellent *School Book Nation: Conflicts over American History Textbooks from the Civil War to the Present* (Ann Arbor, MI, 2003), 23–24, where he rightly warns scholars to distinguish between what adults try to teach the young and how historical knowledge is interpreted by students.

7. Alfred D. Chandler, Jr. and James W. Cortada, *A Nation Transformed: How Information Has Shaped the United States from Colonial Times to the Present* (New York, 2000); Daniel R. Headrick, *When Information Came of Age: Technologies of Knowledge in the Age of Reason and Revolution, 1700–1750* (New York, 2000); and Moreau, *School Book Nation*, 39.

8. Histories of the curriculum often focus on particular subjects but not the entire range of studies. Among the best studies, see John A. Nietz, *Old Textbooks* (Pittsburgh, PA, 1961); and John Elbert Stout, *The Development of the High-School Curricula in the North Central States from 1860 to 1918* (Chicago, 1921).

9. On the ideology of American public schools in the nineteenth century, the standard work is Carl F. Kaestle, *Pillars of the Republic: Common Schools and American Society, 1780–1860* (New York, 1983).

10. Sally H. Wertheim, "Joseph B. Ray," in *Biographical Dictionary of American Educators*, ed. John F. Ohles (Westport, CT, 1978), 3: 1074; David F. Labaree, *The Making of an American High School: The Credentials Market and the Central High School of Philadelphia* (New Haven, CT, 1988), 17–19, 72–76; and Lloyd P. Jorgenson, *The State and the Non–Public School, 1825–1925* (Columbia, MO, 1987), 60–67.

11. William T. Harris, "Textbooks and Their Uses," *Education* 1 (September 1880): 8; and Merle Curti, *The Social Ideas of American Educators* (New York, 1935), chapter 9.

12. Edward L. Youmans, *A Class-Book of Chemistry* (New York, 1851), 6; and David A. Wells, *Wells's Principles and Applications of Chemistry* (New York, 1858), iii. Also see "Edward Livingston Youmans," in *Dictionary of American Biography*, ed. Dumas Malone (New York, 1936), 10: 615–16; and George E. DeBoer, *A History of Ideas in Science Education* (New York, 1991), 4–8. On the multiple benefits of temperance instruction embraced by a range of reformers, see Jonathan Zimmerman, *Distilling Democracy: Alcohol Education in America's Public Schools, 1880–1925* (Lawrence, KS, 1999).

13. J. Dorman Steele, *Fourteen Weeks in Chemistry* (New York, 1867), 37; and Frank Wigglesworth Clarke, "A Report on the Teaching of Chemistry and Physics in the United States," (Washington, DC: U.S. Bureau of Education, Circular of Information, No. 6, 1880). Textbooks commonly highlighted the compatibility of science with the truths of Christianity. For example, read J. L. Blake, *High School Reader* (Boston, MA, 1832), 61; Alonzo Gray, *Elements of Natural Philosophy* (New York, 1851), 15–16, 20; David A. Wells, *Wells's Natural Philosophy; For the Use of Schools, Academies, and Private Students* (New York, 1857), iii; G. P. Quakenbos, *A Natural Philosophy* (New York, 1872), 3; J. Dorman Steele, *Fourteen Weeks in Natural Philosophy* (New York, 1872), 7, 13, 38, 314–15; J. Dorman Steele, *Fourteen Weeks' Course in Descriptive Astronomy* (New York, 1870), 6; J. Dorman Steele, *Fourteen Weeks in Popular Geology* (New York, 1870), 7, 251; and James D. Dana, *Manual of Geology* (New York, 1880), 850.

14. Eric Hobsbawn, *The Age of Capital 1848–1875* (London, 1975), 300.

15. Ebenezer Bailey, *First Lessons in Algebra* (Boston, MA, 1833), 115. See the social-class-oriented problems in the following textbooks: Baily, *First Lessons*, 128, 129, 131, 151; Elias Loomis, *The Elements of Algebra* (New York, 1851), 22, 23, 25, 28, 30, 34, 35, 252–54; Benjamin Greenleaf, *A Practical Treatise on Algebra, Designed for the Use of Students in High Schools and Academies* (Boston, MA, 1854), 80, 83–88; Joseph Ray, *Ray's Algebra* (Cincinnati, OH, 1848), 124, 130; and the several examples of irresponsible workers in Horatio Nelson Robinson, *New Elementary Algebra; Containing the Rudiments of the Science for Schools and Academies* (New York, 1860), 138.

16. Edward D. Mansfield, *American Education: Its Principles and Elements* (New York, 1851), 133; Ray, *Ray's Algebra*, 3; and Nietz, *Old Textbooks*, 174. See the entry on McGuffey in Peter Gordon and Richard Aldrich, *Biographical Dictionary of North American and European Educationists* (London, 1997), 308–9.

17. Lindley Murray, *Abridgement of Murray's English Grammar* (Peekskill, NY, 1830), 64–65. Before the 1840s, Murray (an American loyalist who fled to England after the American Revolution) was the leading author in the field. The values of political economy commonly appeared in lessons on grammar, spelling, and so forth. See, for example, Peter Bullions, *The Principles of English Grammar* (New York, 1846), 134–37 (lessons on syntax). On the importance of hard work and application and criticisms of idleness and dissipation, read Samuel Kirkham, *English Grammar in Familiar Lectures*, 63rd ed. (Baltimore, MD, 1834,), 105–8, 117, 124, 160, 196; Goold Brown, *The Institutes of English Grammar* (New York, 1853), 24, 30, 155, 182, 194, 206; and William H. Wells, *A Grammar of the English Language* (Chicago, 1860), 13, 15, 19, 27, and 108. On the ubiquitous Franklin, see Murray, *Abridgement*, 49; and William Swinton, *A School Manual of English Composition* (New York, 1877), 7.

18. Reese, *Origins*, 136–41.
19. H. White, *Elements of Universal History*, (Philadelphia, PA, 1849), 13–15. For examples of these themes, see S. R. Hall and A. R. Barker, *School History of the United States* (Boston, MA, 1845); Joel Dorman Steele, *A Brief History of the United States* (New York, 1871); Marcius Willson, *History of the United States* (New York, 1855); and S. G. Goodrich, *Modern History, From the Fall of Rome, A.D. 476, to the Present Time* (Louisville, KY, 1847). Also see Agnew O. Roorbach, *The Development of the Social Studies in American Secondary Education Before 1861* (Philadelphia, PA, 1937), 74–75.
20. S. Augustus Mitchell, *A General View of the World* (Philadelphia, PA, 1847), 298; George W. Fitch and George Woolworth Colton, *Colton and Fitch's Modern School Geography* (New York, 1857), 78–79; James Monteith, *Comprehensive Geography* (New York, 1882), 12; William Swinton, *A Complete Course in Geography* (New York, n.d.), 17; Andrew Guyot, *The Earth and Man* (Boston, MA, 1849), 232; and W. Mayo, *Development and Status of Secondary School Geography in the United States and Canada* (Ann Arbor, MI, 1965), 12–15. Racist and ethnocentric views abounded in the geography texts of the period, which offered many observations on the peoples of the world. Nations and races were divided into groups ranging from the most civilized to the most barbaric. See, for example, *Harper's School Geography* (New York, 1874), 18, 116–17; Sarah S. Cornell, *Cornell's High School Geography* (New York, 1856), 13; Mitchell, *A General View*, 21–25; and James Monteith and S. T. Frost, *McNally's System of Geography for Schools, Academies, and Seminaries* (New York, 1866), 7, 118.
21. Paul P. Abrahams, "Tariffs," in *The Oxford Companion to United States History*, ed. Paul S. Boyer (New York, 2001), 761; Douglas Ambrose, "Southern Intellectual Life," in *Encyclopedia of American Cultural & Intellectual History*, ed. Mary Kupiec Cayton and Peter W. Williams (New York, 2001), 1: 476; and Elizabeth Fox-Genovese and Eugene D. Genovese, *The Mind of the Master Class: History and Faith in the Southern Slaveholders' Worldview* (Cambridge, UK, 2005), chapter 10.
22. Francis Wayland, *The Elements of Political Economy* (Boston, MA, 1841), 152. That man was lazy, and forced to labor after The Fall, and that he was selfish, which led to personal and national prosperity, was a mainstay in most texts. See J. T. Champlin, *Lessons on Political Economy* (New York, 1868), 14, 71, 176, 183; and Amasa Walker, *The Science of Wealth: A Manual of Political Economy* (Philadelphia, PA, 1872), 31. In *The Science Education of American Girls* (New York, 2003), 20–30, Kim Tolley highlights the range of justifications for the study of geography after the American Revolution. Its advocates said geography was a subject of great utility, providing useful knowledge, mental discipline, and lessons in patriotism.

23. Francis Wayland, *The Elements of Moral Science* (Boston, MA, 1835), 376. See also Laurens P. Hickok, *A System of Moral Science* (Schenectady, NY, 1853); Francis Bowen, *American Political Economy* (New York, 1870), 15; and Louis Menand, *The Metaphysical Club: A Story of Ideas in America* (New York, 2001), 26, 128.

24. Reese, *Origins*, 248–55.

## Chapter 5   Changing Conceptions of "Public" and "Private" in American Educational History

This chapter has been adapted from William J. Reese, "Changing Conceptions of 'Public' and 'Private' in American Educational History," in *Public or Private Schools? Lessons from History*, ed. Richard Aldrich (London, 2004), 147–66.

1. Bernard Bailyn, *Education in the Forming of American Society* (New York, 1960), 11; Otto F. Kraushaar, *Private Schools: From the Puritans to the Present* (Bloomington, IN, 1976), 1; and Carl F. Kaestle, *Pillars of the Republic: Common Schools and American Society, 1780–1860* (New York, 1983), chapter 1.

2. On the primacy of the family, see Bailyn, *Education*; and Lawrence A. Cremin, *American Education: The Colonial Experience, 1607–1763* (New York, 1970). On child-rearing, see Jerry W. Frost, "As the Twig is Bent: Quaker Ideas of Childhood," *Quaker History* 60 (Autumn 1971): 67–87; and especially Philip W. Greven, *The Protestant Temperament: Patterns of Child-Rearing, Religious Experience, and the Self in Early American History* (Chicago, 1977).

3. James Axtell, *The School Upon a Hill: Education and Society in Colonial New England* (New York, 1974); and Alan Taylor, *American Colonies* (New York, 2001).

4. See especially, Axtell, *The School upon a Hill*; Kraushaar, *Private Schools*, 11, 14; Cremin, *Colonial Experience*; and Carl F. Kaestle, *The Evolution of an Urban System: New York City, 1750–1850* (Cambridge, MA, 1973). On the distinction between private venture schools and academies, which sometimes grew out of the former, see Kim Tolley, "Mapping the Landscape of Higher Schooling, 1727–1850," in *Chartered Schools: Two Hundred Years of Independent Academies in the United States, 1727–1925*, ed. Nancy Beadie and Kim Tolley (New York, 2002), 20–21, 26.

5. Frederick Rudolph, ed., *Essays on Education in the Early Republic* (Cambridge, MA, 1965); and Kaestle, *Pillars*, chapter 1.

6. On the antebellum period, read Kaestle, *Pillars*. There is no single volume on the post–Civil War era, prior to the Progressive Era that matches the quality of Kaestle's volume.

7. Kaestle, *Pillars*, chapter 3; and Donald G. Mathews, "The Second Great Awakening as an Organizing Process," *American Quarterly* 21 (Spring 1969): 23–43.

8. On New York, see especially Vincent P. Lannie, *Public Money and Parochial Education: Bishop Hughes, Governor Seward, and the New York School Controversy* (Cleveland, OH, 1968); Kaestle, *The Evolution of an Urban System*; and Diane Ravitch, *The Great School Wars: New York City, 1805–1973* (New York, 1974).

9. On the role of Protestants in the creation of public schools, and religious compromises made among them in the process, see Timothy L. Smith, "Protestant Schooling and American Nationality, 1800–1850," *Journal of American History* 53 (March 1967): 679–95; David B. Tyack, "The Kingdom of God and the Common School: Protestant Ministers and the Educational Awakening in the West," *Harvard Educational Review* 33 (Fall 1966): 447–69; David B. Tyack, "Onward Christian Soldiers: Religion in the Common School," in *History and Education: The Educational Uses of the Past*, ed. Paul Nash (New York, 1970), 212–55; John R. Bodo, *The Protestant Clergy and Public Issues* (Princeton, NJ, 1954); and Frances X. Curran, *The Churches and the Schools: American Protestantism and Popular Elementary Education* (Chicago, 1954).

10. Michael B. Katz, *The Irony of Early School Reform: Educational Innovation in Mid-Nineteenth Century Massachusetts* (Boston, MA, 1968) and Kaestle, *Pillars*, illuminate the breadth of social changes transforming American society and offer contrasting interpretations of the origins of the American public school system.

11. On mass education, see Kraushaar, *Private Schools*, 30. On higher education, read John S. Whitehead, *The Separation of College and State: Columbia, Dartmouth, Harvard, and Yale, 1776–1876* (New Haven, CT, 1973).

12. Kim Tolley, "Making the Landscape," 22–23; Margaret A. Nash, *Women's Education in the United States, 1780–1840* (New York, 2005); Michael B. Katz, *Class, Bureaucracy, and the Schools: The Illusion of Educational Change in America* (New York, 1975), 23; Theodore R. Sizer, ed., *The Age of the Academies* (New York, 1964); and William J. Reese, *The Origins of the American High School* (New Haven, CT, 1995).

13. Mann quoted in *The Republic and the School: Horace Mann on the Education of Free Men*, ed. Lawrence A. Cremin (New York, 1957), 33, 107. Also see William J. Reese, "Public Schools and the Elusive Search for the Common Good," in *Reconstructing the Common Good in Education*, ed. Larry Cuban and Dorothy Shipps (Stanford, CA, 2000), 16–25.

14. Boutwell quoted in Katz, *Class, Bureaucracy, and the Schools*, 27–28; also see "Common Schools and Public Instruction," *American Journal of Education* 8 (June 15, 1873): 225.

15. David B. Tyack, Thomas James, and Aaron Benevot, *Law and the Shaping of Public Education, 1785–1954* (Madison, WI, 1987), 140–47; Eric Foner, *Reconstruction: America's Unfinished*

*Revolution, 1863–1877* (New York, 1988), chapter 7; Ward M. McAffee, *Religion, Race, and Reconstruction: The Public School in the Politics of the 1870s* (Albany, NY, 1998), 192–96; and Timothy Walch, *Parish School: American Catholic Parochial Education From Colonial Times to the Present* (New York, 1996), 62–63.

16. Dexter A. Hawkins, "Compulsory School Attendance," *American Journal of Education* 30 (1880): 825; and Walch, *Parish School*, 63–65.

17. Edward N. Saveth, "Education of an Elite," *History of Education Quarterly* 28 (Fall 1988): 367–86; and William H. Harbaugh, *The Life and Times of Theodore Roosevelt* (New York, 1975), 128, 216.

18. Joel H. Spring, *Education and the Rise of the Corporate State* (Boston, MA, 1972); David B. Tyack, *The One Best System: A History of American Urban Education* (Cambridge, MA, 1974); Wayne E. Fuller, *The Old Country School: The Story of Rural Education in the Middle West* (Chicago, 1982); and Herbert M. Kliebard, *Schooled to Work: Vocationalism and the American Curriculum, 1876–1946* (New York, 1999).

19. Tyack, "Onward," 212–255; William J. Reese, "Public Schools and the Great Gates of Hell," *Educational Theory* 32 (Winter 1982–83): 9–18; Jerry Falwell, with E. Dobson and E. Hindson, *The Fundamentalist Phenomenon: The Resurgence of Conservative Christianity* (New York, 1981); Edward J. Larson, *Summer for the Gods: The Scopes Trial and America's Continuing Debate Over Science and Religion* (New York, 1997); Joel A. Carpenter, *Revive Us Again: The Reawakening of American Fundamentalism* (New York, 1997); David B. Tyack, "The Perils of Pluralism: The Background of the Pierce Case," *American Historical Review* 74 (October 1968): 74–98; and Kraushaar, *American Nonpublic Schools*, 13–14.

20. Paul F. Douglas, "Keep the Public Schools Public," *Social Frontier* 4 (November 1937): 42–46; Mary Elizabeth O'Connor, "Are Private Schools So Superior?" *Journal of Education* 120 (October 1937): 321–22; "Are Private Schools Better?" *Journal of Education* 131 (February 1948): 47; J. L. Sherman, "Is the Private Secondary School Undemocratic?" *School and Society* 69 (1949): 193–95; Rev. Paul C. Reinert, "Does America Need Private Education?" *Vital Speeches* 16 (April 1, 1950): 372–75; T. D. Martin, "Are Private Schools a Menace to our Democracy?" *Nation's Schools* 46 (September 1950): 28; and Oliver L. La Farge, "We Need Private Schools," *The Atlantic Monthly* 193 (February 1954): 53–56.

21. On Catholicism and the 1960 election, see Walch, *Parish School*, 209; and James T. Patterson, *Grand Expectations: The United States, 1945–1974* (New York, 1996), 439.

22. Christopher Jencks, "Is the Public School Obsolete?" in *School Reform: Past and Present*, ed. Michael B. Katz (Boston, MA, 1971), 243.

23. Joel H. Spring, *The Sorting Machine: National Education Policy Since 1945* (New York, 1976); and Barbara Clowse, *Brainpower for the Cold War: The Sputnik Crisis and National Defense Education Act of 1958* (Westport, CT, 1981).

24. Carl F. Kaestle and Marshall S. Smith, "The Federal Role in Elementary and Secondary Education, 1940–1980," *Harvard Educational Review* 52 (November 1982): 384–409; and Julie Roy Jeffrey, *Education for the Children of the Poor: A Study of the Origins and Implementation of the Elementary and Secondary Education Act of 1965* (Columbus, OH, 1978).

25. While the literature on race and education after 1945 is vast, the starting place on the *Brown* decision is Richard Kluger, *Simple Justice: The History of Brown v. Board of Education and Black America's Struggle for Equality* (New York, 1976); and James T. Patterson, *Brown v. Board of Education: A Civil Rights Milestone and Its Troubled Legacy* (New York, 2001). On segregationist academies, see David Nevin and Robert E. Bills, *The Schools That Fear Built: Segregationist Academies in the South* (Washington, DC, 1976).

26. Harvey Kantor and Barbara Brenzel, "Urban Education and the 'Truly Disadvantaged': The Historical Roots of the Contemporary Crisis, 1945–1990," in *The "Underclass" Debate: Views from History*, ed. Michael B. Katz (Princeton, NJ, 1993), 366–402. On rising expectations, see William J. Reese, *America's Public Schools: From the Common School to "No Child Left Behind"* (Baltimore, MD, 1995), chapters 7–9.

27. On concerns over morality, see B. Edward McClellan, *Moral Education in America: Schools and the Shaping of Character from Colonial Times to the Present* (New York, 1999), chapter 5; and Reese, "Public Schools," 9–18.

28. H.M. Hamlin, "Are We Returning to Private Education?" *Nation's Schools* 55 (March 1955): 63; Bernard J. Kohlbrenner, "Some Practical Aspects of the Public Character of Private Education," *School and Society* 86 (September 27, 1958): 248; E.R. D'Allesio, "Public Policy Implications of Public Assistance to Nonpublic Education," *Religious Education* 70 (March–April 1975): 174–84; and the essays in Edward G. Gaffney, Jr., ed., *Private Schools and the Public Good: Policy Alternatives for the Eighties* (Notre Dame, 1981).

29. On the "child benefit theory," read Diane Ravitch, *The Troubled Crusade: American Education, 1945–1980* (New York, 1983), 30, 33, 41; on private school groups and the Elementary and Secondary Education Act during the Johnson years, see Walch, *Parish School*, 213–14.

30. See, for example, Milton Friedman, *Free to Choose* (New York, ©1979); and John Coons and Stephen D. Sugarman, *Education by Choice: The Case for Family Control* (Berkeley, CA, 1978). Also see an early attempt to document the revival of conservatism in the 1970s,

Alan Crawford, *Thunder on the Right: The "New Right" and the Politics of Resentment* (New York, 1980).

31. Bruce J. Schulman underscores the rising power of the ideology of the market place in *The Seventies: The Great Shift in American Culture, Society, and Politics* (New York, 2001), and Catherine A. Lugg discusses the personalities and policies of the Reagan years in *For God and Country: Conservatism and American School Policy* (New York, 1996). On Reagan and tax credits, see Walch, *Parish School*, 221, 227–28; and James W. Fraser, *Between Church and State: Religion and Public Education in a Multicultural America* (New York, 1999), 178–79.

32. The literature on Catholic education is vast. In addition to Walch, *Parish School*, at a minimum read Andrew M. Greeley and Peter H. Rossi, *The Education of Catholic Americans* (Chicago, 1966); James Coleman, Thomas Hoffer, and Sally Kilgore, *High School Achievement: Public, Catholic, and Private Schools Compared* (New York, 1982); and Anthony S. Bryck, Valerie E. Lee, and Peter B. Holland, *Catholic Schools and the Common Good* (Cambridge, MA, 1993).

33. National Center for Education Statistics, *Private School Universe Survey, 1999–2000* (Washington, DC: U.S. Department of Education, Office of Educational Research and Improvement, 2001), 1–3. On the diversity of private schools in the past, see the overview in Kraushaar, *American Nonpublic Schools*, part 1; and the case studies in James C. Carper and Thomas Hunt, eds., *Religious Schooling in America* (Birmingham, AL, 1984); and in *Religious Schools in the United States K-12*, ed. Thomas C. Hunt and James C. Carper (New York, 1993).

34. National Center for Education Statistics, *Private School Universe Survey*, 20.

35. "Bush Calls Ruling about Vouchers a 'Historic' Move," *New York Times*, July 2, 2002, A1.

36. On the rise of modern conservatism, especially read Rick Perlstein, *Before the Storm: Barry Goldwater and the Unmaking of the American Consensus* (New York, 2001).

## Chapter 6    Soldiers for Christ in the Army of God: The Christian School Movement

This chapter has been adapted from William J. Reese, "Soldiers for Christ in the Army of God: The Christian School Movement in America," in *Educational Theory* 35, no. 2 (1985): 175–194. Reprinted by permission of the University of Illinois.

1. National Commission on Excellence in Education, *A Nation at Risk: The Imperative for Educational Reform* (Washington, DC: U.S. Department of Education, 1983). "A fundamentalist is an evangelical who is angry about something," wrote historian George M. Marsden in *Understanding Fundamentalism and Evangelicalism* (Grand

Rapids, MI, 1991), 1. Fundamentalists, "a subtype of evangelicals," were militantly opposed to secular, humanistic, and liberal values within twentieth-century Protestantism and American society. The word "fundamentalist" was coined in 1920.

2. Joan Richardson, "ACE Fundamentalists' Alternative to 'Pagan' Public School Systems," *Indianapolis Star*, December 17, 1978, A12. Donald Howard, quoted in the text, continued, "The Pilgrims were just like you. They were fundamentalists. They were separatists. They believed in educating their own children." Also see James C. Carper, "The *Whisner* Decision: A Case Study in State Regulation of Christian Day Schools," *Journal of Church and State* 24 (Spring 1982): 281, note 1; James C. Carper, "The Christian Day School in the American Social Order, 1960–1980," in *Religion and Morality in American Schooling*, ed. Thomas C. Hunt and Marilyn M. Maxson (Washington, DC, 1981), 79–101; "The Christian Day School Movement," *Educational Forum* 47 (Winter 1983–84): 135–49; and "The Christian Day School," in *Religious Schooling in America: Historical Insights and Contemporary Concerns*, ed. James Carper and Thomas C. Hunt (Birmingham, AL, 1984), chapter 5; and James C. Carper and Jeffrey A. Daignault, "Christian Day Schools: Past, Present, and Future," in *Religious Schools in the United States K-12*, ed. Thomas C. Hunt and James C. Carper (New York, 1993), 318–19, which estimated enrollments of about one million pupils by the early 1990s, after a slowdown in the "rate of growth" in the previous decade. An early, popular critique of the Christian school movement in the South was by David Nevin and Robert E. Bills, *The Schools That Fear Built: Segregationist Academies in the South* (Washington, DC, 1976.) Falwell is quoted by Adell Crowe and Saundra Ivey, "Church Schools Flourish Here Over Decade," *Nashville Tennessean*, August 4, 1980, A2. Also see Jerry Falwell, *Listen! America!* (New York, 1980); and Ed Dobson and Ed Hindson, *The Fundamentalist Phenomenon: The Resurgence of Conservative Christianity* (Garden City, NY, 1981).

3. Compare Peter Skerry, "Christian Schools versus the I.R.S.," *The Public Interest* 61 (Fall 1980): 18–41; with Nevin and Bills, *Schools That Fear Built*. Also read Paul F. Parsons, *Inside America's Christian Schools* (Macon, GA, 1987), xii.

4. Quoted by Jonathan Roos, "Students Stand Firm in Fight against Order Closing School," *Des Moines Register*, November 11, 1981, B4. The struggles over regulation in Iowa can be traced in the following articles in the *Register*, all written by Jonathan Roos: "More Christian Schools Resist Iowa's Rules," April 4, 1980, C2–3; "Baptist School Chief, Parents Face Charges," November 6, 1980, A8–9; "Church Rally Assails States' School Laws," October 27, 1981, B7; "Churches File Suit To Block School Laws," November 10, 1981, B2–3; and "Fellowship Asks for Meeting With Governor Ray," November 12, 1981, B6. For a critique of the separatist nature of the movement, see

the ethnographic study of one Baptist school in central Illinois by Alan Peshkin, *God's Choice: The Total World of a Fundamentalist Christian School* (Chicago, 1986).

5. The standard history of the rise of fundamentalism is by George M. Marsden, *Fundamentalism and American Culture: The Shaping of Twentieth-Century Evangelicalism, 1870–1925* (New York, 1980). On the interwar period, see Joel A. Carpenter, *Revive Us Again: The Reawakening of American Fundamentalism* (New York, 1997); and Edward J. Larson, *Summer for the Gods: The Scopes Trial and America's Continuing Debate Over Science and Religion* (New York, 1997).

6. The most important early treatment of racial issues was by Nevin and Bills, *The Schools That Fear Built*.

7. On the history of postwar education, see Diane Ravitch, *The Troubled Crusade: American Education, 1945–1980* (New York, 1983); and Joel Spring, *The Sorting Machine: National Educational Policy Since 1945* (New York, 1976).

8. By the 1960s and 1970s, criticisms of the public schools abounded: attacks on low academic standards, falling SAT scores, the end to school prayer, school violence, racial integration, and imperious teacher unions. Many people latched onto the "back to basics" movement. For the diversity of complaint, see at least *A Nation At Risk*; James S. Coleman, Thomas Hoffer, and Sally Kilgore, *High School Achievement* (New York, 1982); and Burton Yale Pines, *Back to Basics: The Traditionalist Movement That is Sweeping Grass-Roots America* (New York, 1982), chapter 4. The historical literature on Protestantism and America's schools is vast; see David B. Tyack, "The Kingdom of God and the Common School: Protestant Ministers and the Educational Awakening in the West," *Harvard Educational Review* 36 (Fall 1966): 447–69; David B. Tyack, "Onward Christian Soldiers: Religion in the American Common School," in *History and Education*, ed. Paul Nash (New York, 1970), 215–55; and William J. Reese, "The Public Schools and the Great Gates of Hell," *Educational Theory* 32 (Winter 1982–83): 9–17. On the rise of Protestant schools, read Henry A. Buchanan and Bob W. Brown, "Will Protestant Church Schools Become a Third Force?" *Christianity Today* 11 (May 12, 1967): 5; William H. Fischer, "Wanted: Protestant Schools," *Christianity Today* 9 (May 7, 1965): 11–12; and Frank E. Gaebelein, "American Education," *Christianity Today* 11 (January 20, 1967): 4.

9. Many local Christian school leaders admitted that the desegregation of the public schools contributed to higher Christian school enrollments. At the same time, they repeatedly argued that desegregation was only one of the many stimuli influencing private school growth. For a sampling of opinion, see the following: Helen Huntley, "In Christian Schools, the Bible Enters All Classrooms," *St. Petersburg Times*, September 2, 1981, B10–11; Deena Mirow, "Religion: The Big R," *Cleveland Plain Dealer*, 8 November 1981, G2–4; Pat T. Patterson,

"Six Families Explain Switch," *Little Rock Gazette*, October 18, 1981, B9–12; Isabel Spencer, "Christian Schools Growing," *Washington Evening Journal*, 28 February 1978, D4–5; Randy McClain and Richard Wright, "Private Parochial School Enrollments Here Soaring," *Baton Rouge Morning Advocate*, August 24, 1981, C3–4; "Two Church Groups Will Open Schools," *St. Louis Post-Dispatch*, August 10, 1980, G14; "Public Schools in Need of Prayer?" *Christianity Today* 18 (October 26, 1973): 67; and Terry Monahan, "City Parochial School Bucks Accreditation System," *Sioux Falls Argus Leader*, December 2, 1979, E8. Even Nevin and Bills asserted that racism alone poorly explained the rise of Christian schools in the South in the 1960s; see *Schools That Fear Built*, 11: "The question is more complicated than the simple racism that marked the 1960s but obviously race is a big ingredient in the new schools."

10. See Michael Disend, "Have You Whipped Your Child Today?" *Penthouse* 13 (February 1982): 60. For a popular critique of the public schools by one of the founders of Moral Majority, read Tim LaHaye, *The Battle for the Public Schools* (Old Tappan, NJ, 1983). For the other quotations, see "Preacher Fights to Control School," *Cleveland Plain Dealer*, July 6, 1975, D4; and Sharon M. Bertsch, "Lansing Christian, Growing New School System in City," *Lansing State Journal*, September 16, 1979, G1.

11. *Tax-Exempt Status of Private Schools*, Hearings before the Subcommittee on Oversight of the Committee on Ways and Means, House of Representatives, Ninety-Sixth Congress, (Washington, DC, 1979), part 2, 949; and John Thoburn, quoted in "The Christian Schools Come Marching On," *Louisville Courier Journal*, October 26, 1975, F2.

12. Quotations from articles by Danny Lewis, "Christian Schools Drawing Greater Number of Students," *Montgomery Advertiser*, February 21, 1981, E10; Joan Richardson, "Education–According to the Gospels," *Peoria Journal Star*, October 30, 1977, C1; and Dick Ulmer, "Christian Schools Buck Trend," *Omaha World Herald*, August 16, 1981, B9 and B10. Also see the comments by the Reverend Leland Kennedy, pastor of the New Castle Baptist Church in New Castle, Delaware, in Isabel Spencer, "Christian Schools Growing," *Wilmington Evening Journal*, February 28, 1978, D4; and LaHaye, *The Battle for the Public Schools*; and Falwell, *Listen! America!*

13. Carper, "The Christian Day School in the American Social Order" and "The Christian Day School Movement." Also read Huntley Collins, "Christian Schools Gain Resurrection," *Portland Oregonian*, July 12, 1981, D8; and Carl F. Henry, "Religion in the Schools," *Christianity Today* 17 (September 14, 1973): 38. Dewey's instrumentalist philosophy, conservative critics (both Christian and secular) often contended, led to the erosion of absolute standards and academic training. Susan D. Rose noted the hostility to Dewey in her case

studies of Christian schools, *Keeping Them out of the Hands of Satan: Evangelical Schooling in America* (New York, 1988), 39. On the collapse of Protestant values in higher education, read George M. Marsden, *The Soul of the American University: From Protestant Establishment to Established Nonbelief* (New York, 1994).

14. Very M. Haley, Secretary of the Christian Academy, cited in Harley R. Bierce, "Faith-Oriented Schooling Shows Rapid Growth among Protestants," *Indianapolis Star*, July 11, 1975, D9. Also see John Wheaton, "Each Parochial School Different," *Casper Star-Tribune*, May 9, 1979, D1; and William J. Reese, "Education," in *Encyclopedia of Indianapolis*, ed. David J. Bodenhamer and Robert G. Barrows (Bloomington, IN, 1994), 84.

15. The primacy of the family was underscored in Falwell, *Listen! America!*; and LaHaye, *The Battle for the Public Schools.*

16. Joan Roesgen, "Will State Put Brakes on Church Schools?" *Billings Gazette*, September 17, 1978, B2. An activist in Arnold, Maryland, asserted that "God in his word has given the responsibility of training to parents primarily." See Nancy Jane Adams, "Stress on Values a Chief Attraction," *Annapolis Evening Capital*, March 3, 1981, G12; Denise Melinsky, "Sooners Protest Church School Closing," *Daily Oklahoman*, 21 October 1982, C2; Art Toalston, "Jackson Schools Grow With Fundamentalist Movement," *Jackson Clarion Ledger* (Mississippi), August 20, 1978, D5; "What About the Becker Amendment?" *Christianity Today* 8 (June 19, 1964): 22, Bert Latamore, "Private School Growth Boom," *Manchester Union Leader*, May 10, 1979, D9; and Gloria Wright, "Christian Schools Prospering," *Syracuse Herald American*, March, 22, 1981, G3.

17. Robert K. Gordon, "Academy for Born-Again Christians Going Strong," *Trenton Times*, June 28, 1981, G3. Careful screening of parents by Christian school administrators was common, since they wanted to attract families that shared a common religious orientation. Some activists boasted that, while public schools admitted children, they admitted entire families to school. Also read Patricia M. Lines, "Homeschooling Comes of Age," *Public Interest* 140 (Summer 2000): 74, which notes the close ties between homeschooling and the Christian school movement. She also points out that originally the homeschool movement in the 1950s and 1960s was led by liberals and activists who believed the public schools were too conservative! In "Home Schooling Grows Up," *Christianity Today* 39 (July 17, 1995): 50, John W. Kennedy estimated that 80 percent of all children schooled at home were Christian. He revised the estimate upward to 90 per cent in "Home Schooling Keeps Growing," *Christianity Today* 41 (July 14, 1997): 68.

18. *Tuition Tax Credit Proposals*, Hearing before the Committee on Finance, U.S. Senate, Ninety-Seventh Congress, Second Session (Washington, DC, 1982), 258; "Christian Schools Come Marching

On," F2; George Hillocks, Jr., "Books and Bombs: Ideological Conflict and the Schools–A Case Study of the Kanawha County Book Protest," *School Review* 86 (August 1978): 632–54; and Jason C. Bivins, *The Fracture of Good Order: Christian Antiliberalism and the Challenge to American Politics* (Chapel Hill, NC, 2003), 80.

19. Excellent studies of state regulation include Carper, "The *Whisner* Decision"; Skerry, "Christian Schools versus the I.R.S."; and Jeremy Rabkin, "Behind the Tax-Exempt Schools Debate," *The Public Interest* 68 (Summer 1982): 21–36.

20. Quoted in Joe Simmons, "Battle Lines Drawn Over Registering Schools," *Montgomery Advertiser*, October 15, 1981, E4; William Stewart, Indiana Director for Accelerated Christian Education, cited in "Private Schools Face Taking Problems," *Indianapolis Star*, 17 December 1978, G10; and Falwell, quoted in L. Kent Wolgamott, "Falwell Predicting Nebraska Will Sanction Christian Schools," *Lincoln Journal & Star*, October 25, 1981, A14. Fundamentalists from across the nation took a similar position. For a sampling of their opposition to state regulation, see Marsha Rhea, "Christian Educators to Fight Encroachment," *Montgomery Advertiser*, October 13, 1978, G3; Barbara T. Roessner, "Enfield Church School Case Targeted for Supreme Court," *Hartford Courant* (Connecticut), February 18, 1979, D12; Megan Rosenfield, "Fundamentalists Challenge State Licensing of Their Schools," *Washington Post*, July 24, 1978, E9–10; Joan Richardson, "1,500 Protest State Involvement in Operation of Church Schools," *Indianapolis Star*, January 17, 1979, E13; Jonathan Roos, "More Christian Schools Resist Iowa's Rules," *Des Moines Register*, April 27, 1980, C2–3; Jerry Moskel, "Rise in Church-Run Schools Confounds State," *Lansing State Journal*, October 11, 1979, A9–10; Roesgen, "Will State Put Brakes"; Maureen Boyle, "Church School Defies State," *Manchester Union Leader*, April 13, 1979, D12–13; and Chuck Raasch, "Control of Schools up to Court," *Sioux Falls Argus Leader*, February 1, 1980, C14.

21. Carper, "The *Whisner* Decision," 281–302; "Christian Schools: Learning in the Courtroom," *Christianity Today* 22 (September 22, 1978): 36–37; Edward E. Plowman, "Alarmed at Government Intrusion, Religious Groups Close Ranks," *Christianity Today* 25 (March 13, 1981): 72–74; Rodney Clapp, "The Police Lock a Baptist Church," *Christianity Today* 26 (November 12, 1982): 52–55, 58; and Bivins, *Fracture of Good Order*, 85–86.

22. Quotations from articles by Richardson, "Education–According to the Gospels," C4; Roos, "Students Stand Firm," B5; and Roos, "More Christian Schools Resist Iowa's Rules," C2.

23. Huntley Collins, "New Students Flock to Christian Schools," *Portland Oregonian*, July 12, 1981, D5; Doug Perry, "Christian School Would Rather Operate without Accreditation from State Board," *Louisville Courier-Journal*, September 26, 1977, D5. The

Louisville paper gave extensive coverage to the local conflicts between fundamentalists and the state; see Richard Wilson, "Carroll Sees School Suit as a Threat," March 24, 1978, F6; Anne Pardue, "2 Christian School Officials Testify They Can't Follow State Standards," June 15, 1978, F6; Ann Pardue, "Non-Accredited Christian Schools Legal, Judge Rules," October 5, 1978, G5–6; and "Christian Schools Applaud Ruling That Limits State Control," October 10, 1979, B4–5. On the situation in Albany, read Frederick P. Szydlik, "Private School Rolls Soar," *Albany Times-Union*, September 6, 1982, G4.

24. Clapp, "The Police Lock a Baptist Church," 54. The *Omaha World-Herald* and the *Lincoln Journal & Star* were consulted to follow the history of conflict in Louisville. Also see Jack Kelley, "Pastor Vows to Keep Church School Open," *U.S.A. Today*, August 31, 1983.

25. Bob Miller, "Is Certification Necessary?" *Anchorage Daily Times*, December 7, 1981, G11; Janice Rombeck, "Schools That Blend Christianity, ABCs Flourishing," *Wichita Eagle*, May 11, 1980, G13–14; and Kurt Hechenauer, "Religious Schools Pop Up in State as Escape from Public Education," *Daily Oklahoman*, March 29, 1982, C13–14.

26. See especially the congressional reports on the IRS. and Christian schools: *Tax-Exempt Status of Private Schools*, Hearings before the Subcommittee on Oversight of the Committee on Ways and Means, House of Representatives, Ninety-Sixth Congress (Washington, DC, 1979), parts 1 and 2. Also read "The I.R.S. Pins 'Badge of Doubt' on Tax-Exempt Private Schools," *Christianity Today* 23 (January 5, 1979): 42; "Private Schools Get I.R.S. Procedure Suspended," *Christianity Today* 23 (October 5, 1979): 58–59; and Tom Minnery, "Religious Schools Rev Up For New Round With IRS," *Christianity Today* 24 (November 21, 1980): 50

27. On the conservative revival, see Bruce J. Schulman, *The Seventies: The Great Shift in American Culture, Society, and Politics* (New York, 2001).

28. See, for example, two books published in 1972: Jonathan Kozol's *Free Schools* (New York, 1972); and Allen Graubard's *Free the Children: Radical Reform and the Free School Movement* (New York, 1972). The Rev. John C. Macon, administrator of the Clinton Christian School in Prince George's County, Maryland, and an activist in the Eastern Association of Christian Schools, was quoted in Rosenfeld, "Fundamentalists Challenge State Licensing of Their Schools," E9.

29. Adams, "Stress on Values a Chief Attraction," G12.

30. Individual Christian schools often attracted pupils whose parents attended a fundamentalist or evangelical church other than the sponsoring institution. For example, a Christian school in Ewing Township in greater Trenton, New Jersey, enrolled pupils who were "Baptists, Methodists, Catholics, and members of the Assembly of God and the Church of the Nazarenes." See Gordon, "Academy for Born-Again Christians Going Strong," G4. Also read *Tax-Exempt Status of Private*

*Schools*, 1979, part 1, 55. James Carper estimated in "The Christian Day School Movement" that "the average number of students per school is probably between 100 and 200 . . . ." (137).

31. *Tax-Exempt Status of Private Schools*, 1979, part 1, 55, 117; *Tuition Tax Relief Bills*, Hearings before the Subcommittee on Taxation and Debt Management Generally of the Committee on Finance, United States Senate, Ninety-Fifth Congress, Second Session (Washington, DC, 1978), part 2, 702; and Skerry, "Christian Schools versus the I.R.S.," 20.

32. "Fundamentalist Schools Multiply," *Chicago Tribune*, 21 September 1981, C7; Stacey Burling, "Private Schools Doing Well Despite Costs," *Norfolk Virginian-Pilot*, 8 September 1980, D4; Skerry, "Christian Schools versus the I.R.S.," 26, 32; *Tuition Tax Credits*, Hearings before the Subcommittee on Taxation and Debt Management of the Committee on Finance, United States Senate, Ninety-Seventh Congress, first session (Washington, DC, 1981), part 2, 63. Compare Joseph Bayly, "Why I'm for Christian Schools," *Christianity Today* 24 (January 25, 1980): 92.

33. Nevin and Bills, *Schools That Fear Built*, 409. The authors continue: "They [the parents] tend to relate to monetary success, to be impatient of those less successful and to see change as a threat. Few of the new school patrons are rich; some are still quite poor and the tuition represents a sacrifice."

34. Mirow, "Religion: The Big R," G2. Also see Rom Rademacher, "Public Schools Lose While Private Schools Gain," *Grand Rapids Press*, October 11, 1981, C1; Jeanne Pugh, "Parents Plan Concert to Raise Funds for Christian Schools," *St. Petersburg Times*, October 29, 1977, A12; Sharon J. Selyer, "Private Schools Are Doing Well Despite the High Cost of Tuition," *Atlanta Journal*, August 9, 1982, C13–14; John Furey, "Private Schools in Salem Bucking Hard Times Ahead," *Oregon Statesman*, November 1, 1981, C4–5; Jon Walker, "S.F. Private Schools Doing Fine Despite Tough Economic Times," *Sioux Falls Argus Leader*, October 28, 1982, E4–5; and Jimmie Covington, "Inflation Ups Private School Costs, But Parents Willingly Pay," *Commercial Appeal* (Memphis, TN), April 27, 1980, C5–6.

35. On school integration and civil rights, there is an enormous literature; see at least Richard Kluger, *Simple Justice: The History of Brown v. Board of Education and Black America's Struggle for Equality* (New York, 1975); J. Harvie Wilkinson III, *From Brown to Bakke: The Supreme Court and School Integration, 1954–1978* (New York, 1979); and James T. Patterson, *Brown v. Board of Education: A Civil Rights Milestone and Its Troubled Legacy* (New York, 2001). On the growth of African American enrollments within Christian day schools, including the rise of black controlled schools, see Carper and Daignault, "Christian Day Schools," 320–22.

36. See Peggy Peterman, "Private Schools: A Growing Alternative," *St. Petersburg Times*, August 29, 1976, G8–9; Spencer, "Christian Schools Growing," D4–5; and Mirow, "Religion: The Big R," G2, who quotes the Rev. Roy Thompson, whose Cleveland Baptist Church sponsored Heritage Christian School: "We could have 1,000 more students if we take them simply to avoid busing. We feel sorry for them, but we can't take them for that reason because our religious convictions are so strong." Also see *Tax-Exempt Status of Private Schools*, 1979, part 1, 385–86.

37. Miller, "Certification: Is It Necessary?" G11; Nevin and Bills, *Schools That Fear Built*, 57 and chapter 8; Richardson, "Education–According to the Gospels," C1–4; and Jimmy Covington, "Private Schools Gear for Rise in Fall Enrollment of Students," *Commercial Appeal*, April 29, 1974, C8. The application form also asked applicants to reveal their thoughts on capitalism, progressive education, the Jesus Movement, creation, and Billy Graham's cooperative evangelism. Also see Bivens, *Fracture of Good Order*, 92–93.

38. Ulmer, "Christian Schools Buck Trend," B10; and Nevin and Bills, *Schools That Fear Built*, chapter 8.

39. The classic historical study is by Raymond E. Callahan, *Education and the Cult of Efficiency* (Chicago, 1962). Also see Michael Apple, "Interpreting Teaching: Persons, Politics, and Culture," *Educational Studies* 14 (Summer 1983): 112–35.

40. Detailed descriptions of ACE are available in the following: Bob Miller, "Jesus Supplies Incentive in Christian Study," *Anchorage Daily Times*, December 7, 1981, G2–3; Richardson, "ACE Fundamentalists' Alternative to 'Pagan' Public School Systems," A11–12; Sharon M. Bertsch, "Do-It-Yourself Package Works for Fundamentalist Schools," *Lansing State Journal*, October 15, 1978, F8–10; Lisa Hammersley, "Church Schools Purchase Christian Education Plan," *Charlotte Observer*, February 28, 1981, F4–5; Gloria Wright, "Christian Schools Prospering," *Syracuse Herald American*, March 22, 1981, G4; Huntley Collins, "Christian Schools on Strict, Individual Effort," *Portland Oregonian*, July 13, 1981, A12; and Rose, *Keeping Them Out of the Hands of Satan*, chapter 6. In *Inside America's Christian Schools*, 64, Parsons estimated in 1987 that about "a third of all Christian schools in the United States operate with the A.C.E. curriculum."

41. Marsden, *Fundamentalism and American Culture*, brilliantly recreates the historical context that gave rise to fundamentalism.

42. Deborah Frazier, "Bible is the Answer for Grand Junction Schools," *Rocky Mountain News*, October 18, 1981, C14; Ulmer, "Christian Schools Buck Trend," B9; and Saundra Ivey and Adell Crowe, "Parents Seek Something Special in Private School," *Nashville Tennessean*, August 3, 1980, B8. Bob Winebarger, principal of the Park West School in Lincoln, Nebraska, wrote that "we base everything on

the Bible, the only source of absolute truth and knowledge. We center our teachings on Christ rather than the child or the academic content." See Anita Fussell, "Standards Split Launches Bible Schools," *Journal & Star*, September 14, 1980, A2.

43. Roos, "Students Stand Firm against Order Closing School," B4; John Carlson, "Boom in Religious Schools: Threat to Public Education?" *Des Moines Register*, September 14, 1980, A11; and Spencer, "Christian Schools Prospering," G3.

44. Spencer, "Christian Schools Growing," D5; and Nevil and Bills, *Schools That Fear Built*, 61, 62; and Huntley Collins, "New Students Flock to Christian Schools," *Portland Oregonian*, July 12, 1981, D6.

45. Carlson, "Boom in Religious Schools," A11; and Nevin and Bills, *Schools That Fear Built*. 61. The subject of scientific creationism is too vast to be explored here, but see Parsons, *Inside America's Christian Schools*, chapter 7. The issue of teaching "intelligent design" is the latest controversy related to the teaching of science in Christian as well as public schools.

46. Timothy D. Crater, "The Unproclaimed Priests of Public Education," *Christianity Today* 25 (April 10, 1981): 45; and Roos, "Students Stand Firm in Fight against Order Closing School," B4.

47. Rombeck, "Schools That Blend Christianity, ABCs Flourishing," G14; Richardson, quoting the state representative for A.C.E in Illinois, in "Education–According to the Gospels," C2; Collins, "New Students Flock to Christian Schools," D5; and Rose, *Keeping Them out of the Hands of Satan*, chapter 9.

48. Frank Beacham, "A Ruling is Near on Dade School's Refusal to Admit Black Students," *Miami Herald*, May 19, 1975, E5; "Ask Jesus To Help You," *Providence Journal*, April 13, 1980, A1; Ward Pimley, "Church Classes Alter Approach to Education," *Providence Journal*, 18 November 1979, F4; and Frank Krzywicki, "Church Schools Find Acceptance," *Delaware State News*, February 12, 1978, C9.

49. Bertsch, "Do-It-Yourself Package," F9; Danny Lewis, "Christian Schools Drawing Greater Number of Students," *Montgomery Advertiser*, February 21, 1981, E11; Pamela Mendels, "Basics, Bible, and a 'Board of Education,' " *Providence Journal*, October 25, 1981, D6; Bob Banta, "Bibles and Backsides," *Austin American-Statesman*, August 1, 1982, B1; and Disend, "Have You Whipped Your Child Today?" On paddling and other forms of discipline, see Parsons, *Inside America's Christian Schools*, 5.

50. See *Tuition Tax Relief Bills*, 702.

51. Rev. Daniel D. Carr, Executive Director of the Organized Christian Schools of North Carolina, cited in John Robinson, "Christian Schools Add Discipline, Doctrine to Learning Routines," Raleigh *News and Observer*, November 29, 1981, F13.

52. Kate Harris, "Public School Officials Fear Proposed Tuition Tax Credit," *Birmingham News*, May 24, 1981, A8–9; Sherry Johnson,

"N.C. Officials Fear Tax Plan Would Destroy Public Schools," *News and Observer*, April 16, 1982, D10–11; and John Furey, "New Debate over Private School Costs," *Oregon Statesman*, May 2, 1981, C14.

53. Livingston Taylor, "Senate Passes Private-School Textbooks Aid," *Louisville Courier-Journal*, March 18, 1978, E13; and Anthony Cardinale, "Tuition Tax Credit Gets Mixed Review," *Buffalo Evening News*, April 17, 1982, D6.

54. "Private Education: A Tax Break?" *Christianity Today* 22 (April 21, 1978): 43; and "School Tax Credits: Making New Converts," *Christianity Today* 22 (September 22, 1978): 37–38. Also see the testimony of various Christian School representatives in *Tuition Tax Proposals* (1982).

55. Statistics are often unreliable, as historian James C. Carper noted in an article by Mary Ann Zehr, "Evangelical Christian Schools See Growth," *Education Week* 24 (December 8, 2004). Also see Mary Ann Zehr, "Vote Sought on Public School Exodus," *Education Week* 23 (May 26, 2004): 1–2; and Mary Ann Zehr, "Southern Baptists Decline to Take Up Call for Public School Exodus," *Education Week* 23 (June 23, 2004): 10.

56. National Center for Education Statistics, *Private School Universe Survey, 1999–2000* (Washington, DC: U.S. Department of Education, Office of Educational Research and Improvement, 2001), 20.

## Chapter 7   Public Schools and the Common Good

This chapter has been adapted from William J. Reese, "Public Schools and the Common Good," in *Educational Theory* 38, no. 4 (1988): 431–40. Reprinted by permission of the University of Illinois.

1. William J. Reese, *Power and the Promise of School Reform: Grassroots Movements during the Progressive Era* (Boston, MA, 1986).

2. The best biography is by Jonathan Messerli, *Horace Mann: A Biography* (New York, 1982). Also read Michael B. Katz, *The Irony of Early School Reform: Educational Innovation in Mid-Nineteenth Century Massachusetts* (Boston, MA, 1968), which recounts the enormous changes that occurred during Mann's lifetime; William J. Reese, "Public Schools and the Elusive Search for the Common Good," in *Reconstructing the Common Good in Education*, ed. Larry Cuban and Dorothy Shipps (Stanford, CA, 2000), 25–31; and Carl F. Kaestle and Maris A. Vinovskis, *Education and Social Change in Nineteenth-Century Massachusetts* (Cambridge, MA, 1980). The standard history of the origins of the public schools is by Carl F. Kaestle, *Pillars of the Republic: Common Schools and American Society, 1780–1860* (New York, 1983). Also read Leon L. Litwack, *North of Slavery: The Negro in the Free States, 1790–1860* (Chicago, 1961), chapter 4; and Howard Rabinowitz, *Race Relations in the Urban South, 1865–1900* (New York, 1978), part 2.

3. *Common School Assistant*, quoted in Lawrence A. Cremin, *The American Common School: An Historic Conception* (New York, 1951), 59; and Horace Mann, "New York State School Convention," *Common School Journal 7* (July 15, 1845): 218. Mann was summarizing, favorably, ideas from fellow reformer Henry Barnard. Some of the themes in this chapter are elaborated upon in William J. Reese, *America's Public Schools: From the Common School to "No Child Left Behind"* (Baltimore, MD, 2005).

4. Numerous references on public-private issues in the nineteenth century are found in an earlier chapter of this book. On New York, especially read Vincent P. Lannie, *Public Money and Parochial Education: Bishop Hughes, Governor Seward, and the New York School Controversy* (Cleveland, OH, 1968); Carl F. Kaestle, *The Evolution of an Urban System* (Cambridge, MA, 1973); and Diane Ravitch, *The Great School Wars: New York City, 1805–1973* (New York, 1974). On church-state issues generally, read Lloyd P. Jorgenson, *The State and the Non–Public School, 1825–1925* (Columbia, MO, 1987).

5. Benjamin Justice, *The War That Wasn't: Religious Conflict and Compromise in the Common Schools of New York State, 1865–1900* (Albany, NY, 2005).

6. On the McGuffey Readers, see Ruth Miller Elson, *Guardians of Tradition: American Schoolbooks of the Nineteenth Century* (Nebraska, IL, 1964); and Elliot J. Gorn, ed., *The McGuffey Readers: Selections from the 1879 Edition* (New York, 1998), 11, 16.

7. Thomas Jefferson, *Notes on the State of Virginia*, ed. William Peden (New York, ©1954), 146; Merle Curti, *The Social Ideas of American Educators* (Totowa, NJ, ©1935), 40–49; Wayne Urban and Jennings L. Wagoner, Jr., *American Education: A History* (New York, 1996), 75; Kaestle, *Pillars*, 6–9, 61, 198–99; and Jennings L. Wagoner, Jr., *Jefferson and Education* (Charlottesville, VA, 2004), 37, 42–43, 131, 143.

8. Kaestle and Vinovskis, *Education and Social Change*, chapter 2; and Curti, *Social Ideas*, 131–32, 138, 199.

9. On the dramatic social changes and the fears (and reform movements) they elicited, see especially Walter Licht, *Industrializing America: The Nineteenth Century* (Baltimore, MD, 1995); Daniel Feller, *The Jacksonian Promise: America, 1815–1840* (Baltimore, MD, 1995); Steven Mintz, *Moralists & Modernizers: America's Pre-Civil War Reformers* (Baltimore, MD, 1995); and Ronald G. Walters, *American Reformers, 1815–1860*, rev. ed. (New York, 1997). On African Americans and Reconstruction, read James D. Anderson, *The Education of Blacks in the South, 1860–1935* (Chapel Hill, NC, 1988); Herbert G. Gutman, *Power & Culture: Essays on the American Working Class*, ed. Ira Berlin (New York, 1987), chapter 6; and Leon F. Litwack, *Trouble in Mind: Black Southerners in the Age of Jim Crow* (New York, 1998).

10. On the Germans in St. Louis, for example, see Selwyn K. Troen, *The Public and the Schools: Shaping the St. Louis System, 1838–1920* (Columbia, MO, 1975), 62–65.

11. The literature on the Progressive Era is vast, but read at least the following: Richard Hofstadter, *The Age of Reform: From Bryan to FDR* (New York, 1955); Robert H. Wiebe, *The Search for Order, 1877–1920* (New York, 1967); David P. Thelen, *The New Citizenship: Origins of Progressivism in Wisconsin, 1885–1900* (Columbia, MO, 1972); Robert M. Crunden, *Ministers of Reform: The Progressives' Achievement in American Civilization, 1889–1920* (New York, 1982); and Michael McGerr, *A Fierce Discontent: The Rise and Fall of the Progressive Movement in America, 1870–1920* (New York, 2003). On the rise of school social services, see Reese, *Power and the Promise*.

12. The standard biography, in a large field of competitors, is by Robert B. Westbrook, *John Dewey and American Democracy* (Ithaca, NY, 1991). Also see Louis Menand, *The Metaphysical Club: A Story of Ideas* (New York, 2001), part 4.

13. On Dewey's years in Chicago and a detailed analysis of his major philosophical ideas about education, read Westbrook, *John Dewey*, and Menand, *Metaphysical Club*. For a sense of Dewey's place in historical context, amid other educational thinkers, see Herbert M. Kliebard, *The Struggle for the American Curriculum, 1893–1958*, 3rd ed. (New York, 2004), 27, where he writes, "The paradox of John Dewey's reputation is that, although he gained worldwide recognition during his own lifetime and has unquestionably earned a place in the panoply of the world's great educators, his actual influence on the schools of the nation has been both seriously overestimated and grossly distorted. It was his fate to become identified with a vague, essentially undefinable, entity called progressive education, either an inchoate mixture of diverse and often contradictory reform or simply a historical fiction." Cf. Menand, *Metaphysical Club*, 316.

14. John Dewey, *Experience and Education* (New York, 1938).

15. Kliebard, *Struggle*, 27, passim; and Joyce Antler, *Lucy Sprague Mitchell: The Making of a Modern Woman* (New Haven, CT, 1987). For a broad view of the linkage of education with the economy over the course of the twentieth century, see W. Norton Grubb and Marvin Lazerson, *The Education Gospel: The Economic Power of Schooling* (Cambridge, MA, 2004); on Dewey's rejection of narrow vocational training, see 9, 40.

16. David B. Tyack's studies of the Progressive Era are indispensable; see especially *The One Best System: A History of American Urban Education* (Cambridge, MA, 1974); and David Tyack and Elisabeth Hansot, *Managers of Virtue: Public School Leadership in America, 1820–1980* (New York, 1982). The sweeping influence of the vocational ideal is explored in Herbert M. Kliebard, *Schooled to Work: Vocationalism and the American Curriculum, 1876–1946* (New York, 1999).

17. On ability grouping, see Jeannie Oakes, *Keeping Track: How Schools Structure Inequality* (New Haven, CT, 1985); and her article, "Grouping Students for Instruction," in *Encyclopedia of Educational Research*, ed. Marvin C. Alkin (New York, 1992): 2: 562–68.

18. Compare David John Hogan, *Class and Reform: School and Society in Chicago, 1880–1930* (Philadelphia, PA, 1985), 180; and Kliebard, *Schooled to Work*, 231–36. On the theory and practice of common schooling, consult Lawrence A. Cremin, *The Genius of American Education* (New York, 1965), 63–64.

19. The literature on the history of scientific testing is huge; see especially Stephen Jay Gould, *The Mismeasure of Man* (New York, 1981); Michael M. Sokal, ed, *Psychological Testing and American Society, 1890–1920* (New York, 1987); and Henry L. Minton, *Lewis M. Terman: Pioneer in Psychological Testing* (New York, 1988). On youth and the workplace, see Selwyn K. Troen, "The Discovery of the Adolescent by American Educational Reformers, 1900–1920: An Economic Perspective," in *Schooling and Society: Studies in the History of Education*, ed. Lawrence Stone (Baltimore, MD, 1976), 239–51.

20. On the history of "progressive education," see Lawrence A. Cremin, *The Transformation of the School: Progressivism in American Education, 1876–1957* (New York, 1961); Patricia Albjerg Graham, *Progressive Education From Arcady to Academe: A History of the Progressive Education Association, 1919–1955* (New York, 1977); and Arthur Zilversmit, *Changing Schools: Progressive Education Theory and Practice, 1930–1960* (Chicago, 1993). On turn-of-the-twentieth-century schools, see Joel H. Spring's *Education and the Rise of the Corporate State* (Boston, MA, 1972). On Mitchell, read Antler, *Lucy Sprague Mitchell*, 15, 259, 276, 313; and Patricia Albjerg Graham, *Schooling America: How the Public Schools Meet the Nation's Changing Needs* (New York, 2005), 55–62.

21. On business models, see Tyack, *One Best System*; and Raymond E. Callahan, *Education and the Cult of Efficiency: A Study of the Social Forces That Have Shaped the Administration of the Public Schools* (Chicago, 1962).

22. On Mitchell, see Antler, *Lucy Sprague Mitchell*, 360–62.

23. V. A. C. Henmon, "Retardation, Acceleration, and Class Standing," *Elementary School Journal* 14 (1914): 283; N. W. Walker, "Joseph Spencer Stewart of Georgia: An Appreciation," *The High School Journal* 18 (January 1935): 15; George Drayton Strayer and N. L. Engelhardt, *The Classroom Teacher at Work in American Schools* (New York, 1920), 124; and John Louis Horn, *The American Elementary School: A Study in Fundamental Principles* (New York, 1922), 302.

24. See Daniel Kevles, "Eugenics," in *The Oxford Companion to United States History*, ed. Paul S. Boyer (New York, 2001), 231–32; Michael S. Olsen, "Margaret Sanger," in Boyer, *Oxford Companion*, 683; and Carl N. Degler, *In Search of Human Nature: The Decline and Revival*

*of Darwinism in American Social Thought* (New York, 1991), chapter 7. While commonly seen as an educational conservative, William C. Bagley of Teachers College was a major critic of intelligence testing; see *Determinism in Education: A Series of Papers on the Relative Influence of Inherited and Acquired Traits in Determining Intelligence, Achievement, and Character* (Baltimore, MD, 1925). Bagley's views on testing are explored in J. Wesley Null, *Disciplined Progressive Educator: The Life and Career of William Chandler Bagley* (New York, 2003), 178–86.

25. On the post–World War II era, contrast Joel H. Spring, *The Sorting Machine: National Educational Policy Since 1945* (New York, 1976) with Diane Ravitch, *The Troubled Crusade: American Education, 1945–1980* (New York, 1983). For critical perspectives on the 1960s and 1970s, see David L. Angus and Jeffrey E. Mirel, *The Failed Promise of the American High School, 1890–1995* (New York, 1999), chapters 6–7; and Diane Ravitch, *Left Back: A Century of Failed School Reforms* (New York, 2000), chapters 10–11. On the issue of standards, see Daniel P. Resnick, "Minimum Competency Testing Historically Considered," *Review of Educational Research* 8 (1980): 3–29; and Daniel P. Resnick and Lauren B. Resnick, "Standards, Curriculum, and Performance: A Historical and Comparative Perspective," *Educational Researcher* 14 (April 1985): 5–20. On violence and drug use, William J. Reese, "*Reefer Madness* and *A Clockwork Orange*," in *Learning from the Past: What History Teaches Us about School Reform*, ed. Diane Ravitch and Maris A. Vinovskis (Baltimore, MD, 1995), 355–81.

26. On the left-liberal battles, see Diane Ravitch, *The Revisionists Revised: A Critique of the Radical Attack on the Schools* (New York, 1978). The rise and fall of liberalism is clearly described in James T. Patterson, *Grand Expectations: The United States, 1945–1974* (New York, 1996).

27. See the many valuable essays on history and contemporary reform in Ravitch and Vinovskis, eds., *Learning from the Past.*

28. Richard Rossmiller, "Financing Schools," in Alkin, *Encyclopedia*, 2: 512–520. For differing perspectives on the history of suburbia, read Thomas J. Sugrue, *The Origins of the Urban Crisis: Race and Inequality in Postwar Detroit* (Princeton, NJ, 1996); and Rosalyn Baxandall and Elizabeth Ewen, *Picture Windows: How the Suburbs Happened* (New York, 2000).

29. On the travails of the New York City schools, consult Jerald E. Podair, *The Strike That Changed New York: Blacks, Whites, and the Ocean-Hill Brownsville Crisis* (New Haven, CT, 2002).

30. Mortimer Adler, an old foe of John Dewey and "progressive education," tempered his views and championed a liberal arts curriculum; see, among his various writings in the 1980s, *The Paideia Proposal* (New York, 1982).

31. See Milbrey Wallin McLaughlin, *Evaluation and Reform: The Elementary and Secondary Education Act of 1965, Title I* (Cambridge,

MA, 1975), vii, 1–5; Robert L. Linn, "Measurement in Education," in Alkin, *Encyclopedia*, 3: 799; and Morris Finder, *Educating America: How Ralph W. Tyler Taught America to Teach* (Westport, CT, 2004), chapter 5. Graham, *Schooling America*, chapter 5, highlights the emphasis within educational policy making on testing and achievement since the early 1980s.

32. On Bush's plans in his second term, see "Bush Urges Rigorous High School Testing," *New York Times*, January 13, 2005, A24.

33. On the great romantic's experiences as a teacher, see Robert D. Richardson, Jr., *Henry Thoreau: A Life of the Mind* (Berkeley, CA, 1986), 5–6, 34–36.

## Chapter 8   Why Americans Love to Reform the Public Schools

This chapter has been adapted from William J. Reese, "Why Americans Love to Reform the Public Schools," *Education Research and Perspectives* 31 (December 2004): 107–119.

1. The best single volume on the history of contemporary school reform is *Learning from the Past: What History Teaches Us about School Reform*, ed. Diane Ravitch and Maris A. Vinovskis (Baltimore, MD, 1995).

2. On how teachers translate reforms into practice, especially see David B. Tyack and Larry Cuban, *Tinkering toward Utopia: A Century of Public School Reform* (Cambridge, MA, 1995.) Also read Larry Cuban, *How Teachers Taught: Constancy and Change in American Classrooms 1890–1980* (New York, 1984).

3. Joel Spring, *The Sorting Machine: National Educational Policy Since 1945* (New York, 1976), 38; and various essays in Ravitch and Vinovskis, *Learning from the Past*.

4. The themes developed in this essay are elaborated upon in my book, *America's Public Schools: From the Common School to "No Child Left Behind"* (Baltimore, MD, 2005), which contains a lengthy bibliography of primary and secondary sources.

5. On the innumerable ways in which reformers reinvent the wheel, recycle old ideas, and try to undo past reforms, see David B. Tyack, *The One Best System: A History of American Urban Education* (Cambridge, MA, 1974); David Tyack and Elisabeth Hansot, *Managers of Virtue: Public School Leadership in America, 1820–1980* (New York, 1982); and David Tyack, "Reinventing Schooling," in Ravitch and Vinovkis, *Learning from the Past*, 191–216. For the example of the kindergarten, see Selwyn K. Troen, *The Public and the Schools: Shaping the St. Louis System, 1838–1920* (Columbia, MO, 1975), chapter 5.

6. Of the vast historiography on the Puritans, see especially John Morgan, *Godly Learning: Puritan Attitudes towards Reason, Learning, and Education, 1560–1640* (Cambridge, UK, 1986); James Axtell, *The School upon a Hill: Education and Society in Colonial New*

*England* (New York, 1974); Darrett B. Rutman, *Winthrop's Boston: A Portrait of a Puritan Town, 1630–1649* (New York, 1965); and the marvelous synthesis by Alan Taylor, *American Colonies* (New York, 2001), chapters 8–9. On Mencken, Terry Teachout, *The Skeptic: A Life of H.L. Mencken* (New York, 2002), 125.

7. Taylor, *American Colonies*, chapter 8.

8. See Rutman, *Winthrop's Boston*, chapters 1–2, on the multiple meanings of the phrase "city upon a hill" as well as the detailed exploration of the subject by Francis J. Bremer, *John Winthrop: America's Forgotten Founding Father* (New York, 2003), 173–84.

9. Axtell, *School upon a Hill*, chapter 1; and Rutman, *Winthrop's Boston*, chapter 6. Alan Taylor argues that the Jeremiad should be viewed as a sign that idealism remained a guiding ideal of Puritan New England. As he writes in *American Colonies*, 185, "Finding the present generation wanting, a jeremiad exhorted listeners to reclaim the lofty standards and pure morality ascribed to the founders of New England. Paradoxically, the popularity of the genre attested to the persistence, rather than the decline, of Puritan ideals in New England." Also read Max Weber, *The Protestant Ethic and the Spirit of Capitalism* (New York, ©1958).

10. Wayne Urban and Jennings L. Wagoner, Jr., *American Education: A History* (New York, 1996), 41; Morgan, *Godly Learning*; and Gerald Strauss, *Luther's House of Learning: Indoctrination of the Young in the German Reformation* (Baltimore, MD, 1978). After completing this chapter, I was fortunate to read James A. Morone's outstanding volume, *Hellfire Nation: The Politics of Sin in American History* (New Haven, CT, 2003), which underscores many of the themes in this section of my essay. See especially chapters 1–3.

11. On the *New England Primer*, see Axtell, *School upon a Hill*, 36–37, 143–44.

12. Garrison Keillor, *Lake Wobegone Days* (New York, 1985).

13. Thomas Jefferson, *Notes on the State of Virginia*, ed. William Peden (New York, ©1954), 146; Jennings L. Wagoner, Jr., *Jefferson and Education* (Charlottesville, VA, 2004), 37, 42–43, 131, 143; Merle Curti, *The Social Ideas of American Educators* (Totowa, NJ, ©1935), 40–49; Urban and Waggoner, *American Education*, 75; Carl F. Kaestle, *Pillars of the Republic: Common Schools and American Society, 1780–1860* (New York, 1983), 6–9, 61, 198–99. Joseph J. Ellis explains that Jefferson's book was written in 1781 and first appeared in France; see *American Sphinx: The Character of Thomas Jefferson* (New York, 1997), 85.

14. On Franklin's influence and presence in school texts, see, for example, Ruth Miller Elson, *Guardians of Tradition: American Schoolbooks of the Nineteenth Century* (Lincoln, NE, 1964), 191–92; and William J. Reese, *The Origins of the American High School* (New Haven, CT, 1995), 39, 97–98, 115, 167, 175, 184, 201.

15. Gordon S. Wood, *The American Revolution: A History* (New York, 2003), xxxiv–xxv, 113–35 and also *The Radicalism of the American*

*Revolution* (New York, 1991). On the slavery question and the Founders, see Joseph J. Ellis, *Founding Brothers: The Revolutionary Generation* (New York, 2000), chapter 3; and the overall reassessment of Jefferson by Sean Wilentz, *The Rise of American Democracy: Jefferson to Lincoln* (New York, 2005), 135–40.

16. Kaestle, *Pillars*, 61, 198–99; and Wagoner, *Jefferson and Education*, 28–29, 128, 145.

17. The best biography of Mann is by Jonathan Messerli, *Horace Mann: A Biography* (New York, 1972). Other references on Mann are cited in earlier chapters of this book.

18. Untitled editorial, *Common School Journal* 3 (February 15, 1841): 63; *Twelfth Annual Report of the Board of Education, Together with the Twelfth Annual Report of the Secretary of the Board of Education* (Boston, MA, 1849), 59; and Curti, *Social Ideas*, 131–32, 138, 199.

19. Tyack, *One Best System*, 66, on elementary school attendance; Edward A. Krug, *The Shaping of the American High School, 1880–1920* (New York, 1964) and Ellen Condliffe Lagemann, *An Elusive Science: The Troubling History of Education Research* (Chicago, 2000), 8, on the boom in secondary enrollments; and Nathan C. Schaeffer, "Educational Interests of the State," *The School Journal* 63 (October 1914): 148.

20. B. A. Hinsdale, *Studies in Education: Science, Art, History* (Chicago, 1896), 148–49.

21. Lawrence A. Cremin, *The Genius of American Education* (New York, 1965), 11. Numerous writers have commented on the social lives of teenagers and the influential role of sports in American secondary schools; see, for example, James S. Coleman, *Adolescents and Schools* (New York, 1965); and Reese, *America's Public Schools*.

22. In *The Genius of American Education*, 11, Cremin noted that "One of my friends likes to remark that in other countries, when there is a profound social problem there is an uprising; in the United States, we organize a course!"

23. Stanley M. Elam, "The 22nd Annual Gallup Poll Of the Public's Attitudes towards the Public Schools," *Phi Delta Kappan* 72 (September 1990): 49–50; and Stanley M. Elam, Lowell C. Rose, and Alex M. Gallup, "The 25th Annual Phil Delta Kappa/Gallup Poll Of the Public's Attitudes toward the Public Schools," *Phi Delta Kappan* 75 (October 1993): 144–45.

24. David Farber, *The Age of Great Dreams: America in the 1960s* (New York, 1994), 113; and James T. Patterson, *Grand Expectations: The United States, 1945–1974* (New York, 1996), 637–38.

25. Lowell C. Rose and Alec M. Gallup, "The 31st Annual Phi Delta Kappa/Gallup Poll of the Public's Attitudes toward the Public Schools," *Phi Delta Kappan* 81 (September 1999): 44.

26. Jefferson's letter is quoted in Wagoner, *Jefferson and Education*, 146.

27. Arthur Schlesinger, Jr., "History and National Stupidity," *The New York Review of Books* 53 (April 27, 2006): 14.

# Index